KU-019-716

CONTENTS

ACKNOWLEDGEMENTS & ABBREVIATIONS		v
INTRODUCTION		1
CHAPTER ONE	*'Arran Water'*	11
CHAPTER TWO	*Planning*	27
CHAPTER THREE	*Not In My Back Yard!*	35
CHAPTER FOUR	*Capital Ideas*	53
CHAPTER FIVE	*The Eagle Soars Again*	61
CHAPTER SIX	*'Arran Water' Returns*	75
CHAPTER SEVEN	*The Visitors Arrive*	95
CHAPTER EIGHT	*The Business*	127
APPENDIX A	*Company Timeline*	151
APPENDIX B	*Expressions*	163
BIBLIOGRAPHY		181
INDEX		183

ACKNOWLEDGEMENTS & ABBREVIATIONS

IN WRITING THIS HISTORY of the establishment and evolution of Isle of Arran Distillers and the distillery at Lochranza I am indebted to a few of the great and the good, some saints and sinners and many who perhaps felt they had little to say, but revealed much with their contributions both great and small. In no particular order of preference my thanks go to:

Dave Broom; Euan Mitchell; Douglas Davidson; the late Hal Currie and his wife Barbara; Andrew Currie; Paul Currie; Jim and Shauna Lees; David Hutchison and Barbara Paulucy; Mark Hutchison; Les Auchincloss; Iain Thomson; Charles Fforde of Sannox Estate; David Boyle; Kevin Ramsden; Hugh Boag and Colin Smeeton of the *Arran Banner*; Gavin D. Smith; Jaclyn McKie; Dagmar Fortsch; James MacTaggart; Alan Reid; Faye Waterlow; Robin and Christine Bell; the staff at the archives of the Ewart Library, Dumfries; James and Linda Brown at Whisky Archives (Scotland); Linzi Smith and Claire Keane at Ayrshire Archives; Iain Russell, archivist at Glenmorangie plc; James McEwan; Ian Buxton; John Currie; David Currie; Ross Peters; Mike Peirce; Andrew Kettles; Louisa Young; Gillian Snaddon; Mark Callachan; Maggie Cornwall; Gordon Bloy; John McMullan; Campbell Laing; Kate and Mhairi Hartley; Ben, Anne and Gerard Tattersfield; Graham Omand; John Dowens; Nicole Lie; Lucie Stroesser; Andrew Bell; Susan MacNeill; Natalie Muirhead; Kamila Panasiuk; Amie Latona; Douglas Coulter; Katie Morrison; Deborah Dunn; William Paton; Peter Dunn; Gareth Gregg; Holly Weir; Richard Wright; Stewart Dunsmuir; Carolanne Anderson; Steve Butler and Alayna Ellis of Border Force National Museum Collection; Tim Rayson, secretary of the Kent and Sharpshooter Yeomanry Association; Gilbert Anderson of the Arran Society of Glasgow; Alex and Liz Dale; Scott Bain; Jan Vissers; Andrew Smith; Sheila Gilmore at VisitArran; the staff of the Douglas Hotel and the Auchrannie Resort Hotel, Brodick; Sandy Rankin; Revd Angus Adamson; Richard Forsyth of Forsyth's of Rothes; Graeme Walker of Scottish National Heritage; Mike Smith and Karen McBride at the Orb Group; Julie Hanna of North Ayrshire Council Planning Department; Chris Pollock of North Ayrshire Council Licensing Section; George Stewart of the Lochranza Hotel; Ronald Zwartepoorte; Terry Crawley; Colin Siddle; Stephen Gibbs of Dougarie Estate; Ewen Fraser of Miltonduff Distillery; Alan Winchester, Master Distiller at The Glenlivet; David Croll; Bob Gibson; Gillian McCreadie; Robbie Porteous; Fiona Wilson; Paul Barnbrook; Stuart Gough of Arran Heritage Museum; Gary Dawson, Gary Doherty and Del Sneddon of Pocket Rocket Creative and the photographers Jonathan Cosens, Allan Wright, Peter Sandground, Martin Shields, Andrew Smith, Christopher Hogge, Teimei Horiuchi and David Kelso.

Finally, a special thank you to Gregor Adamson of Brodick, who graduated from Stirling University in 2015 and whose dissertation *An Examination of Illicit and Licensed Whisky Production on the Isle of Arran from 1700 to the Present Day* was invaluable for primary sources which shed much new light on the history of whisky making on the island.

Abbreviations

The following terms commonly appear in the text and to save repetition, after the first instance they will appear in this form.

alcohol by volume	abv
Cunninghame District Council	CDC
David Hutchison & Associates	DHA
Highlands and Islands Enterprise	HIE
International Wine & Spirits Competition	IWSC
litres of pure alcohol	lpa
No Age Statement	NAS
parts per million	ppm
Scottish Natural Heritage	SNH
Visitor Centre	VC

INTRODUCTION

T HE NOTION OF BUILDING A WHISKY DISTILLERY is probably harboured by more whisky enthusiasts than care to admit it, but very few find themselves in a position to do anything about it. Of those who have done so in the past, many have failed and the history of the Scotch whisky industry is littered with brief mentions in excise records and local history archives of the short-lived concerns that were once the hopes of people of vision who simply did not stay the course. Harold Currie (1924-2016) was one such who managed to achieve this dream.

Harold, or Hal as he was popularly known, was one of five children born to his merchant seaman father in Liverpool. He was a natural entrepreneur who ran errands for local shopkeepers and neighbours. He was educated at St Margaret's Grammar School before going on to Liverpool College of Commerce where he studied economics. As a youthful chorister he learned sign language for the deaf, using it to send messages to his friends during sermons when things were running a bit slow and he even practised semaphore in order to signal goodbye to his father from the quayside whenever he returned to sea. As a young boy he was evacuated to North Wales in 1939 and on reaching the age of 18 in 1942 he joined up, a singular distinction. A fascination with tanks saw him enlist in the Royal Armoured Corps and he subsequently joined the 4th County of London Yeomanry (Sharpshooters) in 1944, after they had returned from the Middle-East with the 7th Armoured Division (the Desert Rats).[1]

---

[1] The title of 'Sharpshooters' goes back to the Boer War when the original 3rd County of London Yeomanry were raised to fight in the Boer War as Imperial Yeomanry. The 3rd were raised specifically to fight the Boers at their own game as light horsemen who were crack shots. They fought in the Great War and were invited to raise a second regiment – the 4th in 1939. Unusually they fought together in the desert, Italy and Sicily before Normandy and were presented by Montgomery to King George VI in Tunis as the best armoured regiment in the desert. There was also a company of Scottish Sharpshooters in the Imperial Yeomanry and their memorial is in St Giles Cathedral, Edinburgh.

The 4th County of London Yeomanry land on the Normandy beaches on the day after D-Day, 7 June 1944. *Currie family*

SS-Obersturmführer Michael Wittmann (The Black Baron), the central figure in the Battle of Villers-Bocage. For his actions during the battle Wittmann was promoted to SS-Hauptsturmführer and awarded the Knight's Cross of the Iron Cross with Oak Leaves and Swords. He was to die in action on 8 August 1944. *Bundesarchiv (Federal Archives of Germany)*

The *Illustrated London News* of 1 July 1944 carried an artist's impression of part of the battle when a Tiger tank is disabled. *Kent and Sharpshooter Yeomanry Association*

A view of three German tanks, including two Tigers, knocked out during the battle in the centre of Villers-Bocage on 13 June 1944. *Bundesarchiv (Federal Archives of Germany)*

Hal was one of the servicemen who took part in the D-Day landings in Normandy, when the Sharpshooters landed on Gold Beach on 7 June 1944 (D+1). Due to the difficulty in getting though the German defences to the north of Tilly-sur-Seulles the Sharpshooters were tasked by General Montgomery with passing through the American forces to the west to exploit a gap in the enemy lines in order to outflank them and sweep round the back towards Villers-Bocage. This was to create an advantage in the advance on Caen to the west. Moving through the night Hal found himself arriving on a sunny morning at 8am on 13 June to be met by a throng of delirious townspeople who threw flowers in their path and offered Calvados and cider to their liberators.

However, all was not as it seemed. As the Sharpshooters led the column out of the town along the road east, followed by a company of 1st Battalion the Rifle Brigade, they were ambushed by a single Tiger tank, commanded by SS-Obersturmführer Michael Wittmann (a household name in Germany and known as The Black Baron), who took out the Sharpshooters' lead Cromwell

cruiser tank and then turned on the rest of the column which was trapped within the embanked road. To put it mildly, all hell then broke loose. Wittman took the bull by the horns and rampaged on down the road towards Villers-Bocage as panic set in amongst the British riflemen who ran to take cover. Other Tigers followed him and as Wittman entered the town he found the Sharpshooters' tank column was trying to reverse (badly). However, some tank units had managed to manoeuvre into side streets off the main road that ran through the length of the town. Hal was in one of them. It was not long before a Tiger tank approached their hiding place and, as soon as it came into view, Hal's crew fired upon it. The Tiger was taken out and ended up embedded in the front of a shop on the other side of the road. The driver and co-driver were killed and the surviving crew rapidly evacuated and made for cover in a nearby building.

Foolhardiness is not a trait that Hal displayed in later business life but at that moment he sprang from the tank and ran towards the disabled Tiger to 'view the damage'. He noticed a discarded Luger pistol hanging from the turret and

3

A typical brew-up in Normandy with a 4th County of London Yeomanry crew in front of their Cromwell tank. Hal Currie was the driver in one such tank during the battle. *Kent and Sharpshooter Yeomanry Association*

grabbing it, he turned and ran back to his tank only then realising that he could have been shot by the Germans hiding nearby.[2] Fortune smiled on him and he remained unscathed but in a little less than a quarter of an hour over a dozen tanks, two anti-tank guns and an estimated 15 transport vehicles had been destroyed by 2 Kompanie schwere SS-Panzer Abteilung. Wittmann accounted for many of these on his own. Military historian Max Hastings stated that it was 'one of the most devastating single-handed actions of the war'. Other commentators, however, considered it a foolish and unnecessary risk, much akin to Hal's action that day.

The ensuing battle that followed after Wittman's withdrawal lasted several hours and Hal recalls that half his regiment was lost. 'I was lucky. There was a lull in the firing and we got as many out as we could into the surrounding countryside. The RAF sent in bombers to cover the retreat. After that I ended up in Hamburg, followed by a move to Berlin, where we entered a zone that the Russians had left. The German population came out and greeted us as liberators.' Ever the entrepreneur he forged a business partnership in the British Zone with a German leather manufacturer and produced handbags for returning soldiers to take home to their wives and girlfriends. Paul Currie told me that his father 'would have stayed on if circumstances had allowed. The war made him see the world in a new light and he saw huge opportunities ahead'.

Hal's contribution to the war effort in France was formally recognised on 16 October 2015 at the City Chambers in Glasgow when he received the Légion d'Honneur from the French Consul General Emmanuel Cocher. Those war experiences must have had a great bearing on his approach to how he tackled the rest of what life had in store for him. After he demobbed he joined the Liverpool and Bristol wine and spirit merchants Rigby & Evans and built up his knowledge of the business, eventually becoming the right-hand man to his managing director, Arthur Stirling. On 27 May 1950 Hal married Barbara Cartwright whom he had met at a dance, and they moved out to Cheshire to live.

[2] The Luger 'was unfortunately thrown away when his mother was moving house', Hal's youngest son Paul recalls.

Four sons followed over the next 13 years: John in 1951, David in 1953, Andrew in 1961 and Paul three years later. Andrew and Paul were to be closely involved in the story of the establishment and early years of the distillery at Lochranza.

In 1960, Stirling was invited by Seagram supremo, Sam Bronfman, to become joint-MD along with Geoffrey Palau, of the London-based UK arm of House of Seagram, a role which he accepted and Hal was included in the team as Stirling's PA. While his career was moving in the right direction, his other passion, football, was also keeping him busy in his spare time. A keen footballer who had had to give up the game after an injury, Hal then trained as a referee in the army and initially took charge of amateur games in his native Cheshire before climbing the ladder to handle professional fixtures. He recalled his first game in charge: 'A disaster. The army had given me a false sense of security. I was hopeless. Afterwards when one of the players asked how many games I had under my belt, I admitted that this was my first.' Despite the setback he persevered and went on to officiate in professional football both at home and overseas. (On his move to Scotland he continued to referee junior professional football until 1972.)

At this time Seagram's emphasis was in maintaining the upward trend in the production and marketing of the Chivas Regal and Captain Morgan brands. He made sure that Chivas was pushed hard as an aspirational purchase in export markets to compete against Johnnie Walker, insisting that it had to be of the highest quality and promoting it with the slogan, 'Come to Chivas Regal when you can afford it'.

But an ill wind blew in Hal's favour when Stirling asked him to take his place at the annual luncheon of the GB Wine and Spirits Association in Manchester. This was an essential networking event and as Stirling was unwell, Hal stepped into the breech. But it did not end there as Stirling was off work for several months, leaving Hal in control. Meantime Palau was noting how well Hal was doing and suggested to Sam Bronfman that he and the rest of the Seagram board attend a meeting in London where Hal could present his vision for the company in the UK.

Hal Currie in Berlin just beyond the Brandenburg Gate, posing next to a Russian traffic controller, July 1944. *Currie family*

Hal with the Légion d'Honneur
which he received at Glasgow City
Chambers on 16 October 2015 from
the French Consul General
Emmanuel Cocher.
Martin Shields Photography

Bronfman was impressed by the presentation and ensured that Hal sat beside him at the lunch that followed. He was then duly invited over to the States for a three-month spell where he observed the corporation's management style and structure, prior to taking over the Seagram operations in Scotland as MD of Chivas Bros based in Renfield Street, Glasgow. In 1971 Sam Bronfman died and his son Edgar took over the reins but left the UK operations under Hal's control. By this time Seagram had moved out of Glasgow to Paisley where a major blending and office facility had been constructed prior to Hal's arrival in Scotland. Home for Hal, his wife Barbara and family, was in the village of Dalry, later moving to the Kilmarnock area. His attachment to Scotland was now almost as well rooted as a native's.

Much of Hal's later working life was to be spent in international travel, building the brands he managed. One memorable trip was to war-torn Beirut where he crossed the city from the airport to the Christian sector to visit his sole customer and only avoided a certain kidnapping thanks to the quick thinking of his taxi driver. Hal was rewarded with a 4,000-case order from Monsieur Laoun and a hug from the cabbie whom Laoun had made sure was also well rewarded! After that experience Hal decided to sail directly from Larnaca in Cyprus into East Beirut.

Those trips were also put to good use as Hal often called the FA before he went abroad to see if there were any international fixtures available for him. This resulted in him refereeing some games while he was on business trips overseas on more

Andrew, Barbara and Paul Currie with Hal at the ceremony. *Martin Shields Photography*

than one occasion. His passion for football had not gone unnoticed at St Mirren FC in Paisley where he was invited to join the board of the Love Street club which was then struggling in the second division of the professional leagues. He agreed to become chairman and promptly decided to recruit a young manager called Alex Ferguson who was making a big impression at the helm at East Stirlingshire. Ferguson was eventually convinced to take on the St Mirren job by Jock Stein and from 1974 to 1978 he created a thrilling young team which gained promotion to the Scottish Premier Division in 1977 with the loss of only two games. The rest, as they say, is history.

Just as Ferguson joined St Mirren, Hal's career took a new direction. The French drinks giant Pernod acquired the Scotch whisky brand House of Campbell and asked Hal to become the MD with a view to increasing sales throughout the world. A year later, in 1975, rivals Pernod and Ricard merged to form Pernod-Ricard SA and commenced the building of a trade giant. Hal was promoted to head of UK operations and he remained in that position until he retired. During that time he converted the bulk exports of Scotch whisky into cased bottle sales and drove the worldwide demand for House of Campbell in particular, witnessing 70% growth in the brand in France in the first ten months of 1982 as the Scotch market there expanded 17% as a whole between 1980 and 1982. However, other producers were not experiencing the same trading conditions and massive overstocks built up in the 1970s meant that the Distillers Company Ltd began a rationalisation plan in 1983 which saw the mothballing, and often total loss, of many malt distilleries throughout Scotland including the much admired Port Ellen on Islay.

To accommodate this expansion in sales House of Campbell moved to a new site at Kilwinning, Ayrshire. However, having stepped down as chairman of St Mirren (succeeded by Willie Todd, the only man ever to have sacked Alex Ferguson) and with Pernod-Ricard wanting to move the House of Campbell HQ south to London, in December 1982 Hal decided to step aside as MD to remain in Scotland while being retained by the group on a consultancy basis. In 1985 he viewed a dilapidated house on the Ballochmyle estate of Sir Claud Hagart-Alexander with his Glasgow architect friend David Hutchison (who had carried out industrial work for Hal while at Pernod-Ricard) who believed it could be renovated. The result was the charming rural Currie family home of Pathhead nestling above the banks of the River Ayr.

Hal's time working as a consultant for Pernod-Ricard (ironically the group acquired the Chivas business in 2001) lasted into the early 1990s when he finally called it a day. Soon after he retired, however, Dato Terry Lee, with whom Hal had been working in developing business in Malaysia, tracked him down to Pathhead where it was arranged that they should resume their dealings. This resulted in a mutually beneficial business relationship which continued until Hal's death on 15 March 2016, with particular emphasis on exports to Papua New Guinea.

However, his most public achievement only took seed after David Hutchison attended the annual dinner of the Arran Society of Glasgow on Saturday 8 March 1991 in the Trades House, Glassford Street. The Arran minister Revd Elizabeth Watson spoke to members and their guests as did Peter Morrison, the noted Scottish baritone, who regaled the diners with the history of whisky-making on the island, stating that when the last legal distillery at Lagg in the south of the island closed in 1837, its spirit had been considered to be the best in Scotland. In fact, in 1824 the geologist and Hebridean traveller John MacCulloch recorded that Arran was 'in the older days … the Burgundy of all the vintages'. David, whose family on his mother's side go back seven generations in the Whiting Bay area, had property on Arran and had often wondered why the trade had died out. The fact that there was also the site of what he believed was an illicit still on his croft at Knockenkelly kept the question burning in his mind. He left the dinner that night with a growing determination that if Arran whisky had once been so good, why could it not be great once more? All that was needed was a distillery …

Not long after this David and his wife were invited down to have dinner at Pathhead where he posed the same question to Hal, knowing full well that it would intrigue him. Why didn't they join forces and create a brand new distillery on Arran? After all, David had all the skills required to design it and Hal had fantastic and longstanding contacts in the whisky industry, so they would make a good partnership. And that is the beginning of the story of how the distillery at Lochranza was born.

The Hutchison family croft at Knockenkelly, above Whiting Bay, where David Hutchison believes there is an old illicit still site located in the grounds. It appears on the 1869 OS map as an 'Old Kiln'. *Neil Wilson*

CHAPTER ONE

'Arran Water'

MORE GENERICALLY KNOWN AS AQUA VITAE or *usquebaugh* ('water of life') 'Arran Water' was revered in 19th-century Ayrshire, its main market across the Firth of Clyde when sufficient supplies allowed the smugglers to make the often precarious crossing, frequently undertaken at night. It was good business when they got away with it, but it was in their blood and even in 1845 was still considered 'an honourable occupation' which brought much needed cash back into the island. To the smuggler, the exciseman and the customs officer were instruments of authority preventing him from undertaking his birthright, and the tradition of smuggling in the area went back for as long as excise regulations and the imposition of customs duty constrained what is now considered to be 'free trade'.

Prior to 1707, when England and Scotland were joined by the Treaty of Union, each country operated as a foreign market towards the other for the import and export of goods. Excise duty was imposed on these goods in order to raise revenue for the respective governments and had been in existence on the Continent since the early 17th century, the most successful being the '*accius*' imposed in the United Netherlands ('excise' may well be a corruption of the Dutch term). In 1626 Charles I attempted to introduce an excise based on this system but parliament rejected it, fearing that it would destroy the nation. It was not long before they changed their tune when a war had to be funded and on 22 July 1643 excise duty was imposed in England and Wales on ale and spirits to payroll the parliamentary army. It was supposed to be temporary, but after a year was extended for the duration of the war and after that ended it remained, and has done so in one shape or form, ever since.

Scotland followed suit in 1644 with an excise duty on 'everie pynt of aquavytie or strong waterris sold within the country', again to payroll the army. Beer, or 'biere' was also taxed at 4d a Scots pint. The collection of the excise duty was 'farmed' out to lairds and landowners who paid a standing monthly or quarterly sum to the Treasury in lieu of this arrangement. This meant that there was no need to directly manage remote areas with collectors and gaugers who would have been costly. These revenue 'farmers' employed their own staff and in Scotland the landowners used their senior tenants or 'tacksmen' to make the collections. In 1649, the Marquis of Argyll had the 'Tak of the Excyse' throughout the entire country, essentially sitting at the top of a revenue-generating pyramid system.

However, despite the 'farmed' excise system in Scotland, the results were poor due to the very remoteness of many areas and the vagaries of access and weather. Headquartered in Leith the Scottish Excise was described in 1655 by Thomas Tucker, the Registrar of the English Excise, as ineffectual and in some instances fraudulent amongst the tacksmen. Total annual revenue rarely exceeded £25,000 until the early years of the 18th century. In 1683 the farming of the excise in England ceased and a Board of Commissioners was appointed in London which strictly managed the collections throughout the country. Scotland's excise remained 'in tack' until 1707, excepting Islay where it continued to be farmed out until 1797, largely due to the fact that the sole laird, Daniel Campbell, was a Justice of the Peace and Member of Parliament and was better placed to manage excise collection in the whole of Islay and Jura.

The Treaty of Union of 1707 was the beginning of a gradual move to equalise import duties between England, Ireland, Scotland and Wales. The aim was:

… that there will be the same Customs and Excise and all other taxes and the same prohibitions, restrictions and regulations of trade throughout the United Kingdom of Great Britain.

One of these, the tax on malt, was to be the source of much social disorder when it was finally imposed on Scotland six years later. Scotland's excise duties were, at this time, collected in a different manner to England's where meticulous monitoring and gauging were the norm. In Scotland 'composition' was used whereby an estimate was made of how much dutiable spirit and ale were made in a half-year, with few or no checks to verify this. But adopting the English system was considered too great a task over the whole country so Edinburgh and certain ports and large market towns were to use the English method while the rest of the country continued with composition until the situation allowed the formal nationwide adoption of the proper system. By 1710 there was a staff of 30 at HQ in Leith, 25 supervisors and gaugers dealt with Edinburgh, and 190 other officers were stationed throughout the country. Within two years Collectors had set up in Aberdeen, Ayr, Berwick, Dumfries, Dundee, Fife, Glasgow, Inveraray, Linlithgow, Elgin, Perth, Scrabster, Selkirk, Ullapool and Wigtown.

The excise regulations governed inland trading solely, but in the execution of his duties the exciseman would find himself recovering goods smuggled in from abroad, and also those traded within his jurisdiction. Customs duty was imposed on goods imported from abroad. The extent of the excise regulations covered every aspect of daily life with licences issued to the traders and commercial enterprises involved in the manufacture and retail of exciseable goods and related services. If you were an auctioneer, you needed an excise licence as you may have sold an estate, furniture, wool or even made the first sale of 'Foreign Produce'. Then the goods that were manufactured or bought and sold by the licensee were dutiable.

In the 18th century every port, harbour and canal terminus quay of significance in the United Kingdom levied these duties and each had a permanent Custom House. Excise duty was collected on commodities such as beer (of varying strengths), bricks and tiles, candles, cereals, coal, coffee, cider and perry, fish, glass, hides and skins, hops, kelp, leather, malt, mead, paper and 'printed goods', salt, soap, spirits (including 'Maidstone Geneva') starch, stone bottles, sugar, sweets, tea, timber, tobacco, vinegar, wine, wire and wool. In other words, almost every commodity which had an impact on daily life and living had duty imposed upon it. However, soon after George III asked William Pitt the Younger to form a government in September 1783, a preliminary report of a parliamentary committee, appointed under Lord Shelburne 'to enquire into the illicit practices used in defrauding the revenue', landed on Pitt's desk. Its findings were horrendous. Having taken on a huge debt burden to finance the American War of Independence, the Treasury needed revenue from every possible source. But even the Excise, by far the most efficient and well set-up office of revenue collection, could only generate 30% of what it was legally entrusted to raise. In order to deter the smuggling of foreign goods such as tea and brandy, duties were slashed in the hope that this would encourage legal trading and fill the government coffers. But would this initiative work when the government's attention turned to home-produced commodities such as whisky? In short, it did not. Illicit whisky from the Highlands and Islands retained a status far greater than any legally produced spirit from the Lowlands and the London government would struggle with the introduction of rational, coherent legislation for the next four decades as it battled with the massive Lowland distilling dynasties until 1823.

The first form of income tax had not been introduced until 1798 by Pitt the Younger to help balance the books, so government revenue during the 18th century was largely dependent on sources such as the Window Tax and the tax on salt. Excise and customs duties were major earners for the Treasury and remained so until reforms of customs and excise regulations followed in the early 19th century. They were, in some ways, equivalent to VAT, which was also imposed on a 'temporary' basis only to remain to the current day. These impositions were therefore largely responsible for the social conditions under which most ordinary people tried to survive or live and prosper in 18th- and 19th-century Scotland and Arran's geographic position made it of special interest to the Excise. It would be almost impossible to imagine how such a set of regulations could not have led to wholesale smuggling into and out of Arran. In particular, the Wash Act of 1784 was to have as profound an effect on the encouragement of illicit distilling across the Highlands and on Arran, as the Excise Act of 1823 was to have on helping to stamp it out.

Before the middle of the 18th century, *aqua vitae* made in Scotland was not recognisably what we would now regard as whisky. It was often a coarse brew, derived from available grains to which other ingredients, such as local herbs, were added to 'soften the blow'. The pioneering Gaelic traveller Martin Martin (the Alan Whicker of his day) described the hooch that was distilled on Lewis around 1700 as follows:

Their plenty of Corn was such, as dispos'd the Natives to brew several sorts of Liquors, as common *Usquebaugh*, another call'd *Trestarig, id est Aquavitae*, three times distill'd, which is strong and hot; a third sort is four times distill'd, and this by the Natives is call'd *Usquebaugh-baul, id est Usquebaugh*, which at first taste affects all the Members of the Body: two spoonfuls of this last Liquor is a sufficient Dose; and if any Man exceed this, it would presently stop his Breath, and endanger his Life. *The Trestarig* and *Usquebaugh-baul*, are both made of Oats.

His observations while he was on Arran are particularly revealing when he states that, 'natives think a dram of strong waters is a good corrective'. Clearly the island's distillate was of a different order. It would be another half-century before the local barley strains of bere and bigg were used to create the fermented wash that, when distilled, produced a malt-derived spirit – the precursor to modern whisky.

In 1713 the Malt Tax had been extended from England to Scotland at a rate of sixpence a bushel. First imposed in England in 1693 as a purely wartime measure during the War of the Spanish Succession, under the terms of the Treaty of Union it had been agreed that this tax would not be extended into Scotland until at least seven years had passed, however, this was later altered to 'the duration of the war'. Home brewing was a common practice in Scotland and the populace did not consider that the English would renege on their agreement and extend the tax to their own ale when peacetime returned, particularly when it had been assured that the tax was temporary.

There was huge opposition to the imposition and the Duke of Argyll, no less, stated that, 'If this tax were to be collected in Scotland it must be done by a regiment of Dragoons.' Several Scottish Lords requested audience with Queen Anne in order to argue the Scottish case which they insisted was a …

… violation of one article of the Act of Union, that levying such an unsupportable burden as the Malt Tax upon them was likely to raise their discontents to such a height as to prompt them to declare the Union dissolved!

The Act scraped through parliament and the duty was imposed from 24 June but it proved almost impossible to collect and many Justices of the Peace refused to deal with criminal proceedings against defaulters. In June 1725, the picture changed once more, and it was much worse. Although Walpole's government reduced the duty in Scotland to three pence on a bushel of malt, the duty was to be collected by means of force, if necessary. The ensuing civil insurrection led not only to the demise of brewing in Scotland but also to riots in Glasgow which would have a profound effect on another island famed for its distilling culture – Islay.[1] Ultimately it also led not only to an increase in smuggled spirits from abroad, such as Dutch genever and French brandy as they replaced the reduction in ale drinking, but also a huge increase in the production of distilled spirits in Scotland which had been exempted from the Gin Act of 1736, designed to reduce consumption of that particular spirit.

Ships would be met in the Firth of Clyde and the goods sold to smugglers who had the means to move them on. But it was not always a benign stretch of water and could wreak havoc on shipping. One notable weather event on 14 January 1739, a hurricane, brought devastation to shipping along the coasts of Scotland with many losses in the Firth of Clyde. Any smuggler who wanted to 'jink the gauger' also needed to be a skilled sailor to ply his trade between Arran and Ayrshire.

The volume of the smuggling of imported goods in the mid-18th century was huge, if only when judged by the successful seizures made by the customs officers. The *Edinburgh Courant* of 30 October 1750 reported:

They write from Campbeltoun, that Mr. Fraser of the Custom House there lately took a Smuggler, near the Ile of Sanda, with about 180 Casks of Rum and Brandy; and that Capt. Crawford of the King's Wherry took another, near the Ile of Arran, with about 120 Casks of said liquors, and two Hogsheads of Wine, all which are lodged in the King's Warehouse there.

This also confirms that smuggling activity at that time dealt with the inward-bound movement of goods and it was not until the transformation of *usquebaugh* into a purely malt-derived distillate after this time that it became a commodity of high repute and value which could be sold on the mainland.

Salt was also another dutiable commodity that was readily smuggled into Arran. First taxed in 1693 by William of Orange, by 1702 a Salt Office was established at the Treasury and throughout the century and into the next, duty on salt increased until it was 40 times its cost. (In 1798 it was a staggering five shillings a bushel). This made it a hugely profitable import for the Arran smugglers. But it was not just profit that drove so many men and women into the trade. The prevailing social change of the mid-18th century on Arran was one of agrarian reform and land tenancy changes, or put another way, land clearances. After John Burrel, the 'Special Commissioner' appointed by the tutors of the young 7th Duke of Hamilton, arrived on Arran in 1766, he set about a complete survey of the landholdings in order to begin a total revision of the rural economy of the island. The long,

[1]On 24 June 1725 a mob, enraged by the Malt Tax, rioted in the centre of Glasgow. They sacked Shawfield Mansion on Glassford Street, the property of Daniel Campbell, the local MP who had voted for the imposition. The compensation he received from the city allowed him to convert the mortgage he held on the islands of Islay and Jura into an outright purchase. During his lairdship of Islay (which enjoyed a complete lack of direct excise regulation as this was 'farmed' out to the landowner until 1797) legal distilling was encouraged and created the basis of the industry on the island today.

drawn-out result over the next 70 years would be the throwing together of the old runrigs and the amalgamation of clachans and other communal landholdings into fewer and more efficient farm units, all of them paying larger rents to the ducal estate. Arrears were a frequent problem for the tenantry as rents simply could not be met with the proceeds made from the land.

While private distilling remained legal until 1781, it was unlawful to sell any of the spirit produced and smuggling and illicit distillation offered a far more lucrative 'get out'. Instead of growing barley and selling it to millers and maltsters, enterprising families and syndicates (it was rarely a solitary undertaking) could finance a remote bothy still or secrete a stillroom within their premises and, by turning their excess grain into spirit, had a much more valuable commodity to sell, particularly to the lucrative mainland market. Kelp harvesting also offered them some means of raising cash legally but it was not a crop that could be easily harvested and by the end of the 18th century smuggling and illicit distillation were rife on Arran.[2]

MacBride states that in 1784 there were 32 stills on Arran of which 23 were operating in the south end. In the same year the Wash Act was passed which had a major effect on the activity with 26 stills being collected and taken to Brodick Castle. There were two main features of the act as described by Gregor Adamson:

Firstly it reduced the level of duty on spirits, as the imposition of high duty levels throughout the 1700s were blamed for the increase in illicit whisky production. Secondly the Act established a precise geographical 'Highland Line', which separated the Lowlands from the Highlands for the purpose of differential excise levels. The Highlands were defined as the 'several counties of Orkney, Caithness, Sutherland, Ross, Inverness, Argyll, Bute, Stirling, Lanark, Perth, Dumbarton, Aberdeen, Forfar, Kincardine, Banff, Nairn and

Moray.' Thus, Arran was included in this Highland zone, as a part of the county of Bute. Distillers in these Highland areas paid a lower licence fee and lower rates of excise duty were applied to small-scale distilleries which used locally produced barley. The Act aimed to stimulate legal distilling in the northern part of the country and reduce smuggling activities. The Act was successful in one respect as the number of smaller licensed distilleries did increase, however illicit distillation remained rife in Highland areas.

In the *Old Statistical Account of Scotland* (1791-99) the minister John Hamilton of Kilmory parish also noted:

A considerable quantity of barley is also exported to Greenock, Saltcoats, Irvine, Ayr and Campbelltown; but 3 licensed stills have lately been erected in the island, which will exhaust a great part of the barley that can henceforth be spared.

Confirmation of this comes in correspondence from the Arran exciseman William Stevenson to the Collector in Ayr on 19 December 1792:

… there are three inland Distilleries in the Island of 40 Gallons each which for two years past have consumed annually half of that quantity of Barley[3] and the rest has been exported to Campbelltown, Ayr, Saltcoats and Greenock.

One of those licensed stills was at Whitehouse, Lamlash, and sold whisky between December 1793 and November 1794 for four shillings a gallon. Gregor Adamson expands on this:

Another of the Arran distilleries from 1793, was located at Glenshant, near

---

[2] Kelp harvesting died out after the Napoleonic Wars when cheaper barilla was imported from Spain. It was loaded on to ships that sailed to Greenock and Liverpool where it was used as an ingredient in the manufacturing of soap and glass. It was also used as a fertiliser on farmland.

[3] 600 bolls, equivalent in 'Argyll measures' to about 100 metric tonnes today.

Brodick Castle. A document titled, *Account of sundry, outputs and utensils and other documents made by Alexander McKinnon of Glenshant distillery from 1 Dec 1790 to 1 Jan 1793*, recovered from the Arran Estate Office, provides vital insight into the workings of this licensed Arran distillery. The primary document reveals that the total outputs for this period were £91 8s 10d, including £11 for a still and boiler from Campbeltown. The record also reveals curious information regarding those employed at the distillery. It is stated that Peggy Donaldson was employed as a brewer and paid £6 for her employment over two years, more than any other employee at Glenshant. Women were known to have played a key role in illicit production throughout Scotland and on Arran, however this document also demonstrates that they were significantly involved in licensed distilling.

Lamlash Bay from an early 19th-century engraving with Duchess Anne's Quay right of centre and Holy Isle beyond. *Arran Heritage Museum*

Arran consisted of two large parishes, Kilmory and Kilbride and the law stated that a maximum of two stills per parish were allowed and given that the Whitehouse and Glenshant stills were located in Kilbride, the third licensed still must have been in Kilmory at this time as the distillery at Lagg was not operating until around 1825. Its location, however, is a mystery.

By 1797 it was estimated that there were another 50 active illicit stills operating in the south of Arran, consuming all of the island's output of bere which MacBride claims was '500 to 2,000 quarters'. The Revd Hamilton chose not to mention this at all, perhaps wishing to deny the distillers the oxygen of publicity but more probably to draw a veil over a social arrangement prevalent at that time. While the law demanded that the rules and regulations were to be adhered to, the realpolitik then was that the landowners had an interest in allowing illicit distilling to discreetly flourish. Why? First, their rents were more likely to be paid if their tenants had ready cash in hand, and second, they were often amongst the smugglers' and distillers' best customers. It was a social symbiosis that suited everyone – except the excisemen and customs officers. The irony of this relationship was that the lairds were often the Justices of the Peace who found themselves passing judgement in court on some of their tenant-suppliers who had unfortunately been caught in possession.[4] Gregor Adamson reveals the extent of the illicit industry in the south end by quoting from a 1796 letter from Mr MacLeod Bannatyne of the Customs and Excise Board, Edinburgh, to the Arran factor, Mr Stevenson.

It appears to me that your islanders being so closely connected with each other and so generally interacted in protecting offenders that nothing is likely to be effected by sending an officer and party to Brodick or Lamlash, because they are no sooner arrived than their objective comes to be known, and intelligence will of course be conveyed to the persons meant to be seized, long before the party can reach their places of residence … unless the party is strongly supported by an Armed force.

This first-hand account from 1796, clearly emphasises that there was a sophisticated local smuggling network in place, making it difficult for law enforcers to detect illicit activities and prosecute those involved. This in turn made the eradication of illicit production almost impossible, and paved the way for its continuation into the 1800s.

Later on in 1796, Mr Stevenson also requested that twenty military men be stationed on the island in order to combat whisky production and smuggling. These actions by the Arran factor reiterate the assertion that illicit distillation was rife on Arran, and that it continued to thrive in the face of restrictive measures implemented by local and national law enforcers.

In July 1802, 41 Arran residents appeared in Rothesay Excise Court, 29 of them to face charges related to illicit activities and the remaining 12 to give evidence.

Five of them were women confirming how involved the activity was in domestic affairs. Gregor Adamson again:

One of the women called to answer for a supposed crime before the Excise Court, was a Mrs Adams of Lamlash. The lack of a forename suggests that she was in fact a widow, and was engaged in some form of illicit distillation activity. There is further evidence to support the assertion that widows on Arran were involved in the unlicensed production of whisky. This can be found in a letter to James Lamont, the Arran factor, from John Murphie, the tenant of West Bennan, located to the south of the island. In the letter, Murphie claims that, 'lately a poor woman, a widow … having a small quantity of malt to make up her rent, used her freedom to put her distilling utensils into a new house built by your factor which was without doors and windows, and that in your factors absence and without asking his liberty.'

This correspondence hints at the fact that women, and in particular widows, were directly involved in the distillation of illicit whisky. However, it must be stated when considering this evidence, that Murphie was a notorious illicit distiller himself, and he was tried for assaulting and deforcing Officers of the Revenue in 1811. Therefore, it could be inferred that he was attempting to pass on the blame for his own misdemeanour. Nonetheless, the Excise Court record coupled with the testimony of Murphie, reveals that illicit production was widespread and that all members of the community, including women, were implicated in the efficient distilling and smuggling network present on Arran during this period.

Another primary document which shows that illicit activities were carried out throughout the island is the warrant for the arrest of John Hendry of Mosend (Machrie), Hugh MacKenzie of Shedog, Hugh Kerr of Lochranza and Neil MacCook of Sliddery, for alleged transgressions against the laws of the Excise in April 1803. Hendry, MacKenzie and Kerr were convicted and fined £3 3s, whilst MacCook was fined £2 2s. This court

[4] In 1811 the population of Arran consisted of 1,123 houses occupied by 1,143 families. Of these 1,021 were 'chiefly employed in Agriculture', while only 100 were 'chiefly employed in Trade, Manufacture or Handicraft' and 22 were employed in neither of these two classes. The population of 5,704 was made up of 2,673 males and 3,031 females. There were only six uninhabited buildings. In 2014 the resident population was 4,650.

document demonstrates that distillation was common throughout Arran, as the men found guilty lived in settlements located from one end of the island to the other. Furthermore, the record states that MacKenzie was the miller at Shedog and Kerr was employed as the assistant miller at Lochranza. This suggests that millers throughout Arran, who had access to vast quantities of grain, were predominately involved in the malting process. This would have allowed them to sell the malted barley to other Arran tenants, to be utilised in the illicit distillation of whisky. The conviction of MacKenzie and Kerr also reveals that respectable members of the community were heavily involved in unlicensed whisky distilling.

Another curious factor was the proximity of Robert Armour, the plumber in Campbeltown. Between 1797 and 1817 there was no legal distilling undertaken in Kintyre and this meant that servicing illicit stills was a major part of his business; he moonlighted as a stillmaker and repairer, his skills being put to good use wherever they were needed, be it on Gigha, in Kintyre or in the south end of Arran. Indeed, such was the extent of this 'black' market that he maintained meticulous account books from 1811-17 of his many illegal transactions. Gregor Adamson summarises Armour's accounts:

Over the six-year period, Armour produced around four hundred stills, carrying out work amounting to the value of £2000. In relation to Arran, fifty-three transactions were carried out, involving the construction of bodies, heads and worms, the repair of excising equipment and the sale of old stills. Armour's equipment was transported across the Kilbrannan Sound to Arran by boat and the majority of his Arran clients were tenants in the south end of the island.

From his records, 17 distilling locations in the south end of Arran can be identified and prominent amongst Armour's clients were Malkom Cook of Margrioch,

William McKinnon and Daniel Kerr of Western Bannen, John Nicol whose location is simply 'Kilmorie', Robert Black of Coreravie, William Currie ('Alexander Currie's son') of Corcrave, and John Cook and James McDonal of West Bannen. These placenames have been irregularly spelled throughout the accounts and many that are similar are probably the same place. Western Bannen and West Bannen would equate to Bennan at the very south of the island where a member of the Cook family was involved in one of the last seizures made on the island which is described towards the end of this chapter.

In about 1814 tenantry improvements were attempted by the Duke of Hamilton on Arran, but there was public opposition to this and to associated road-building. At that time access to much of the island outside Brodick was only possible by boat and the roads, such as they were, were merely rough tracks for pony and cart. The measure was effectively a further round of clearances and was particularly relentless against the runrig clachans. Robert Brown, the duke's factor, stated that people were especially defiant in districts where smuggling was endemic. Illicit distilling was barely existent in the north of Arran because fishing was more important, but the aforementioned tenants in the south end, like those in Tiree, where the Duke of Argyll battled constantly against illicit distillation, were alleged to be in close contact with the Irish. Road tools were carried off and new houses vandalised as they were being built. The Duke of Hamilton eventually threatened to expel them from the island but this did not come to pass.

The illegal trade prospered, but the forces that were gathered against it became more and more determined to root it out at any cost. The records may show the successes the Excise had in suppressing smuggling and distilling on Arran, but rarely is mention made of their failures. The *Caledonian Mercury* of 22 March 1817 reported:

There was seized, on 7th current, near Irvine, by Messrs Isaac Buchanan and John Hall, officers in Excise, Kilmarnock, and a party of military, a horse and cart, with eight ankers Arran whisky, containing about sixty gallons.

On other numerous occasions 'wretched' lives were lost for the sake of a boatload of salt or a few bales of tobacco. Just four days after the above seizure, a pitched battle took place on Arran as the *Scots Magazine* related:

> In the afternoon, a boat, with smuggled whisky on board, set sail from the south end of Arran. After proceeding a short way, the crew observed a revenue cutter[5] lying off, and put about. This was noticed by the cutter, and instantly a boat was manned with ten hands, and sent in pursuit. The smugglers reached the shore, and were in the act of carrying the whisky inland, when they were overtaken, and the spirits seized. Before the cutter's men could return to the boat, a number of islanders collected, attacked them, and attempted to rescue the spirits. A dreadful scuffle ensued, in the course of which, two men and a woman were shot dead on the spot, and a boy and a girl wounded. The two men killed are named McKinnon, a father and son; and the woman's name is Isabel Nichol.

The resultant trial of the cutter's mate, John Jeffrey, in Edinburgh in September, recorded that:

> After an impartial investigation, from which it clearly appeared that the conduct of Mr. Jeffrey, who had been distinguished for firmness and forbearance, was occasioned solely by the violence and outrage of a misguided multitude, and was absolutely necessary to defend the lives of those who were under his command, the jury, with the entire approbation of the Court, returned an unanimous verdict of Not Guilty.

The Excise Collector in each region reported to the Scottish Board of Commissioners in Leith on a quarterly basis and the records for the Port of Air (Ayr) reveal something of how they operated. Up to Christmas 1821 the record shows

[5] *The Prince Edward.*

Bennan appears in numerous references to illicit distilling on Arran. This early 20th-century postcard of Craigdhu reveals ruined habitations, thatched crofthouses and a more modern farmhouse of stone and slate construction. *Stuart Gough*

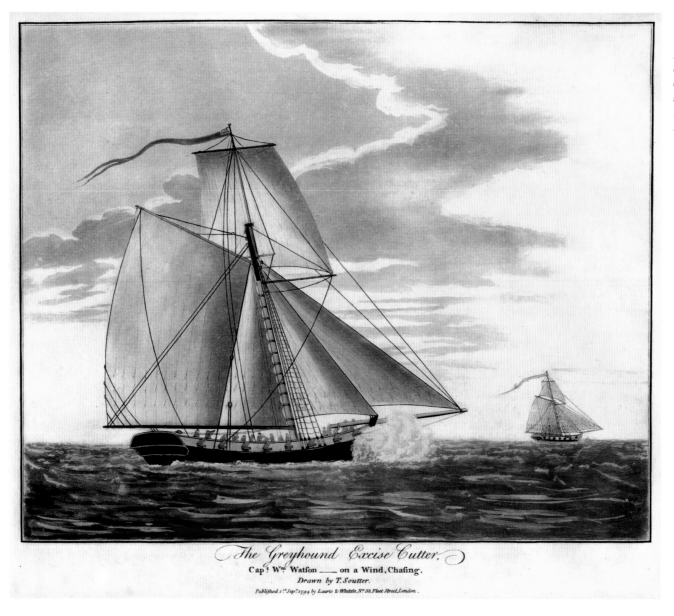

The Greyhound Excise Cutter.

Cap.t W.m Watfon _____ on a Wind, Chafing.

Drawn by T. Soutter.

Published 1.st Sep.t 1794 by Laurie & Whittle, N.º 53, Fleet Street, London.

A late-18th century excise cutter, *The Greyhound*, typical of the type used in the waters around Arran at that time.
Border Force National Museum Collection

seizure of one 'open boat and materials', and '1 cask 1½ gallons whisky' which were subsequently sold by public roup[6] on 22 February to members of the public for £5 6s and £1 1s 9d respectively. In the quarter up to Lady Day (5 April) 1822 '1 cask 8 gallons whisky', '1 Small Cask 2 gal whisky' and '1 Jar 1¼ gal whisky' fetched £7 4s, £1 15s 6d and £1 2s 6d. Against this income an account of expenses amounts to 10s 6d for the Justice of Peace Clerk, 1s 6d for the Town Crier who would have called the roup in Ayr and 3s for 'Yard Rent' where the goods had been stored.

In the quarter after Lady Day 1822, there was a much larger haul of four seizures amounting to a sale of £85 2s 7½d at public roup with expenses totalling £1 5s. The smuggler's boat was bought for £5 by James Telfer of Ayr and a few of his fellow townsmen bought all the whisky which went for between 16s 6d and 18s per gallon. The Town Crier's fee was down to 1s.

But instances such as these were to diminish after the Excise Act was passed in 1823 and the Salt Tax repealed two years later, resulting in many illicit distillers going legal in Kintyre, Arran and throughout the Highlands. Gregor Adamson explains:

The building reputed to have served as the grain store for the Lagg Distillery which closed in 1837. *Neil Wilson*

Landowners were encouraged to invest in licensed distilleries throughout Scotland due to the slashing of annual licence fees for legalised production. This clearly motivated the Duke of Hamilton on Arran as Brown commented in 1823, that, 'In the island of Arran we are now ready to establish a legal distillery, with a view of consuming the barley, and getting the people to give up illicit distillation'. These measures meant that illicit distilling was virtually non-existent by the early 1830s. The factor of the Duke of Hamilton, John Paterson, alludes to this in 1834, stating that, 'illicit distillation, which prevailed to a great extent, has now nearly altogether ceased'.

Paterson also stated in 1834 that, 'A legal distillery has been in operation at Torrylin for several years past, which makes spirits nearly equal to the famous Arran Water.'

[6] auction

This distillery is reputed to have started sometime in 1825 and according to published Parliamentary Papers for the period from 10 October 1823 and 10 Oct 1826, produced 11,187 gallons of proof spirit from 4,922¼ bushels of malt. In the quarter to 5 January 1827 it produced 967 gallons of proof spirit from 509¼ bushels of malt under the ownership of Charles McAlister Shannon & Co before being taken over in 1830 by Matthew Spiers. Adamson reveals a little more about the previous owner:

> During his time running the distillery McAlister Shannon was convicted by the Courts of Exchequer and fined £5. Information regarding what he was fined for is not stated, nonetheless the conviction hints at continuing illicit activities in the Kilmory area after 1823. The Parliamentary Papers reveal that Lagg distillery manufactured whisky from malt grain only. From 1825 to 1826, the distillery produced 3336 gallons of malt spirit, with this figure rising to 6105, between 1827 and 1828. In addition the distillery was charged £13 13s 4d in duty on the amount of whisky produced in 1826. When Spiers took over the amount of whisky produced remained relatively similar, with outputs recorded as 2561 gallons in 1831, rising to 4568 for 1832.

Increased vigilance towards the local maltsters also meant that it became more difficult to procure malted barley from them to conduct illicit distilling. For those who did continue, it must have proved profitable. On Bute in 1826 a family were convicted and fined the huge sum of £60. Despite bearing 'the appearance of great destitution' within a few days they had paid it in full.

But the economic forces that gradually brought an end to legal distilling on Arran were more widespread. In 1830 there were 37 legal distilleries in South Ayrshire producing 18,000 gallons of spirit a year and in Campbeltown nine distilleries had opened in the two years since 1823; by 1837 that figure was 28. Competition had had the final say.

In the Statistical Account of 1834-45 the Revd Alan McNaughton of Kilbride parish on Arran had recorded:

> The practice of illicit distillation prevailed very generally not many years ago. But the heavy fines imposed of late on convicted delinquents, and the diminution of the gains of smuggling by the improvement of the spirits manufactured by the licensed distiller, have in a great measure put an end to this demoralising traffic.

By the first quarter of 1836 the amount of whisky smuggled to the mainland from Arran was considered by the Excise to be 'very inconsiderable' and after this there was 'no smuggling' reported in the quarters throughout 1837 and into 1838. In July 1838 the Excise reported:

> The only case of Smuggling within the precincts of this port which has come to our knowledge in quarter ended 5th Instant is that of a small cask Eight Gallons Aqua seized by the Officers of the Revenue on the morning of the 5th Instant and which has in conformity with directions by Your Honours' Order of 30th June 1830 been handed over to the Officers of Excise with a report of all the circumstances attending the Seizure. R.R

Perhaps the problem was finally being eradicated? Any illicit distillation that did continue must have been on a much reduced level for the Excise to have considered it hardly worthy of comment. In the other Arran parish, Kilmory, Revd Angus Macmillan made the following observation:

> Illicit distillation prevailed till a very recent period, to a very considerable extent, but within the last ten years, very decided measures were taken for its suppression, and it is now almost entirely done away. Its demoralising effects were not developed here so prominently, as in other places, from the

circumstance of its not being considered a disreputable pursuit, and there being few, if any, in the parish, who, at some period in their lives, were not engaged in some department of smuggling. To the smuggler no stigma was attached on account of his employment: on the contrary, it was considered rather an honourable occupation, as exhibiting an intrepidity and art that acquired for their possessor a distinction in the minds of his companions. It was in the darkest night, and in the most tempestuous weather, when no cruiser would stand the gale, that, in his little skiff, the smuggler transported his cargo to the opposite shores of Ayrshire.

But the Excise was not solely involved in seizures. Loss of cargo lost overboard in a wreck was also dealt with if the goods were no longer subject to claim by insurers as was the disposal of 'overtime goods' and 'sale of samples'. The former were goods on which the owner had failed to pay duty in time and the latter were samples taken for assay or gauging and not returned. In all cases the roups were attended by Ayr men of means who profited from the knock-down prices available to them. On 31 December 1850 almost a half-gallon of whisky was auctioned for 3s 11d and a half-gallon for 4s 6d.

Eventually the illicit industry on Arran petered out but subsequent rises in duty still made the craft attractive to those prepared to take the risk. One of the last major detections by the Excise described in the *Glasgow Herald* of the 8 December 1858:

On Tuesday week quite a sensation was created in the Island of Arran. The active and resolute officer of the preventive service, Mr. Evans, and his two assistants, Andrew McMillan and Murdoch Mathieson, on the morning of that day made a seizure at Port-Bennan, before dawn of morning. In a wild and dangerous place of the coast, they descried what turned out to be a temporary bothy, fixed over the rock. Mr. Evans, leaving his assistants above, slung himself down into the midst of the party, when he was immediately knocked down by one of the smugglers, but quickly seizing his musket, with the butt end he knocked over his assailant, who staggered and rolled over and down the precipitous incline of the hill to about 100 feet. The other parties meanwhile made good their escape. The assistants, McMillan and Mathieson, jumped after the man who had been stunned by Evans' blow. Some blank shots were fired at the others, but the only one taken was the smuggler Cook, who had been rendered faintish by the blow from the musket of the officer. The others, meanwhile, though escaping, cannot elude the vigilance of the preventives. In the bothy were found all the apparatus used in the making of whisky. The copper still-head and worm were taken to Lamlash, and a considerable quantity of wash and feints was destroyed upon the spot. The prisoner was taken to Rothesay jail, where, we learn, he suffers an incarceration of three months. It must be allowed that ever since the increased duty has been placed upon spirits the temptation to illicit distillation has, in proportion, greatly increased; and in such places as the wild hills of Arran, where the chances of detection, from the remoteness of the dwellings, are lessened, the pains and penalties of the law are braved, though the risk run is very great where such activity is found by the officers of the service. Doubtless this detection will act as a beneficial warning to others who may contemplate incurring such risks. Rumour says that on this occasion one of the parties implicated was soon to have been married, and that the preliminary manufacture of 'aqua vite' was to give éclat to the hymeneal ceremonies – the social and genial influences of the 'fiery god' being deemed an almost indispensable requisite to prolong the festive moments and bacchanalian enjoyments.

The Excise officers thereafter were solely involved in dealing with inward smuggling of whisky from the mainland with the final seizure taking place in 1860 when three casks of whisky were landed in the south end of the island. The officers were diverted by the brother of the innkeeper at Lagg (whose whisky it should

A rare view from the late 19th or early 20th century of the Lagg Inn, prior to it having chimney pots added to the top of its stacks. *Stuart Gough*

have been) to share a convivial drink, but on returning to their haul they found the casks had been filled with seawater. Ironically, it was the smugglers who seemed to have had the last word in the story of 'Arran water'. Or had they? To close this chapter, I offer evidence which proves the opposite. Kate Hartley, who retired from employment at Isle of Arran Distillery at the end of 2015, is quoted in Gregor Adamson's dissertation when she recalled a childhood adventure from Lochranza which shows that although the mass practice of illicit distillation died out in the mid-19th century on Arran, it was still carried out discreetly into the 20th century when circumstances allowed.

As a young girl Mrs Hartley remembers finding, 'a bit of a stone dyke, there were jars, pots and bottles all lying about, it was a bit like a wee house'. After finding the structure she informed her great Aunts who told her that she, 'was never ever, ever to go up the hill behind the house again because there was a bad man up there'. Mrs Hartley explained that after she reported her findings, the house gardener, Jimmy Stronach, was sent to destroy what remained of the still. This incident hints that illicit production continued on Arran into the 20th century. This old still found in the 1950s was probably in use during the late 1930s and during World War II, when there was a great shortage of whisky and consequently a vast increase in price. The site of this still also reveals important information concerning the location of distilling activities on Arran. The still was situated in a wooded area next to a source of running water. In addition, it was located on the hillside, strategically overlooking the shoreline and possible signs of detection. Furthermore, the site was located in close proximity to the local peat road, providing easy access to a source of fuel necessary for distilling activities.

The remains of the old illicit still site which Kate Hartley discovered as a child in the woods above Lochranza. *Gregor Adamson*

What history does this old bottle hold? *Gregor Adamson*

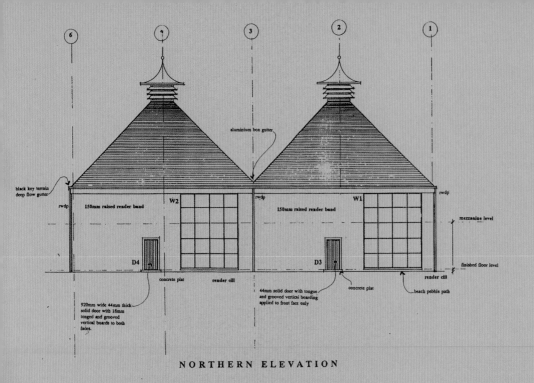

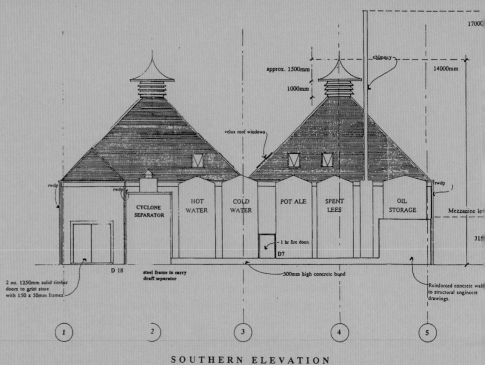

NORTHERN ELEVATION

Northern Elevation labels:
- black key terrain deep flow gutter
- rwdp
- 150mm raised render band
- W2
- aluminium box gutter
- 150mm raised render band
- W1
- rwdp
- mezzanine level
- finished floor level
- D4
- concrete plat
- render cill
- 920mm wide 44mm thick solid door with 18mm tonged and grooved vertical boards to both faces.
- 44mm solid door with tongue and grooved vertical boarding applied to front face only
- D3
- concrete plat
- render cill
- beach pebble path

SOUTHERN ELEVATION

Southern Elevation labels:
- 17000
- chimney
- approx. 1500mm
- 1000mm
- 14000mm
- velux roof windows
- rwdp
- rwdp
- CYCLONE SEPARATOR
- HOT WATER
- COLD WATER
- POT ALE
- SPENT LEES
- OIL STORAGE
- rwdp
- Mezzanine le...
- 315...
- 1 hr fire door
- D7
- D 18
- steel frame to carry draff separator
- 2 no. 1250mm solid timber doors to grist store with 150 x 50mm frames
- 300mm high concrete bund
- Reinforced concrete wall to structural engineers drawings.
- 1 2 3 4 5

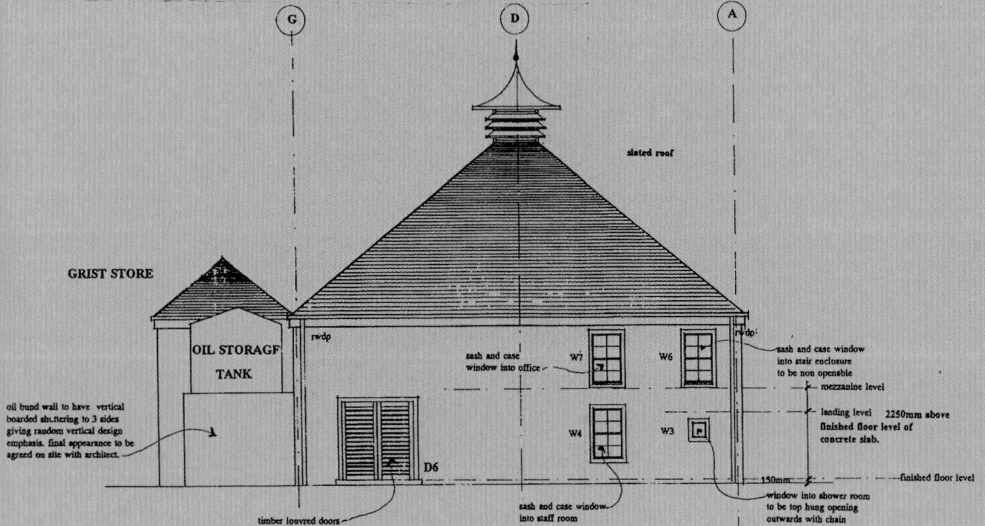

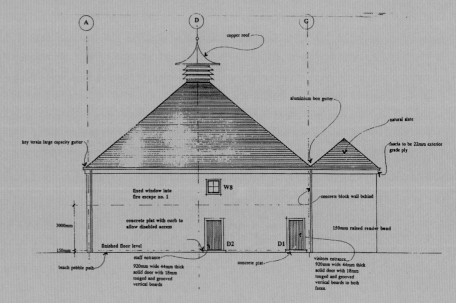

EASTERN ELEVATION

Eastern Elevation labels:
- G D A
- slated roof
- GRIST STORE
- OIL STORAGE TANK
- rwdp
- rwdp
- sash and case window into office
- W7
- W6
- sash and case window into stair enclosure to be non openable
- mezzanine level
- landing level 2250mm above finished floor level of concrete slab.
- W4
- W3
- finished floor level
- oil bund wall to have vertical boarded shuttering to 3 sides giving random vertical design emphasis. final appearance to be agreed on site with architect.
- D6
- timber louvred doors 2500 x 1250mm with 150 x 50mm frame.
- sash and case window into staff room
- window into shower room to be top hung opening outwards with chain
- 26

WESTERN ELEVATION

Western Elevation labels:
- A D G
- copper roof
- aluminium box gutter
- natural slate
- fascia to be 22mm exterior grade ply
- key terain large capacity gutter
- fixed window into fire escape no. 1
- W8
- concrete block wall behind
- 3000mm
- concrete plat with curb to allow disabled access
- 150mm raised render band
- 150mm
- finished floor level
- beach pebble path
- staff entrance
- 920mm wide 44mm thick solid door with 18mm tonged and grooved vertical boards
- D2
- concrete plat
- D1
- visitors entrance. 920mm wide 44mm thick solid door with 18mm tonged and grooved vertical boards to both faces.

CHAPTER TWO

Planning

WHEN HAL CURRIE RETIRED from Pernod-Ricard he harboured a vision to own his own distilling operation. He had often discussed the possibility with his sons Andrew and Paul as they pondered where would it be best to build. What would it be called? How big would it be? Where could they find the best water? On one visit to the Lake District in the 1980s, Hal had been impressed with the quality of the water he was drinking in a restaurant and commented on it. 'This might be the place to look,' he told them. After that Andrew and Paul kept an eye open for any opportunities that might arise but nothing came over the horizon. However, it was David Hutchison who arrived somewhat circuitously at the answer after that dinner he attended in Glasgow in March 1991.

David Hutchison is one of Glasgow's best-known architects; now 70 years old and 'almost' retired, his career involved working for the Irvine New Town project in the 1970s before joining Michael Hyde & Associates as their director in Scotland in the mid-1980s. He first met Hal Currie when he worked on industrial projects for White Heather Distillers (part of the Pernod-Ricard group) and remembers his early dealings with Hal's French bosses.

They would fly into Abbotsinch in a private jet, then decant to the Malmaison at the Central Hotel where most of the Glasgow whisky trade lunched back then. There were two of them, one, Thierry Jacquillat, was always impeccably turned out, and was Director General of the company while the other, Monsieur Methvet was more of the working, hands-on director type. They only drank whisky throughout their meals and I had to follow suit so as not to offend them, although I hardly ever touched the stuff.

David's work for White Heather Distillers revolved around the construction of an unremarkable bottling plant in Irvine but it was the Pathhead house project for Hal that was more memorable. 'It was the first and only time I was threatened with violence on site by a contractor. Hal somehow defused the whole situation, much to my relief.' After David had sown the seed of the distillery idea at dinner at Pathhead, Hal was actually a bit sceptical as the industry had gone through a spate of closures in the early 1980s with many distilleries under the ownership of the Distillers Company such as Port Ellen, Dallas Dhu and North Port closing. Was the creation of new capacity in the industry the smart thing to do? But when he reconsidered the proposal it was clear that the closures had been due to an oversupply of fillings for the blending side of the industry and that David's idea might be worth a second look.

There were a number of further overriding factors that then made him reconsider the viability of the project. First, any distillery established on Arran would not be some anonymous production unit lost in the glens of Speyside. Second, Arran was prime tourism country and attracted thousands of tourists each year; a visitor reception facility could be built at the distillery to bring in much needed cash and offer tourists a wet-weather facility which the island desperately needed. Third, if the output was solely for bottled single malt sales, then a boutique brand could be established and built up. Arran's proximity to the central belt was also attractive when compared to the far-flung Outer Hebrides, Orkney and Shetland. The mild climate was also another factor as that would lessen the rate of evaporation from the warehouses containing maturing stocks.

Making whisky alone costs money, a lot of money, especially on an island. Transport costs for raw materials are higher than on the mainland and when matured stocks are shipped for blending and bottling, costs increase again. If you are starting from scratch, as the Curries were, the financing of a new distillery and associated warehousing alone was a daunting challenge. And if you do manage to kickstart production, the stocks are lying in bond for three years before they can be exploited, so a huge hole in cash flow exists that has to be filled somehow. They had to come up with a plan of how to fund the project quickly and it was Andrew who had a flash of inspiration when climbing on Ben Nevis in the early summer of 1991.

West Ham football club were financing the building of a new stand by offering fans 'The Hammers' Bond', a debenture which gave their fans the right to a seat for 150 years for a fixed upfront cost. It dawned on me that we could help to finance the distillery by offering the public the same sort of thing. The 'distillery bond' would be sold to members of the public in return for future supplies of Arran whisky at a substantial discount.

After the Curries took legal advice from Brodies WS in Edinburgh, it was cleared as a legal business model. Andrew and Paul then started to brainstorm how the project would progress. After graduating Paul had taken a job setting up BP's marketing arm in Poland and Russia after the fall of the Berlin Wall while Andrew was working for the BBC World Service in London. As the project progressed, Andrew took off to see Paul in Krakow to work on some initial sales and cost figures based on the bond idea – all very speculative – but it was a start. David Hutchison meanwhile enlisted the help of his son Mark, an undergraduate geologist, and together they started trying to find some suitable locations around the island that would also be near a decent water source. It became clear to them that while some suitable locations for construction were identifiable, the associated water sources were a far greater problem. Mark was eventually sent off on his own to reconnoitre the island using his own specialist knowledge to see what he could turn up. He takes up the story.

Geologically speaking, Arran can broadly be divided in two. The northern portion is dominated by granite creating the distinctive peak of Goatfell and its neighbours. The southern part of the island (divided roughly where the String road runs east-west) is comprised more dominantly of sedimentary rocks. I looked at these concepts in the context of established whisky making in Scotland. Put simply, the flavours of mainland malts differ from those of the islands in that the mainland distilleries catchment areas are very strongly dominated by granite, a rock which is almost entirely absent from the Scottish islands (with the exception of Arran). In addition to the solid-rock geology, another factor is clearly apparent, and that is the soil. In the case of the peaty character of, for example, an Islay malt, the flavour derives from the phenolic levels of the malted barley. However, the water itself is very peaty, as is evident from simply turning on a tap. Likewise, in Arran, peat is an integral part of the landscape.

So a number of water-related questions arose. Firstly, which waters were safe to drink? This simplest question was deferred to later chemical testing. It was felt unnecessary to conduct a costly review of all likely water sources on the island because knowing the generally high quality and fresh taste of Arran water (for which it already had a reputation), a shorter list of sites would in any case likely pass any chemical quality control. So this took us back to the question of geology. Which catchment areas would seem most interesting?

The geology and topography of Arran are such that the island has been described ad infinitum as 'Scotland in miniature'. Covering an area of 432 square kilometres, and rising to 874m at the summit of Goat Fell in the north, its landscape covers the gentler aspects of the southern coastal fringes, where New Red Sandstone and other sedimentary rocks abound, to the rugged mountain cirque of the north where the ancient granite mountains intrude into the surrounding Devonian sandstone. Twelve thousand years ago, Arran was covered in an ice sheet which scoured the landscape as it receded. Glens were carved such as can be seen at Catacol and Chalmadale and corries gouged out like Coire na Ciche. The ice also left behind clues as to its presence with large boulders dumped incongruously on the land such as the huge Cat Stone outside Corrie. Mark's search through this geologically fascinating landscape was thorough.

We looked at Blackwaterfoot, generally low-lying, soil-rich water with a sandstone and carbonate foundation. This appeared likely to have too much of an agricultural influence. We considered Whiting Bay, perhaps deriving from the conifer-rich slopes. We expected the acidic soil through which such water flows would present a problem for wash management. Strong deviations from a neutral pH can leach components from other ingredients and the distillation hardware and can give rise to unwanted or hard-to-replicate flavours. We considered Corrie and Sannox but again active land use was thought likely to be detrimental. Besides, in this area there was a history of mining which I felt could taint the water at the very least, representing a compromise on taste. With all these sites at our disposal there was another which stood out. That was Lochranza.

He explained the area he investigated to me.

The Easan Biorach burn running through Creag na h-Iolaire into the village taps a huge area of the north of the island. A large area is good because it means any strong flavour inputs from local idiosyncrasies are strongly diluted. So a large catchment presents a higher chance of a smoother taste.

Furthermore, immediately before the village the burn falls steeply through a narrow channel from a high and protected plateau. Thus the watercourse through agricultural land stands out as being very short. Human activity is best kept to a minimum because even if land use at the time of build is benign, future land use may not be. The upland areas are fairly inaccessible and high enough in elevation for there to be almost no human activity. So

29

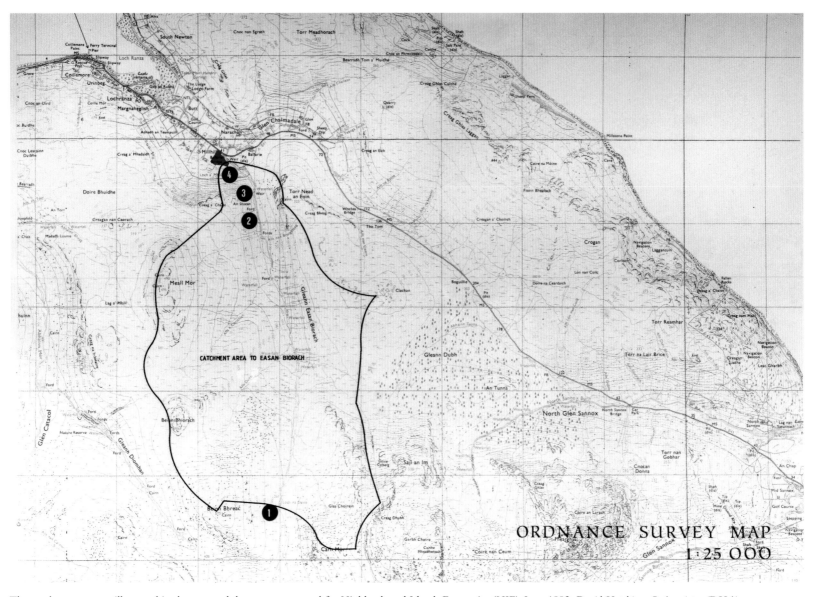

The catchment area as illustrated in the proposal document prepared for Highlands and Islands Enterprise (HIE), June 1992. *David Hutchison & Associates (DHA)*

this physical protection of the longer-term integrity of the water quality was also attractive. The Easan Biorach presented itself as a candidate for very natural water. The plateau and surrounding mountains comprising the north side of Goatfell are almost entirely granite and the parallels with mainland malts were therefore clear at this point. However, the crux was that while the underlying rock is granite, approximately fifty per cent of the surface cover of the catchment area is peat, ie, typical of the water sources for many island malts. So the Lochranza water presented a very unusual set of circumstances where the water comprised the critical elements contributing to the making of the classic Islay malts and the classic Speyside malts combined. This concept presented the possibility of generating a unique whisky.

As Mark prepared a formal report of his findings, Jim Lees, a Corrie-based antiques dealer and rental property owner, was brought into the picture. A longstanding friend of Hutchison, his local contacts were to be put to good use in making the introductions to landowners and other interested parties in order to sound out access to viable water sources and construction land. As the vice-chairman of the then Isle of Arran Tourist Board, Jim was extremely enthusiastic about the proposal.

A trip to the island was arranged in late August 1991 during which Jim advised David and Hal about possible sites in an effort to finally shortlist them or strike them off altogether. As we have seen, historically most of the distilling activity had been in the south end of the island and it seemed a logical place, but Mark's observations that the land had been agriculturally influenced discounted it. That took the search to the relatively undeveloped north of Arran. Lees thought that a location near his home village of Sannox might be a possibility. There was a sand extraction plant in Glen Sannox which he thought was going to stop soon because the lease was due to run out. The water sample tested well although with the site being outside the village envelope, planning permission might prove problematic. A lunch meeting at the Ingledene Hotel (now the Sannox Bay) was then

The Easan Biorach catchment area above Lochranza. *DHA*

The view over the site at Lochranza prior to the granting of planning permission. *DHA*

31

The Easan Biorach looking upstream to its source at Loch na Davie at around 360m/1182ft altitude. *Neil Wilson*

arranged with local estate owner Charles Fforde, Hal Currie, David Hutchison and Jim Lees at which Fforde confirmed that he was happy with the principle of a distillery but not at the Sannox location as the site was not actually going to be available. Jim's recollection of that meeting was that Fforde suggested an alternative site at Lochranza. He confirmed that Sannox Estate had some flat, grazing land at the east end of Lochranza where the Easan Biorach burn passed under Ballarie Bridge. The meeting ended positively and David recalls that when he and Hal had a quiet moment together afterwards they were, 'absolutely convinced that we would make it happen'.

The first wind Arran residents got of the project was in the *Arran Banner* of 31 August 1991 after Jim Lees had persuaded Hal and David to 'be up front' about the whole thing as Arran was 'too small a place to keep a secret'. A meeting of the editor, John Millar, two local councillors for Arran (one of whom was Evelyn Sillars), Jim Lees, Hal Currie and the chairman of the Isle of Arran Tourist Board, Ronnie Mann, then took place at the Tourist Information Centre at Brodick pier, at which Hal presented the concept of the distillery stating that the likely location would be at Lochranza with the water being drawn from the Easan Biorach (assuming it passed the purity tests and could supply the necessary volumes of water for the distillery). The project remained extremely conditional and there were a lot of 'ifs', including 'the feedback from the local people'. Hal also stated that a 'share ownership' scheme might be involved which would include publicans in the West of Scotland. The nascent 'Arran Bond' was not mentioned at this time.

Jim Lees recalls the tenor of the meeting as being one of delight, but Evelyn Sillars cautioned at the time: 'My first reaction is it's another small industry that will bring employment. My second reaction is that it's an awful long way to go before it's achieved. The idea is great. The people sound good. But we've had a lot of people with a lot of ideas.' The *Banner* concurred that, 'This is a point of view which meets most new proposals and only time and perseverance can see those through from an idea to being reality.' It was a point well made. To date there had been much talk, discussion and many meetings but to take everything forward

Above: Mr. Hal Currie of Mauchline on the left, architect David Hutchison on the right and centre, Mr. Jim Lees who has been their guide round the intricacies of Arran places and personalities in their search for the best distillery location.

hopes they will make up the majority of shareholders, but among publicans throughout the West of Scotland. A feeling of part ownership after all is a powerful incentive to promote 'your

The first public knowledge of the project as it appeared in the local newspaper.
Arran Banner

the project had to become an official entity. The decision to create a company called Isle of Arran Distillers Ltd was taken by Hal Currie and David Hutchison and registered on 11 November 1991 with two £1 ordinary shares each as their initial holdings. A head office was then set up at The Cross in Mauchline, close to Pathhead, from which Hal Currie would run operations.

Perhaps the most curious aspect of going public with the proposal now became apparent, or rather did not. In contrast to what would happen a year hence, the local reaction to the announcement appeared to be … precisely nothing. No letters in response arrived at the *Banner*, either for or against. If it was discussed publicly at all, it was in passing at the shops, on the ferry and in the pubs. Unknowingly Hal Currie and the team had gained a year of peace from public inquisitiveness to get on with the job in hand. At the monthly Tourist Information Board meetings Jim Lees was often asked by other members how things were progressing, but the island as a whole seemed to have forgotten about it.

The rights to draw water from the Easan Biorach burn just above Ballarie Bridge were eventually agreed with Sannox Estate but only, according to David Hutchison, after it withdrew a request to charge the distillery for consumption of the process water. (In the 19th century the Duke of Argyll had a similar arrangement with the distillers in Campbeltown who drew vast quantities of water for processing and cooling from Crosshill Reservoir and which netted the Argyll estate a very tidy sum over the Victorian boom years.) Some time later Hal was informed by Glasgow University geology department that the Easan Biorach burn was the best possible water source for making whisky in the entire island. They had chosen the perfect location. Curiously, Mark Hutchison also recalled how his report for the company almost disappeared.

As it turns out, this became a document with some history … (some years later) my father's office in the centre of Glasgow was very heavily damaged by a devastating fire. This gutted the Victorian building right next to Central Station which it occupied. Considerable numbers of plans and documents were lost. I remember my father's description of eventually being permitted entry by the firemen, once it was deemed reasonably safe. He discovered that the office, on the fourth floor or thereabouts, had almost completely lost its floor. However, a small ledge remained on which sat a filing cabinet. In this was my report on the water for the distillery. I remember my father showing it to me, dark blue card cover, heavily charred at the edges and with some water damage.

On the land question, Sannox Estate agreed the sale of 2.33 hectares at Ballarie Bridge for a sum which David Hutchison states as £12,000 on condition that if planning permission was denied, the land would simply revert to the estate. Now that the two main foundation stones – water and land – were in place the real work to make the distillery a reality could begin.

CHAPTER THREE

Not In My Back Yard!

FOR DAVID HUTCHISON the period from November 1991 into early 1992 was one of intense preparation and planning. In order to have the whole project taken seriously by all the interested parties, an 80-page, A3, landscape-format development proposal was prepared by Michael Hyde Associates for Isle of Arran Distillers Ltd and Highlands and Islands Enterprise which included input from Ronnie Anderson at quantity surveyors Poole Dick Associates and the original consulting engineers, Derick Sampson & Partners. The elevations and ground plans in the proposal show that the distillery buildings and the internal arrangement of plant differed from the all-under-one-roof layout that was eventually built in 1995. Similarly, the Visitor Centre (VC) and the sole warehouse were of markedly different design to the ones that were erected. On this basis the initial costs and estimates for the total build were put at a total of £1.422m with the breakdown as follows:

• Warehouse	£352,000	• Pump House	£2,500
• Distillery	£263,000	• Plant Installation	£7,500
• Visitor Centre	£445,000	• External Works	£206,000
• Yeast Store	£10,000	• Signage	£10,000
• Filling Store	£40,000	• Contingencies	£65,000
• Evaporation House	£21,000		

Following meetings in Inverness between Hal and Andrew Currie and HIE, the company failed to raise any interest in the project as the employee numbers

The original artwork rendering of the distillery created from the first set of plans in June 1992. *DHA*

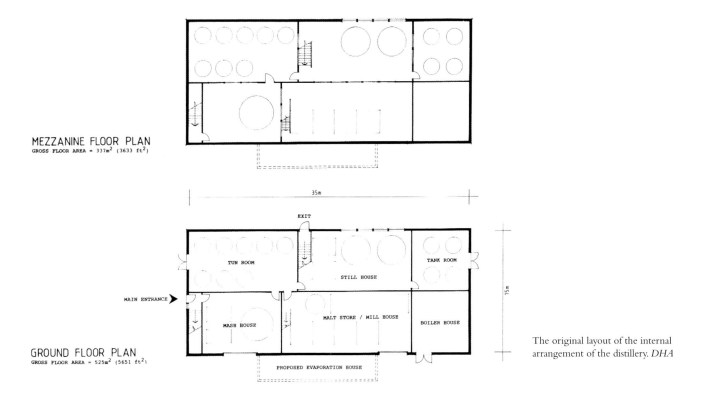

MEZZANINE FLOOR PLAN
GROSS FLOOR AREA = 337m² (3633 ft²)

35m

EXIT

TUN ROOM

STILL HOUSE

TANK ROOM

15 m

MAIN ENTRANCE ▶

MASH HOUSE

MALT STORE / MILL HOUSE

BOILER HOUSE

GROUND FLOOR PLAN
GROSS FLOOR AREA = 525m² (5651 ft²)

PROPOSED EVAPORATION HOUSE

The original layout of the internal
arrangement of the distillery. *DHA*

promised were not great enough.[1] The samples that had been taken from the Easan Biorach burn at the point where the distillery would draw its process water were analysed at the laboratories of RR Tatlock & Thomson at 156-160 Bath Street, Glasgow. The full certification dated 1 June 1992 was also published in the proposal document. The news was good … it was perfect water for making whisky.

Once completed and revised the build costs were estimated at around £1.5m with £600k of that being the cost for the distilling plant, the rest being structure.

Armed with the plans and costs, the company began a series of meetings with what was then Cunninghame District Council (CDC). The response was not wholly enthusiastic, but it was not a 'no' so Hal and David kept moving the project forward.

In the meantime Hal, Andrew and Paul Currie worked on the financing options for the project. Hal also spent time contacting colleagues and friends in the whisky industry to bounce his ideas off and generate feedback. The first way of raising finance, the Arran Bondholder scheme, would be a binding contract between the company and a Bondholder whereby the latter purchased an option to buy whisky

[1] Later some funding would be forthcoming from HIE for the VC and subsequent warehousing.

R. R. TATLOCK & THOMSON
ANALYTICAL & CONSULTING CHEMISTS
MINERAL SAMPLERS
PUBLIC ANALYSTS LABORATORY

Partners
J. W. GRAY, M.Inst.E., C.Chem., F.R.S.C.
D. F. WITHINGTON, B.Sc., M.Chem.A., C.Chem., F.R.S.C.

Registered Office:
156-160 BATH STREET
GLASGOW G2 4SX

Telephone: 041 - 332 0491
FAX: 041-332-6164

Registered Number 2245 (Scotland)

Michael Hyde and Associates,
RWF House,
5 Renfield Street,
Glasgow G2 5EZ.

Our Ref:1475
Received:26.5.92
Date:1st June 1992

Lochranza Distillery, Isle of Arran, Easan Biorach Burn, Lochranza

Appearance	normal	pH	6.1
Odour	none	Conductivity	
Colour, mg/L Pt/Co scale	5	(as uS/cm)	53

MILLIGRAMS PER LITRE

Oxidisability	3.6	Magnesium	1.5
Free Ammonia (as NH_3)	0.06	Iron	0.05
Sulphate (as SO_4)	8	Zinc	0.05
Fluoride	0.2	Copper	nil
Chloride	16	Manganese	0.03
Nitrate	0.3	Lead	nil
Nitrite	nil	Aluminium	0.03
Alkalinity	10	Potassium	0.4
Total Hardness (as $CaCO_3$)	10	Sodium	6.5
Calcium	1.6		

The results of analysis show that the amounts of the chemical constituents
determined satisfy the requirements of the Water Supply (Water Quality)
(Scotland) Regulations 1990.

R. R. Tatlock & Thomson

R. R. TATLOCK & THOMSON
ANALYTICAL & CONSULTING CHEMISTS
MINERAL SAMPLERS
PUBLIC ANALYSTS LABORATORY

Partners
J. W. GRAY, M.Inst.E., C.Chem., F.R.S.C.
D. F. WITHINGTON, B.Sc., M.Chem.A., C.Chem., F.R.S.C.

Registered Office:
156-160 BATH STREET
GLASGOW G2 4SX

Telephone: 041 - 332 0491
FAX: 041-332-6164

Registered Number 2245 (Scotland)

Michael Hyde and Associates,
RWF House,
5 Renfield Street,
Glasgow G2 5EZ.

Our Ref:1476
Received:26.5.92
Date:1st June 1992

Lochranza Distillery, Isle of Arran, Easan Biorach Burn, Lochranza

Number of Organisms per 1ml capable of growing on Agar at 22°C in 3 days	6	Probable number of coliform bacilli per 100 ml. 0
Number of Organisms per 1ml capable of growing on Agar at 37°C in 1 day	0	E. Coli 0

The bacteriological results are satisfactory.

R. R. Tatlock & Thomson

The water analysis of the Easan Biorach as supplied by Tatlock & Simpson, June 1992. *DHA*

from the distillery in the future at an agreed price which would result in major savings on the market price at the time of supply. In early July 1992 leaflets were dropped through the letterboxes of Arran residents informing them of the Bondholder scheme and asking anyone interested merely to register that interest. David Hutchison recalls that he and his wife spent a lot of time driving around Arran, dropping them off at boarding houses, hotels, pubs and anywhere else they could think of. The offer was pitched to the locals at a discounted £400 per bond to secure five cased dozens of blended Scotch at five years and the same volume of single malt at eight years of age. The costs of bottling, customs and excise duty and VAT were to be added at the rates current at the time of exercising the option. The *Banner* reported that market research about establishing a distillery on Arran had been undertaken and this revealed that 'people not only think it is a good idea, but would be prepared to invest in it'. At this point, Hal Currie stated publicly that there would be an official launch in September but there was still no certainty that the distillery would be built.

In the *Banner* of 28 July 1992, the editorial leader began to get to grips with what

Clyde River Purification Board

Director: Desmond Hammerton FRSE

Our Ref: RK/SM/T47-A   If calling please ask for: Mr Kerr

Your Ref: EF/YB   3 June 1992

Derick Sampson and Partners
Consulting Engineers
Doges Palace
Templeton Business Centre
62 Templeton Street
Glasgow
G40 1DA

Dear Sirs

Proposed Isle of Arran Malt Distillery, Lochranza

I refer to your letter of 1 May 1992 requesting an indication of the consent levels for two possible discharge volumes arising from the proposed distillery at Lochranza. Following your letter, Mr Frazer in discussion with Mr Kerr asked that the consent levels be calculated for a discharge to the Chalmadale Water instead of the Easan Biorach as this latter watercourse has an emergency pumping facility used by the Water Department should there be problems at their high level intake.

From low flow estimates for both the Easan Biorach and Chalmadale Water and taking account of the water abstracted for public supply, the volume available for dilution in the Chalmadale Water downstream of the Easan Biorach confluence is approximately 23 litres/second. Therefore the probable dilution factor for the two possible discharge volumes into the Chalmadale Water is as follows:-

Spent lees and wash water discharge of 0.2 litres/sec = 115:1

Pot ale, spent lees and wash water discharge of 0.58 litres/sec = 39:1

The long term water quality data we have on the Chalmadale Water indicates that the quality is excellent and of course my Board would require that any discharge would not give rise to a significant deterioration in quality. In addition, in calculating the likely consent levels we have assumed that cooling water will be recycled and only small quantities of water will be required for make up purposes.

Based on the above we would probably impose conditions as indicated below:-

Suspended solids = 60 mg/l

Biochemical Oxygen Demand = 40 mg/l

pH = 5 to 9

Temperature = not greater than 20°C or incremental on stream background

Rivers House, Murray Road, East Kilbride, Glasgow G75 0LA   Tel. East Kilbride (03552) 38181   Fax. (03552) 64323
District   2, Alloway Place, Ayr. KA7 2AA   Tel. Ayr (0292) 264047   Fax. (0292) 611130
Offices 45, Chalmers Street, Ardrishaig, PA30 8EY   Tel. Lochgilphead (0546) 602876   Fax. (0546) 602337

2

Copper - we have no background levels for the receiving watercourse but conditions would be imposed to keep the level within the required environmental quality standard for fresh water of 5µg/l dissolved copper.

I should also point out that depending on the timescale of the developments and the discharge volume it is possible that the discharge may qualify in terms of the EC Municipal Waste Water Directive 1991 in terms of population equivalent for identified industrial discharges as specified in the Directive.

The discharge will of course require my Board's formal consent in terms of the Control of Pollution Act 1974. The application for consent will be advertised for public comment in accordance with Section 36 of the Act and the Board would take account of any valid representations received on the proposed discharge. For your information I attach the relevant application form.

If you feel a meeting would be helpful to discuss the proposal please contact Mr Kerr or Mr Livingstone at Ayr.

Yours faithfully

Divisional Inspector (South)

Enc

The Clyde River Purification Board's requirements regarding effluent discharge sent to the original consulting engineers Derick Sampson & Partners, June 1992. *DHA*

was being proposed and felt that while the offer was 'very attractive' it also wondered if the successful sales of Bonds would be the sole means of funding the distillery. It was a perceptive analysis because the Bonds were indeed the only funding vehicle being made public by the Curries at that time. If the distillery was to be purely locally funded, they would need to sell almost 4,000 Bonds at £400 each to begin the match the funding costs of £1.5m and as the entire population of Arran was not far off that figure, it was clear that a more professional, widespread and properly funded marketing plan would be required. In any event,

the company soon lodged their formal planning application on 29 July 1992 and this was registered by CDC on 3 August.

It is after this date that the reaction to the plans began to manifest itself amongst the Arran community and the spectre of 'nimbyism' rose to cast a shadow over the project for the next ten months. The first indication of how some felt on the island was when a petition was organised by Mrs Lorna Halliburton of Lochranza who wanted to get a discussion going, while stressing that she was not taking sides. However, the 60 petitioners who had signed, the *Banner* claimed, 'did not like these implications'. Three main areas of concern were recorded. First, it was claimed that the Easan Biorach burn had some septic tank effluent in it. Second, that there was a lack of water pressure in Lochranza 'at times', and third that 'distillery smells' would waft over the village. Jim Lees responded.

That is the reason we went about it in the manner we did. We felt the people of Arran and Lochranza should know. Almost a year ago we went public. The general feeling from everyone I've spoken to is that it would be a great thing for the island … It was always going to be that some people who would be affected would be unhappy – the NIMBY factor if you like. I would doubt if anyone signing against is in business on the island and needs to rely on the economy of the island.

A week later a Lochranza resident, James M Lynch, described the proposed distillery as an 'environmental disaster' and that the 'beautiful and peaceful village of Lochranza could be destroyed overnight'.

In his regular 'Money Matters' page of the *Banner* of 22 August 1992, David Henderson, a Lochranza resident, in a well-considered article, decided the proposed distillery business might not be economically viable.

Up until now, I have deliberately avoided entering the debate over the proposed plan to construct a distillery at Lochranza, but before going any further I must admit to having a major interest in the venture. I would hasten to add that I have no involvement whatsoever with the group planning the project. No, I presently use the site as a practice golf range!

There is a considerable groundswell in Lochranza opposed to the development and I can understand and fully share the sentiments expressed, particularly the distillery-associated smell argument. On the other hand, from an employment point of view, we have been told that a number of jobs will be created but, on closer examination, it is likely that a high percentage of these jobs will have to be filled by those with experience of the industry rather than by taking on unskilled local labour which can then be trained up.[2] I understand that a similar situation developed in Lamlash with Arran Provisions.

From an economic point of view, there is little to justify the construction of a new distillery. At present, whilst whisky sales are reasonable buoyant, the industry is generally reducing output with a number of distilleries being offered for sale or, if no buyer can be found, being closed. The major producers are certainly not planning any new distilleries. It has been said that the Isle of Arran association will help to promote sales of a further island single malt but, as things stand at present, sales of other single malts such as Jura and Orkney's Highland Park are struggling and are certainly not sufficient to take all the output, the bulk of which continues to go in fillings for leading brands such as Grouse and Bell's. In addition, the marketing effort required to promote such brands is very considerable indeed and I would just question whether a start-up situation, which would obviously be struggling financially, would have the cash available to carry out much in the way of promotional marketing. It strikes me that substantial grants will no doubt be made available for such a construction but that, at the end of the day, the consortium would have no option but to look to sell on the distillery to another party within the industry who would then have the capacity and resources to utilise a high proportion, of the output, coupled with marketing the product as a single malt. On the subject of output, at this stage it is impossible to predict with any great accuracy what type of malt will be produced. It is unlikely to be the peaty malt of Islay, as I would have thought that the water quality at Lochranza was such that its greater purity would produce a product more akin to the Speyside output, but obviously only time will tell. The initial financial requirement to fund the project will be substantial and, the consortium's cash-flow problem will

---

[2] This proved not to be the case when operations began.

remain for at least three or four years until the quality of the output becomes clear, and only then can sales be made thus generating cash.

The project appears to have a long way to go before it gets off the ground.

His reflections must have made sanguine reading for Hal Currie unless he knew something about the proposed financing of the distillery that Henderson did not. In the event, now somewhat mobilised, a meeting of objectors was called for Monday 24 August at short notice and, not being advertised outside the village, no one from the distillery company was able to be there. Jim Lees had been asked to attend but stated that there wasn't any point in going. Over 40 people did attend, none of whom, the *Banner* reported, were in favour of the distillery. Joe Trickett, a former Lochranza postmaster, was in the chair and unwittingly became the punchbag for the objectors even though he appeared to sympathise with them. According to the plans that he had seen at Lamlash, he said that the distillery 'would dwarf other buildings in Lochranza'.[3] Mr Forbes Bramble, a non-resident, raised the point that if the distillery venture failed, a valid planning consent would be 'lurking on your back door for industrial use'. He then wondered if the motives of the company were not to build a malt whisky distillery at all, but 'a bulk grain distillery' instead.

The meeting continued with contributions from the floor which did little to clarify the situation and, to be fair, there was little clarification to be had due to the lack of firm information available. Concerns regarding the nature of any public financing of the project and the increase in heavy haulage on Arran's narrow northern roads were also voiced. Mrs Bramble asked for a show of hands to 'hold the thing up while a consultation meeting took place' which was unanimous. It was then agreed that Colin Siddle, newly arrived in the village but with an Arran family heritage, would front the village action group.

By 5 September Hal Currie and Jim Lees decided that a co-ordinated response was required not only to David Henderson's 'Money Matters' article, but also to

[3] The original plans were indeed for larger structures than were actually built.

the paper's questioning of Lees after the meeting as to why he had not bothered to attend. I quote Jim's response in full here as it reveals how measured and considered it was, delivered with a little characteristic humour.

Sir,

I feel I must comment on your article of last week headlined 'Lochranza says no'. On the question of my non-attendance at the meeting, may I say that it was my impression that it would be a protest meeting organised for those people in Lochranza who were opposing the proposed distillery. This impression may have been wrong. However it has been reinforced by the fact that the meeting was not publicised outside of the village. I saw no useful function in entering the lion's den without the benefit of fellow Christians.

I feel I should clarify my involvement in the distillery. I do not have, at present, a financial interest in the distillery. However I certainly do intend to purchase a bond, as I am greatly taken with the notion of ten cases of quality whisky quietly maturing, and awaiting my attention.

My involvement stems from the fact that David Hutchison, the project architect and a personal friend of long standing, asked if I could assist him with some local information. This I was delighted to do as I thought then, and even more so now, that the proposed distillery would be of great benefit to the economic wellbeing of the island. This benefit does not only come from the employment in the distillery, although that in itself would commend it, but also in the enhancement of the tourist product of Arran. Who can argue after last week's weather that another all-weather attraction on the island would not be welcome. Another Arran product, marketed outwith the island, would help raise the island's profile as sown by the success of Arran Provisions and Arran Aromatics.

In your article I am quoted as saying 'that the island view was in favour while the Lochranza view was against', but that I could provide no proof of the former. It is true that I do not carry signed petitions in favour on my person, however I can offer a few facts. At a meeting the company had with the then local councillor, the tourist board chairman, the tourism officer and the Local Enterprise Company representative, all were enthusiastic about the project. The fact that no island business refused to display the company leaflet and indeed many wished the project success. Also the many indications of support I have had personally throughout the island, including Lochranza.

I never said the Lochranza view was against. I said 'there was a view in Lochranza against', a subtle but important difference, however I do know that view is far from unanimous.

Which brings me to my main comment on last week's article, the headline 'Lochranza says no'. Since when does 40-odd people out of an electoral roll of 178 constitute a unanimous 'no' on behalf of the village. I spoke to one of the 40 who attended the meeting and found he actually supported the project. He voted with the others because the motion only asked for consultation, a not unreasonable request.

It must be said that not all the people at the meeting were on the electoral roll since a proportion of the objectors are owners of holiday houses. I have found, certainly in Corrie and Sannox, that the owners of second homes can add to the social and economic activity, and are an asset to the village. Many houses that may have fallen into disrepair have been saved by second homeowners. However I do feel that along with the privilege of owning a second home must go the responsibility of knowing that local people are entitled to an economic livelihood.

James Lees, Sannox

Likewise, Hal Currie's response to David Henderson's comments is reproduced here in full.

Sir,

It is always interesting to read David Henderson's Money Matters column but I must take issue with him over some inaccuracies in his comments on the proposed new distillery at Lochranza, many of which are simply based on conjecture.

As Managing Director of the company planning to set up the distillery, I am aware of opposition to it from some quarters in the village, but on the other hand a large number of Arran residents including a good proportion of people living in Lochranza have not only signified their support, but have expressed an interest in being involved in the enterprise.

I note that Mr Henderson practises golf on the proposed site and I wonder whether his comments have been coloured somewhat by the possible loss of this facility, whereas he should perhaps, as an impartial observer, be more concerned about the wider issues such as the prospect of additional employment on the island.

The only job to be filled from outside Arran will be that of an experienced manager, otherwise the entire workforce will be recruited locally.

I am sure that most people would agree that the smell from a distillery (generally very much localised within the immediate vicinity), is not at all unpleasant and in any case, because of the prevailing wind, the village would not be very affected, if at all.

There are no distilleries for sale in Scotland at the present time. On the contrary a number of distilleries have been reopened during the past two or three years,[4] reflecting the increasing demand in export markets for Scotch whisky and particularly for single malt whisky, for which there continues to be a strong consumer interest.

A new malt whisky from Arran can only benefit this trend and our

[4] Linkwood reopened in 1990 as did Deanston and Ben Nevis.

intention is to concentrate on production and bottling of single malt at the distillery rather than selling to other sectors of the industry for blending, and this plan will of course create many jobs in the future.

With many years of experience in the whisky industry as Managing Director of Chivas Brothers and House of Campbell, and now a consultant in the trade, I know full well that we cannot expect to immediately penetrate the market with our own branded single malt, but I can assure Mr Henderson that the company will have a number of other contributions to a positive cash flow. We have no intention of selling out to a larger company. The new distillery has a robust business case and I would not even consider the proposals unless I was convinced that it was a viable project.

I do however agree with Mr Henderson as to the likelihood of the whisky's quality. The purity of the water is indeed exceptional and the geological surveys very favourable. The ideal conditions at the site convince me and others in the industry that Lochranza will become the home to one of Scotland's truly great malts, and that can only be good for the Isle of Arran.

Harold Currie, Mauchline

The reaction to Jim Lees' letter was somewhat bizarre in that a letter published a week later in the *Banner* was from a regular visitor to Arran, a Mrs L Goodwill from Yorkshire, whose line was very much a case of, 'Just who does he think he is?' She stated categorically that if the distillery went ahead, 'we will no longer be visiting Arran, because to us, it just wouldn't be the same. The same feeling applies amongst our family and friends too … after all it is only going to create about twelve jobs isn't it? Not exactly John Major's answer to dramatically reducing the dole queue!' She then prosecuted an argument that the distillery would create a loss of revenue from tourism by revealing that her family's ostracising of the island would lose it £4,000 a year. If other tourists followed suit, she concluded, '… well, it speaks for itself, doesn't it?' She summed up:

Lastly a suggestion to Mr Lees and his friends. Why don't you go to Glasgow or Bradford or somewhere, where there may be a grotty slum, just waiting to be bulldozed, and build your precious distillery there?

Unfortunately for Mrs Goodwill a response soon arrived at her home from an anonymous resident of Whiting Bay, much of the content of which she described in her next letter to the *Banner* of 19 September. The missive she had received was not kind to her and revealed a fair degree of not only anti-English feeling, but also anti-Yorkshire. The matter, it seemed, was getting a little bit out of hand. Coincidentally, on Friday 18 September, many Brodick residents received a leaflet through their letterboxes from Lochranza Action Group, quantities of which had, according to the *Banner*, apparently been photocopied by Joe Trickett.

Resident of Brodick
Do you realise that if
Lochranza Distillery
Is built, you will be treated to:
30 ton Grain delivery Trucks
30 ton Fuel Oil delivery trucks
30 ton Sherry Casks Trucks
30 ton Smelly Draff Trucks
5 ton Smelly Draff Trailers
leaking Draff Ale thro' village
ALL DAY LONG!

The editor suggested that 'no campaign is likely to benefit from such hyperbole', before humouring the readers with … 'But then, perhaps we are being naïve.'

Hal Currie was quick off the mark and managed to get a response in before the paper went to press. The traffic would actually amount to one malt and barley truck per fortnight, one fuel truck per fortnight and one lorry-load of casks every three weeks, he stated. Draff would be collected by local farmers to feed to cattle and pot ale would be used as fertiliser, replacing some fertilisers currently shipped from the mainland.

In the same issue another letter from a Mr G Febry of North Nibley, Gloucestershire, declared that the £400 Bond would not be a sound investment, but it took him 13 long paragraphs to say so, concluding with a heartfelt declaration that 'the planning authority for Arran must be bonkers to allow such a development in so lovely an area. I really feel it is a criminal act'.

Meanwhile pen and ink were being readied amongst the naysayers in the village and much valuable time taken up preparing letters for the *Banner* editor's scrutiny. It was a daunting task but the issue of 26 September allowed voice to Mr Bert Gratton, whose holiday home at Ballarie Bridge would abut the distillery site and be, quite literally, in *his* back yard. This letter is possibly the longest I have ever come across in a Scottish community newspaper filling almost six columns over one-and-a-half pages of A4 format and I do not intend the reader to suffer it in full, but given that the distillery would be built beside him, his understandable concern, far from being considered and objective, betrayed a mindset that was having none of it, no matter what. He did attempt to cloak his abhorrence of the distillery by trying to deal with a number of issues, namely Jim Lees and the nimby factor, water requirements, effluent disposal, draff disposal, transport requirements, sherry casks, malted barley, Scots Whisky Association [sic], financial considerations, conservation and finally 'the development'. To précis his arguments, the gist of them was as follows:

Jim Lees: *He was right, it's Not In His Back Yard it's In Mine!*

Water: there would never be enough and a holding tank of 200,000 gallons capacity would be required. Furthermore, the water authority would need to build a dam and the cost would be passed on to the ratepayers.

Effluent: A foul-smelling green slime would pervade the burn to the head of the loch. *This will be the FRONT yard to avoid in years to come.*

Draff: It will degrade after a few hour's exposure to the sun, become 'viciously rancid' and will leak all over the island as an 'evil swill' from the draff trucks. *'Not in my backyard, eh!' No, in everybody's backyard and back kitchen too!*

Transport: The 'thunder' of the trucks lurching from Brodick pier to Lochranza *ALL DAY LONG* would make *the relief of Mafeking … look like a nursery rhyme.*

Sherry casks: Mr Gratton was convinced the casks would arrive as staves and a cooperage would need to be built. *The smoke, the smell and noise of an efficient Cooperage is not for the faint-hearted. 'Not in my back yard, eh!' Just in your hair, clothes, favourite moggy and food.*

Malted barley: Mr Gratton saw no evidence of a maltings plant in the site plans, ergo, the company must be building one somewhere else on the island. *Could this be a surprise for the people of Shiskine? Maybe a site beside a mustard factory in Lamlash would be more suitable as the smells associated with malted barley could be refreshed with the tang of Arran Mustard. 'Not in my backyard, eh!'*

The Scots Whisky Association [sic]: A rant that is too entertaining and revealing not to reproduce here.

The Scots are justifiably proud of their association with whisky as a part of their national heritage. I am puzzled at the level of indifference displayed when confronted by the possibility of an addition of another source of history. One would have thought that the immaculate conception of another fine son of Scotland would have the bagpipes skirlin', the flags flying and an open season at the haggis shoot. The truth is, sir, the Scots have no more need of a new whisky or more quantities of a product which is difficult to market now, and is less of an investment than a Post Office savings account. I think it is encumbant [sic] for the erstwhile directors of this charade to show us that their proposed entry into this market is welcomed by the Grants, Gordons and Invergordons of this land.[5]

Financial considerations: Mr Gratton asked some valid questions on how the

---

[5] I leave the informed reader to make of this misnomer what he or she will.

distillery would be financed while denigrating not only the concept of the Bond, but also ignoring the fact that the investors would not be left out of pocket, but have an option to purchase 10 cases of blended and single malt Scotch at prices very much below the market value. He preferred to place £400 on deposit with the Post Office and get a £100 profit after eight years. Each to his own.

Conservation: He asked why Sannox Estate, whom the author considered that *last bastion of conservation*, would allow *a 73 foot high, Tesco-type spire, together with monstrous warehouse blocks obliterating the beautiful backdrop behind Lochranza* challenging Charles Fforde to *deny the developers the opportunity of ruining our glen, by refusing to sell them the land*. Little did Mr Gratton know that the estate, according to David Hutchison, did not have high expectations that planning permission would be approved.

The Development: A proposition that Hal Currie had concealed the Lochranza location for 30 years after Arran had been investigated by *a well-known Scots Whisky Distiller* in 1961 and discounted. He concluded:

No, Mr Currie, you might be able to fool some people, but you do not fool me, and thank God you do not fool the good people of Lochranza. The whisky community might be prepared to sit back and laugh but I can assure you the only laughs that you will hear will be the echoing from Lochranza Hall on the night we hold the celebration dance. I am glad you have had the foresight to omit my cottage from the Elevation Drawing of your Project as I can assure you that your distillery will never feature on the landscape of Lochranza.

Given the extensive space that the *Banner* gave over to Mr Gratton, Hal Currie had no option but to reply quickly and the paper permitted a similar amount of leverage to allow him to do so. A letter from him and a full response was published on 3 October which dealt with Mr Gratton's concerns. In his opening paragraphs, Hal tried to allay a general assumption many had made:

Distilleries are not anything like huge factories belching out noxious fumes as one or two of your correspondents from England seem to have implied; on the contrary they are generally well designed to blend in with their rural settings and most people regard the aroma (which is generally confined to the building) to be very pleasant.

Water: On the basis of 250,000 litres of spirit production, the claim that a 900,000-litre (200,000 gallons) holding tank would be required was not true. No dam would be required to be built either. Furthermore, the distillery supply would be downstream from where the local public supply was taken.

Effluent: Stating that Clyde River Purification controls and future EC legislation would be adhered to, Hal Currie explained that a treatment plant to convert effluent to animal feed was planned. He suggested Mr Gratton asked the fishermen on Speyside and the residents of Islay and Jura if they had any knowledge of his green slime.

Draff: Dismissing Gratton's description of rancid, leaking draff trucks as 'derogatory' and a 'figment of his imagination', Hal Currie stated there would be a maximum of one farm tractor load every two days in the first few years, rising to two per day at full capacity.

Transport: To make 250,000 litres of spirit a year, the distillery would require one 20-ton truck of malted barley every fortnight, one fuel road tanker per fortnight and one 20-ton cask transport every three weeks. Increased production would result in proportionate increases in transport. There would be no cooperage as the distillery was too small to justify it.

Malted barley: Hal Currie reiterated that this would be shipped from the mainland. No maltings plant would be built.

Scotch Whisky Association: *Mr Gratton is regrettably becoming more supercilious as his letter goes on.*

Financial considerations: *He has also missed the point regarding the concept. My colleagues and I will be investing substantially from our own funds in the project, so reflecting our utmost commitment and confidence in the viability of the enterprise.*

Conservation: *To refer to a 'well-known distiller' having considered the viability of a distillery on Arran in 1961 and relate it to the situation prevailing in 1992 is ludicrous … the fact is that I have been working on the project for only 18 months.*

If the cavalry from the ranks of the silent majority on Arran had not yet arrived to assist the company, at least Janet Primrose of the Lochranza Store did put forward some more moderate comments the following week on 9 October.

Sir,

Without going into the pros and cons of the Lochranza Distillery it has struck me that the writers so strongly against the Distillery may not on the whole be well acquainted with the rest of Scotland.

As a child I was taken all over Scotland and distilleries pointed out with pride as places helping to maintain the economy not only of Scotland but also of beautiful spots in which they were situated. This is why the first paragraph of Mr Hal Currie's article struck me as so very true.

After all you don't have to look in history books but can hear first hand of a thriving Lochranza with 5 steamers a day, several shops (amazingly!), and of course the famous Lochranza Dances of not-so-long-ago. You can ask several of the present inhabitants.

We do not differ from other small beautiful villages in that a local employer of even a few people can make for a balanced population and a viable economy within the village.

The next month was taken up with the Curries, David Hutchison and their team preparing for a public meeting in Lochranza to gauge the reaction of the local community. This was held at the village hall on the evening of Friday 6 November 1992 and was attended by around 90 people, just over half the electoral role in the village. With Sam Gooding of CDC Planning Department in the chair, he stated at the outset that he would brook no nonsense and deny interjections.

'Everybody's educated,' he said.

Hal Currie started with a little attempted flattery saying that the best whisky in Scotland must have come from Arran, 'because the best people come from Arran'. It fell flat. He moved on and put the economic case for the distillery assisted by David Hutchison and consultant engineer Ewen Fraser. Hutchison dealt with some of the design issues and did mention that the Sannox site had been looked at but discounted. Ewen Fraser concerned himself with environmental matters and the effluent issue. When Gooding opened the discussion to the floor, the spokesman for the objectors, Colin Siddle, stated that they had no objection to a distillery, simply to the site proposed. He then asked if the site could be used for another purpose, should the application be approved. Rob Lonie, planning director, said no and that any other use would require further planning permission.

John Lowe returned to the issue of the Sannox site. What was wrong with it? David Hutchison replied that the Sannox burn had a lead seam across it and that the water was not so good. Lowe then claimed that the Easan Biorach burn also had a lead seam running across it? 'I'm told there isn't,' said Hutchison. 'I'm told there is,' said Lowe.

Mrs May Lowe asked that the Sannox site be reconsidered to shouts of 'Hear, hear!' and was followed by Joe Trickett who asked as to why recent changes in the plans (a reduction from six warehouses to one and its height reduced as well) had not been communicated to the objectors? Were the goalposts being moved? Other matters were raised covering the smell, the road access and fire cover. 'Fires in a distillery are almost unheard of. Fire risk is minimal,' Hal Currie stated, to which someone responded from the floor, 'Mr chairman, the *Titanic* was unsinkable.' Ewen Fraser recalls that, 'some of the objectors were convinced that there would be acrid, black smoke belching from the distillery chimney and that the effluent would smell. I assured them that their fears were unjustified, but the atmosphere early on was not good.'

Rob Lonie then confirmed that the access and narrow bridge at Ballarie Farm next door to the site were acceptable to Strathclyde Roads Department, a contention that drew 'gasps of disbelief'. The *Banner*'s reporter then felt that, as the 'questions hotted up', Hal Currie 'was clearly wilting a little under the opposition. With 'a mixture of anger and sadness in his voice' he appealed to the meeting, 'We're not some monsters imposing on you some unattractive development'. But then something happened. The *Banner* again:

> And then, quite suddenly, when it was least expected, it all changed.
> A Mrs McMillan [*sic*] spoke. She said she loved Arran and Lochranza.
> She wanted to stay there and her children to stay there but they could not
> do so without jobs. Mr John Neil whose previous question had appeared to
> be against said he just sought information and was not against it. There was
> a clap from the rear. Hal Currie said the jobs would be for local people.
> 'This is where we are going to get the best people.' And even he got a clap.

David Hutchison recalled that episode in more comic terms. 'Things were really not going well until a "wee wumman" stood up and got stuck into everyone. She had children growing up on the island and wanted to make sure they had a future and the distillery would do nothing but good for Arran.'

The 'wee wumman' in question was actually Diane McMullan who was married to John and had three school-age children. John was to become one of the first of the original distillery employees.

Andrew Currie also recalled that one of the objectors had asked the question, '*Why* Lochranza?' But Diane McMullan had got back at them with, 'Why *not* Lochranza?' 'That got everybody clapping,' David recalled, 'and she encouraged others to get up and speak out.' Iain Johnston of the Auchrannie Hotel contributed from the rear of the hall.

> I would like to support Mr Currie in what he's just said and to say that the
> Isle of Arran Tourist Board is very much in favour of this project. I've spent
> a lot of my working life in distilleries and most of the objections in the

David Hutchison reviewing his archival material of the original distillery plans, January 2016. *Neil Wilson*

Banner are totally spurious. Many of my guests tell me that Arran is now considered rather run down. People like Mr Currie should be encouraged.

This brought a loud round of applause and many of the objectors decided enough was enough and started to leave the hall. The *Banner* reported that this was the moment when, 'The tide had turned.'

Joe Trickett, 'obviously saddened at the turn of events, indicated some distaste that he (as a member of the Tourist Board) was being told that he now supported it'. Sam Gooding decided that only one further question would be allowed and someone asked what he could expect to get in the VC. Gooding replied in a drôle manner, 'A dram to start with!' The *Banner* concluded that, notwithstanding various environmental considerations that still required to be addressed, 'It now seems likely that a distillery will be built at Lochranza and that Arran will, in the future, be providing its own dream dram.'

The planning committee returned to the mainland and four days later on the 10 November 1992 determined that the application had to be referred to the Scottish Office under the terms of the Town and Country Planning Direction (Scotland) 1987, due to the fact that consultation with Scottish Natural Heritage (SNH) was required 'about certain types of development which would affect a National Scenic Area'. The Direction also required councils to notify the Secretary of State about any planning applications which SNH had advised against granting.

In the meantime the objectors had regrouped and were carrying on the fight. The *Banner* of 21 November carried another letter from James M Lynch of Lochranza.

Sir,
Anyone reading your report of the recent meeting in Lochranza hall, regarding the proposal to erect a malt whisky distillery at Gleann Easan Biorach, might be forgiven for concluding that the majority of those present were in favour of the project. Nothing could be further from the truth.

Your reporter's assessment of the mood of the audience was obviously clouded by her/his enthusiasm to see this assault on the environment materialise. I feel sure that had your reporter had a new bungalow built near the entrance to Gleann Easan Biorach, as several people have, then a different reaction would be evident. These folk, after a lifetime in the hurly-burly of the industrial mainland, were looking forward to a retirement of peace and tranquillity. What a slap in the face! I think it was very unfair of Sannox Estate to sell the ground for a distillery in the proximity of plots that they had recently sold for house building.

To return to the meeting … from the start, the pedantic attitude of the chairperson, who headed a substantial entourage from Cunninghame, made it clear that no angry interruptions, however justified, would be tolerated. This resulted in a subdued reaction among the dissenters in the assembly. The whole atmosphere of the meeting suggested that the plans for a distillery had already received the 'go ahead' and the meeting was just to 'put a face on things' … a cosmetic exercise and of course a nice little junket for councillors and officials.

Local democracy received a 'kick in the pants'. The objections of seventy-five per cent of Lochranza householders were studiously ignored. Speakers from far and away places like Brodick, Shiskine and Machrie, thought a distillery would be a great idea … isn't that cheek for you? Not in my backyard Jock but in Lochranza's front garden. There were irrelevant discussions about the height of the proposed complex. The fact is, the caring people of Lochranza don't care what height the walls are … they just don't care if it's made of gold and studded with precious stones, they don't care if it rivals the Taj Mahal … they just don't want an industrial complex in their midst.

The old argument about jobs is of course trotted out. A maximum of ten labouring situations is promised. What a price to pay for the destruction of a scenic gem that has existed since the beginning of time. A mother spoke about jobs for her children; quite understandably but what parent would condemn their siblings to a life of drudgery in a whisky distillery, with all the risk of them developing into alcoholics.

The Isle of Arran is not really a place for industrial development. It is, in all truth, a Geriatric Nirvana. It is a nice place to be born, a nice place to go to school and a nice place to die. In between it's a nice place to leave and come back to for your holidays!

His views received stern ripostes from three Arran residents, one of whom was 'on a once in a lifetime trip' in Australia at the time. Mr Lynch's last paragraph clearly had Hazel Mackenzie of Kings Cross annoyed. In the *Banner* of 28 November she replied: *Just who does he think he is … who does he think is running all the businesses, staffing shops etc on this island?* After berating him further she concluded:

I am one of the lucky ones. I have a job and a home here but I have many friends who have had to leave the island. I am also a true native of the island and have as much right to an opinion as all the incomers that think they can come to this island and run it to suit their needs.

Mrs Main McAllister of Lochranza continued the theme, questioning Mr Lynch's assertions that 75% of the village's residents objected to the distillery and that Arran was no place to spend one's entire life.

How dare Mr Lynch suggest that after schooling the young should leave until retirement age. Agreed, that is the choice many willingly take, many not so willingly. Who gave Mr Lynch the authority to suggest what path should be taken?

As for a job in the distillery being a life of drudgery, perhaps Mr Lynch thinks a life on the dole would be preferable, a job is often what you make it and if it gave some people the choice of whether or not to leave the island I think they might see things rather more differently than Mr Lynch.

And from Tamara, New South Wales, Graham Dobson sent a letter that the *Banner* published on 5 December.

I was utterly appalled at Mr Lynch's letter which refers to 'these people after a lifetime in the hurly burly of the industrial mainland were looking to a retirement of peace and tranquillity. What a slap in the face!' Sir, I ask you, a slap in the face for whom? I have been away from Arran for nearly a month now, has so much happened that people no longer need jobs? Mr Lynch refers to 'a mother who spoke about jobs for her children' and then in the stroke of a pen asked 'what parent would want their sibling to work in a distillery and risk becoming an alcoholic?' Mr Lynch seems to have dismissed the fact that a fair percentage of local tradesmen and their apprentices (parent/child) would be used in construction of such an installation, not to mention the haulage of the materials which could benefit such companies as Arran Haulage, Thomson's, etc. He also refers to a maximum of labouring situations. Well to me that is 10 more jobs for people who perhaps don't just view or feel for Arran 'as a nice place to be born, a nice place to go to school and a nice place to die. In between it's a nice place to leave and come back to for your holidays.'

The same issue of the *Banner* reported that the objections of SNH, the final hurdle for the company in the planning process, meant that the Secretary of State, the Rt Hon Ian Lang, would determine whether it was an issue for his office or was to be decided purely at the local council level. The council planners had already given approval if SNH had no objections. The local councillor for Lochranza, Tom Knox, stated, 'I have made myself clear. I voted as an Arran councillor. I've every sympathy for the views of Lochranza, but I felt it was a good thing for Arran and I voted for it.'

A week later Iain M Roberston of Lochranza Golf explained the real crux of the matter from the point of view of the local community.

… it is clear Lochranza needs something of a boost. Is a distillery the best it can expect? Should the decision be made simply upon the objectives of the proposal, or should it be made in the interests of the village? As one who has a particular history of Lochranza may I plead with those who have an interest in, for, or against the distillery to take very great care to ensure that Lochranza gets what is right for Lochranza. The people, indigenous and incomer alike, are merely custodians of the village but, as such, they have a responsibility to its future as well as its past. Many people must decide if Lochranza Distillery is to be part of the future and, if so, they must plan carefully how it is to fulfil that promise RIGHT from the START.

At a meeting on 17 December SNH decided to sustain their objections regarding the impact of the National Scenic Area (NSA) and the proximity of breeding golden eagles and the decision was therefore removed from the local planning committee to the office of the Secretary of State. Neil McGillivray of SNH also preferred that the developers find another site on the island. Jim Lees was upset at the decision and said, 'This site was the result of a careful scientific decision about where the best water was.' He also felt that any further delays to the project might mean the cancelling of the project. At the end of January 1993 councillor Tom Knox stated that, 'They seem to be spending an awfully long time on something that is fairly straightforward.' By the end of February the Secretary of State decided no public enquiry was required and sent the application back to CDC. However, he also ordered that a full environmental assessment needed to be carried out by CDC 'in terms of EU regulations'. CDC challenged this on a legal basis stating that such a delay would probably mean the end of the project.

For David Hutchison, there was an end of another kind at this time as Michael Hyde & Associates decided to close their Scottish office and he struck out on his own, as a sole practitioner, in January 1993, taking the Arran project with him and moving to a third-floor office at 72 Waterloo Street, Glasgow, as David Hutchison & Associates (DHA). The success of his practice was to be founded not only on the

The distillery location looking towards Ballarie Bridge in 1992. *DHA*

Bert Gratton's holiday home which abutted the proposed site of the distillery, 1992. *DHA*

Lochranza distillery project, but forthcoming commissions for Ken McCulloch's Malmaison boutique hotels in Glasgow and Edinburgh. He also began to rethink the design of the distillery. He was adamant about one thing: 'I wanted everything under one roof, all the processes in the same space, not strung out in separate areas.' That meant any future visitors to the distillery would see every process from mashing, through fermentation to distilling in one room, something which Strathclyde Regional Council fire authority was not initially agreeable to, although they certified the arrangement in the end.

For the next five months the project was in limbo with the company unable to take anything forward. However, on Friday 7 May, Ian Lang visited Arran and attended the Conservative and Unionist Association's annual afternoon tea at which he fielded questions on many matters related to Arran excepting anything regarding the distillery. The following Monday his office withdrew the demand for the full environmental assessment and on Tuesday the planning committee approved the application in full, formally registering it on 19 May 1993. Hal Currie's immediate comment was, 'It's all systems go.'

Ironically, just after Lang left the island, a golden eagle was discovered dead by two Brodick walkers on the Bouguille in the north of the island. It was thought that there were only two breeding pairs on the whole island at the time and poisoning was a possibility. In just over a year's time other eagles would play their part in the beginning of the distillery. From this point forward, the main challenge was to raise the finance to make the project a reality.

Colin Siddle commented in February 2016 on his part in the community objection to the distillery proposals.

I was approached by a few elderly people, some of whom I had known for a long time, living in the vicinity of the proposed building. They were concerned about the impact it would have on themselves and their properties. Effluent, noise and the size of the structure were their main worries. I attended a meeting, along with other objectors and supporters, arranged by the local council and the proposers. It seemed, at the time, that the objectors held very little sway and planning permission would be granted irrespective. I believe that we managed to extract a promise that effluent would be negligible and nothing would be done that could be considered detrimental to the village. This was a long time ago and my memory is not as sharp as it was. In hindsight I now believe our fears were unfounded, however, it seemed the right thing to do at the time. The distillery has proved to be an asset for the village and, indeed, for the island as a whole. Visitors to the distillery have spent time and money in many other places around the island which can only be beneficial to the local economy.

CHAPTER FOUR

Capital Ideas

IT HAD ALWAYS BEEN AGREED amongst the Curries that if the building of the distillery was approved then both Paul and Andrew would be actively involved in it. Paul agreed to quit his job at BP in Poland and return to become managing director of the project. Andrew was to be the marketing director and would begin to investigate the options for developing a visitor centre; with no money available to construct one from scratch, these were limited. Both of them would operate off-island from their respective bases in England.

In late July 1993 the Bondholder scheme was made public as a well-designed, landscape-format brochure, designed by Barrow Parkhill Associates Ltd of London, dropped through the letterboxes of respondents. The offer to subscribers was that a single payment of £450 would secure them six cases of blended Arran whisky after five years and a further six cases of single malt after eight, with all taxes, duty and shipping to be paid at the time of supply. The offer saved Bondholders £550 on the retail prices of the day. Anyone who purchased before 6 December also got a 10% discount, taking the price down to £405, so it was a very tempting offer for whisky enthusiasts.

On the rear of the offer form were 13 clauses that constituted the 'Terms and conditions of Sale'. Needless to say, the solicitors earned their fees during this part of the process, but they had to get it right, as a mistake at this stage might have endangered the whole project. Bondholders would also automatically be enrolled in the Arran Malt Whisky Society which would become the firm's mail-order means of creating revenue by selling other bottlings of Scotch as well as quality Arran provisions. However, in the event of the company failing to raise sufficient

I have spent a lifetime in the whisky industry and always, my dream was to create a new single malt.

I am now realising that dream here at Lochranza on the Isle of Arran, a place of clear water, clean air and striking beauty. Behind me lies the site of the distillery. Work on it started in 1994 with the first spirit off the still due to flow early in 1995.

Ours will be the first legal distillery on the island for over 150 years. Arran was once a major whisky producing centre, but the biggest proportion of its output was illegal. (The hills around here were alive with illicit stills until the Excise men finally put an end to them.)

Single malt whiskies are a wonderful – and wondrous creation. Ever since the first 'uisge beatha' (water of life) was produced in Scotland, every whisky has had its own unique and distinct character. Perhaps it is this that makes the romance and mystique of the single malt so appealing to so many people.

What can I tell you about our new whisky? Arran is known as 'Scotland in miniature', a combination of Highland, Lowland and Island. Our new whisky should also combine the exquisite tastes from all the whisky regions of Scotland, and with the quality of Arran's air and water, I'm confident that Isle of Arran will be one of Scotland's great malts. And it will be ready to savour in the year 2001.

As well as telling you about our new venture, the purpose of this brochure is to introduce you to our Arran Bonds. These have been a tremendous success since they were launched in the autumn of 1993 and demand has continued to surge.

The Bonds give you an opportunity to invest in our malt whisky, Isle of Arran Single Malt, and to be involved in our new distillery

from the beginning, as a member of our Isle of Arran Malt Whisky Society. You can buy a Bond, either on your own or with friends. (And what is good whisky for, if not sharing with friends.)

I have pleasure in inviting you today, to become one of our new Arran Bond holders.

CÉUD MÍLE
FÁILTE

A HUNDRED
THOUSAND WELCOMES

Harold Currie
Harold Currie
Chairman of Isle of Arran Distillers Ltd.
Former Managing Director of Chivas Brothers and
House of Campbell and former council member of the
Scotch Whisky Association.

The introductory page to the official Arran Bond offer brochure from July 1993. *Neil Wilson*

capital, Bondholders were assured that their money would be returned. The build costs were quoted as being £2.5m (including the purpose-built VC) and Hutchison was adamant that building would commence at the end of 1993 stating that, 'We're confident that the whole thing will be built in a oner.'

A national advertising campaign in the *Daily Telegraph* and *The Times* was soon to follow with associated PR. Once again Hal Currie was the front man for the campaign and in the press releases. Testimonials came from former industry heavyweights Jimmy Lang and Stewart McBain.

The target was to raise over £1m of the start-up costs required to commence operations. I was one of the respondents and decided to have a punt on the project, purchasing Arran Bondholder certificate number 0479 at the discounted price of £405. A further offer in January 1994 offered 'units' of single malt in 2001, a 'unit' being a case of 12 x 70cl bottles. Prices started at £75 a unit, reducing to £66 for the purchase of seven units or more. The saving equated to around £73 per case. This Bond also included membership of the Arran Malt Whisky Society.

However, even although the offer document expressly stated that the Bond solely

The accounting of the stock held for the Bondholders and the income from it was explained in the accounts for 1995 as:

Bonds are contracts between the company and for the delivery of specified quantities of whisky at a specified future date. The arrangements are administered by the Isle of Arran Malt Whisky Society on behalf of the Bondholders. Money received from the sale of Bonds is credited to an Isle of Arran Malt Whisky Society bank account, which is separately controlled by the Trustees of the Society.

On production of the malt whisky in immature form and its storage in separately identified casks, the Trustees make a payment to account from the Society to the Company's bank account. The Trustees retain sufficient funds to allow them to ensure that the contract with the Bondholder is capable of being fulfilled by the application of those funds.

The amount transferred from the Malt Whisky Society is recognised as a liability and treated as deferred income in the books of the Company.

The Company will recognise profit on the contract when whisky is delivered to the Bondholders.

represented an option to purchase future stocks of whisky, Mr HJ Gordon of Bearsden had a letter published in the *Banner* of 28 August 1993, which inadvertently confirmed this, by arguing that the mistaken impression most people had gained was that they would be investing in some sort of shareholding or part-ownership of the distillery. He felt that the Bondholder offer was therefore 'misleading'.

Jim Lees responded the next week in characteristically combative style. *If you invest in French wine Mr Gordon, it does not entitle you to a share of the vineyard.* He went on to make sure the nature of the scheme was crystal clear.

However, what Mr Gordon failed to tell us in his epistle was that the whisky purchased by the bond represented a saving of £549 over the current retail prices. I am sure that we who are partial to a dram will feel more than adequately compensated for our loss of interest on our £450 or £400 [*sic*] if purchased before 1st October [*sic*].

A confession: I was one of the islanders who put up £30 in prepurchasing the *Banner* all those years ago. I still get a wee glow when I read the *Banner* (except last week!) knowing I was one of the many who made its continuation possible. But I'll tell you something, it will not be a patch on the inner glow I will experience in 2001 when I sip the first of my Arran malt from the comfort of my rocking chair.

While the sales of Bonds gathered pace and David Hutchison sent out documents for tenders for the construction and installation of plant, there was a further delay in proceedings brought about by SNH. In order to allow the eagles in the area of the site to have an undisturbed breeding season, no construction or preparation of the site would be done between February and May 1994. Hal Currie stated that the overriding concern of the company was 'the need to preserve the environment and we don't want to upset the ecology of the island'.

In reality, the Curries were also dealing with a shortfall in financing so the delay was fortuitous as they were in no position to begin construction in the spring of that year. In the meantime DHA implemented a redesign of the distillery to reflect the financial situation. Those amended plans included the original design of the VC and a single warehouse of conventional design. They were submitted on 24 August by DHA to CDC Planning Department.

By the end of August 1994 the *Banner* confirmed that only £600,000 had been raised from the sale of Bonds and that the construction schedule had been revised stating that, 'we hear work will start next month on a smaller building'. The Curries' expectations had been that over £1m in start-up capital would have been raised by then, but, behind the scenes, Hal Currie had been making progress over the course of the past year to create a shareholder base that would properly finance the whole project.

Ross Peters, an acquaintance of Hal's through business and social contacts in the West of Scotland, now came into the funding picture and proved to be the crucial element in creating a broad shareholder base in the company. A Ford Trust Scholar and honours graduate in Natural Sciences from Cambridge University he began his professional career in his native Renfrewshire with the Rolls-Royce Aero Engine division at Hillington before moving on to the company's Derby and East Kilbride operations. His work in developing a parts monitoring system for stress analysis in aero engines has been a core factor in the airworthiness of the world's jetliners ever since. A spell at McLintock Moores & Murray was followed by a move into the world of finance when, in 1973, he joined fund managers Murray Johnstone where he was to spend the next 19 years. His understanding of electronic micro-circuitry and data systems allowed him to analyse the investment potential of emerging Silicon Valley companies and a fact-finding trip to California with chief executive Raymond Johnstone in 1983 was the start of the highly successful Murray Technology and Murray Electronics investment trusts, shares of which were traded on the main market of the London Stock Exchange

In 1994 Peters was headhunted by fund managers Greig Middleton and moved to Guernsey, where he built up a private client investment arm of £100m in 18 months. Peters was by that time aware of the Currie family's distillery project and their acute need for more capital investment so he invited Hal Currie out to Guernsey in the summer of 1994 to meet some potential investors, one of whom was Les Auchincloss, originally from Kilmarnock, who had made his fortune largely in industrial enzymes with Biocon Biochemicals of Cork, Ireland. In 1978 his company became a 30% shareholder in Biocon India and he eventually sold his interests in 1989 to Unilever. At that time Auchincloss was looking to invest in other ventures and distilling held an interest due to his previous ventures. Following that introduction Peters took on a finder's role over the next year to generate investment through the uptake of new share issues from a number of interested

Isle of Arran Distillers Ltd

Mr

Glasgow
G62

18 November 1993

Dear Mr

Thank you very much for your enquiry about our unique offer in the Scotch whisky market, the 'Arran Bond'.

For centuries the Isle of Arran was renowned for its malt whisky, but since the last distillery on the island closed down in the 1830's, the world of whisky connoisseurs has been unable to sample the product, once described as Scotland's finest malt.

Now at Lochranza, an Arran whisky is to be produced once again and through the Arran bond you will be able to share exclusively in this; not only in the Isle of Arran Malt but also in Lochranza blended whisky.

The Arran Bond is not only an opportunity to be involved with a distillery from its inception but also represents an outstanding saving in the cost of the Bondholders whisky. I attach an outline of how this saving is made up. You will see that at present rates you will save nearly £550.00 for an equivalent amount of whisky at today's retail prices. You do not need to take delivery of your whisky all at once; we would be happy to keep in store any number of your purchased cases for ca £2.50 per case per year, if you would like your whisky to age further.

I am also pleased to add that as you are one of the earliest to apply for the bond details, the price to you will be reduced by ten per cent to £405 if you purchase a bond before the 6th December 1993. This will ensure your bond is received before Christmas.

But the Arran Bond represents much more than just a financial saving. I invite you to look through the enclosed brochure and hope you will wish to share in our 'dream dram'.

Yours sincerely,

Andrew Currie
Bond Secretary

Head Office: 1 The Cross, Mauchline, Ayrshire KA5 5AB
Telephone: 0290 552282. Fax: 0290 550177
London Office: Telephone: 071-731 3425. Fax: 071-736 9454
Directors: Harold Currie, David Hutchison
Registered No. 134963 Scotland. Registered Office: as above.

Prospective Bondholders received letters such as this from Andrew Currie after the offer was formally launched in the summer of 1993. Whisky Archives (Scotland)

Isle of Arran Distillers Ltd

FINANCIAL SAVINGS ON THE ARRAN BOND

	ARRAN OFFER		NORMAL UK RETAIL
BLENDED			
	1.95	PRICE OF WHISKY	3.81
	5.55	DUTY	5.55
	1.31	VAT	1.64
	—		—
	£8.81	TOTAL PER BOTTLE	£11.00
	£528.60	TOTAL PRICE FIVE CASES	£660.00
		SAVING: £131.40	
MALT			
	5.55	PRICE OF WHISKY	11.47
	5.55	DUTY	5.55
	1.94	VAT	2.98
	—		—
	£13.04	TOTAL PER BOTTLE	£20.00
	£782.40	TOTAL PRICE FIVE CASES	£1,200.00
		SAVING: £417.60	
		OVERALL SAVING: £549	

Head Office: 1 The Cross, Mauchline, Ayrshire KA5 5AB
Telephone: 0290 552282. Fax: 0290 550177
London Office: Telephone: 071-731 3425. Fax: 071-736 9454
Directors: Harold Currie, David Hutchison
Registered No. 134963 Scotland. Registered Office: as above.

The real attraction of the Bond was … cheap malt whisky! Whisky Archives (Scotland)

private individuals and companies. On the annual return dated 11 November 1995 the list of shareholdings in the company numbered 30, ranging in size from 1,000 to 312,000 controlled by Auchincloss, compared to Hal and David's sole £1 shareholdings two years before. Over the life of the company, Auchincloss has become its major stabilising influence on the financial side.

However, on 22 September 1994, just before a contractor was appointed, the project hit another hurdle. SNH had sent an eight-page fax to CDC Planning Department (copied by letter to DHA) concerning the amended plans submitted by David Hutchison's firm. SNH stated that these were grounds for a further objection. According to the *Banner*, David Hutchison was not a happy man. 'I'm not sure they have objected but they have raised points they want information on. If SNH had not put their oar in, we would have had a contractor by now.' The amendments had actually reduced the size of the distillery building by one-third, with a resultant reduction in height of five metres. Hutchison thought that SNH should have welcomed the alterations, instead they had asked for a number of points to be answered even down to what type of pebbles would be used for the

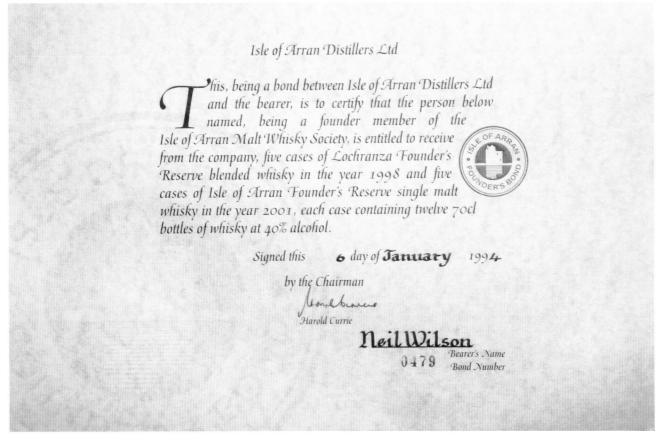

Isle of Arran Distillers Ltd

This, being a bond between Isle of Arran Distillers Ltd and the bearer, is to certify that the person below named, being a founder member of the Isle of Arran Malt Whisky Society, is entitled to receive from the company, five cases of Lochranza Founder's Reserve blended whisky in the year 1998 and five cases of Isle of Arran Founder's Reserve single malt whisky in the year 2001, each case containing twelve 70cl bottles of whisky at 40% alcohol.

Signed this **6** day of **January** 1994

by the Chairman

Harold Currie

Neil Wilson

0479   *Bearer's Name*
        Bond Number

The author's
Bondholder certificate.
Neil Wilson

paths around the building. Hutchison considered the whole matter a stalling operation in the hope that the distillery would just go away. 'I think that common sense will prevail at the end of the day. No one is going to stop this.' Planning officer Mick Lee concurred. With the as yet unchosen contractor due to start on the site on 10 October, a further delay was now inevitable as SNH's concerns were addressed.

On 10 October a 10-page response was sent by Hutchison to the CDC Director of Planning which covered the following areas about which SNH had raised concerns: effluent treatment works, employment and the finishes to the distillery, VC, warehouse and car park. This last section covered concerns over curbs, beach pebble paths ('all pebbles to blend with naturally occurring local colours, textures and sizes, sourced locally'), paths/paving, entrance plats/ramps, gates and signage. Finally the proposed cooling tower was mentioned but at the time Clyde River Purification were considering the cooling water and possibly effluent disposal to be routed by a pipe to beneath the confluence of the Easan Biorach and the Glen Chalmadale burns and then discharged below water level.

Isle of Arran Distillers Ltd

28 January 1994

Dear Mr

You recently requested information on a unique new offer in the Scotch Whisky market, the "Arran Bond", which we launched last autumn. This will continue to be on offer until the spring. Following its tremendous success, we are now launching a second alternative bond, offering the opportunity to buy individual cases of Arran malt whisky.

Accordingly, we would like to offer you our new "Arran Single Malt Bond" as the perfect gift. This will supply exactly the same Isle of Arran Single Malt Whisky in 2001 as the main bond, bringing together the various characteristics of the whisky regions of Scotland to create a truly great malt. This brand will not be on sale to the general public, but will be exclusive to bondholders. However, whereas the previous offer included a total of ten cases of whisky, our new bond allows you to decide how much whisky you would prefer to purchase. You are able to buy one case or more - the choice is yours to take as many as you wish. You do not need to take delivery of your whisky all at once; we would be happy to keep in store any number of your purchased cases for ca £2.50 per case per year, if you would like your whisky to age further.

Each unit offers one case (twelve 70cl bottles) of Isle of Arran Single Malt Whisky in 2001, at the following prices:

1 unit	**£75** excluding duty and VAT.
5-6 units	**£67.50** per case excluding duty and VAT.
7 units or more	**£66.00** per case excluding duty and VAT.

Duty and VAT will be payable on delivery in 2001.

As you will see on the attached sheet, each unit offers you a saving of over £73 per case based on current duty and VAT rates.

With this bond you will also become a member of the Isle of Arran Malt Whisky Society, giving you the opportunity to continue buying whisky at distillery prices as well as other whisky offers. All other relevant information about our new whisky is included in the brochure previously sent to you. If you would like a further copy of this, please call us on one of the numbers shown below.

We look forward to welcoming you as an Arran bondholder, to share in Scotland's newest single malt whisky.

Yours sincerely

Andrew Currie

Head Office: 1 The Cross, Mauchline, Ayrshire KA5 5AB
Telephone: 0290 552282. Fax: 0290 550177
London Office: Telephone: 071-731 3425. Fax: 071-736 9454
Directors: Harold Currie, David Hutchison
Registered No. 134963 Scotland. Registered Office: as above.

Never one to sit still, Andrew Currie was back marketing another offer to respondents in January 1994. Whisky Archives (Scotland)

Isle of Arran Distillers Ltd

FINANCIAL SAVINGS ON THE ARRAN MALT BOND

	ARRAN OFFER		NORMAL UK RETAIL
£s	£75 per case		
per bottle	6.25	PRICE OF WHISKY	11.47
	5.55	DUTY	5.55
	2.06	VAT	2.98
	-----		-----
	£13.86	TOTAL PER BOTTLE	£20.00
	£166.32	TOTAL PRICE PER CASE	£240.00

SAVING: £73.68 PER CASE

Head Office: 1 The Cross, Mauchline, Ayrshire KA5 5AB
Telephone: 0290 552282. Fax: 0290 550177
London Office: Telephone: 071-731 3425. Fax: 071-736 9454
Directors: Harold Currie, David Hutchison
Registered No. 134963 Scotland. Registered Office: as above.

Another not unattractive offer. Whisky Archives (Scotland)

SNH felt that their concerns had been misrepresented by the *Banner*. John Burlison responded on 22 October.

Whilst we understand the concern of the developers to now get works quickly under way, we have offered full advice to the Council in the interests of ensuring that the project is constructed in harmony with the surrounding landscape in what is a designated National Scenic Area.

Burlison also stated that SNH's involvement had meant 'many positive suggestions' but could not qualify these. At the end of October he returned to clarify the issue once and for all:

I was concerned to read that Scottish Natural Heritage was considered to be the cause of delays connected with the Lochranza Distillery proposal (October 1st). The situation is considerably more complex than your report would indicate. When planning consent was granted by Cunninghame District Council in May 1993, there was a requirement that prior to starting building work on site the applicants should supply specific information for the council's consideration and approval. This information, which includes a number of changes from the original proposals, has only been provided to the District Council recently, and the council has sought SNH's views on the changes. We have treated our response as a matter of urgency. Whilst we understand the concern of the developers to now get works quickly underway, we have offered full advice to the Council in the interests of ensuring that the project is constructed in harmony with the surrounding landscape in what is a designated National Scenic Area. Contrary to the impression given in your report, our approach has involved many positive suggestions as to the best way to proceed. It is surely to the benefit of all living and working on the island that where new developments are to be introduced in an area of natural beauty, efforts should be made to do so without destroying the character of the landscape which is itself so important to the local economy.

Hal Currie was adamant that, come what may, the contractor would be appointed imminently with a timescale of completion of the distillery building by spring 1995. The funding was outlined at this stage as '1600 Bonds sold at £400' (£640,000), a number of 'grants and loans' plus £200,000 'from the principals'. In reality, over the course of the late summer and autumn of 1994, largely through the efforts of Ross Peters, £861,002 of capital had been raised from share issues to fully fund the construction of the distillery building. SNH's concerns were satisfied in November and in the same month the tender for construction went to John Thomson Construction Ltd of Lamlash.

Isle of Arran Distillers Ltd

Autumn 1994

Arran Malt Whisky Society

During the last year you have enquired about our unique new offer in the whisky industry, the Arran Bond. This has proved a tremendous success since its launch, but will continue to be offered only until early in 1995. If you are still interested in purchasing a bond please let us know.

In our brochure we gave details about our *Arran Malt Whisky Society*, for which bondholders receive free membership. This is also available to non bondholders, and we would now like to introduce you to what the society offers.

From our contacts in the whisky industry, we source speciality whiskies for members, as well as other quality products from Arran and the rest of Scotland. These offers will be detailed in regular newsletters, the latest of which we have pleasure in enclosing.

The normal membership charge is a one off fee of £20, but as a special introduction you can:

- join <u>free</u> if you purchase two or more items from our current offers
- join for only £10 if you purchase one item

On joining the society you will then be able to benefit from all future offers through our newsletters, and be able to buy our product at distillery prices in the years to come.

We look forward to welcoming you into the Society.

Yours sincerely,

Harold Currie
Chairman

Head Office: 1 The Cross, Mauchline, Ayrshire KA5 5AB
Telephone: 0290 55Z282. Fax: 0290 550177
London Office: Telephone: 071-731 3425. Fax: 071-736 9454

Directors: Harold Currie, David Hutchison
Registered No. 134963 Scotland. Registered Office: as above

And later that year, anyone who had not bought a Bond was offered membership (at a price) to the Arran Malt Whisky Society.
Whisky Archives (Scotland)

CHAPTER FIVE

The Eagle Soars Again

'THERE'S A REASON the site at Ballarie Bridge had never been built on,' builder Iain Thomson told me, 'the wind that comes down off the hill can sometimes be really destructive'. That would become very apparent, as we shall see. But before Mother Nature dealt her hand, the ground had to be prepared and the first sod for the access road into the site was dug up on Monday 28 November 1994. On Wednesday David Hutchison's assistant Mandy Thomson made the first of her fortnightly site visits to see things get started as Hal Currie made public that the income from the Bonds would be used to fund the initial production of whisky and not any of the physical structure. 'It's been a long haul,' he said. 'There have been so many obstacles, but we've overcome them all now.'

Of course, there is sod-cutting and then there is sod-cutting. Officially, Brian Wilson, MP for Cunninghame North, cut the 'first' on Friday 16 December as around 20 people looked on, none of them objectors, although some had been expected. There was not a single protest. Among those in attendance were councillor Tom Knox, Jim Lees, Hal Currie, David Croll, David Hutchison, Mandy Thomson, Iain Thomson and Andrew Currie. The building constructors began to move equipment, Portakabins and plant on site and preparatory work was begun. But with further construction due to be delayed through the four-month period starting in 1 February to allow the eagles above the site to breed in peace, Hal Currie approached CDC on Friday 27 January arguing that the downtime alone would amount to an extra cost of some £20,000 to the company. He asked for them to reconsider the restriction and the next Monday

Brian Wilson MP cuts the first sod on 16 December 1994. From left to right: Ronnie Mann (Chairman of the Isle of Arran Tourist Board), Tom Knox (local councillor), Hal Currie, David Hutchison, ?, Mandy Thomson, David Croll, ?, ?, Andrew Currie, Iain Thomson. *Arran Banner*

Mandy Thomson of DHA in front of the site as clearing begins. *Arran Banner*

All systems go!

David Hutchison sent a letter to the CDC Director of Planning requesting a relaxation of condition 15 of the original planning application of 19 May 1993. In it he stated:

We have examined the programme of works for the distillery building, filling store and pumphouse and do not envisage at this stage that there will be any noise which could be considered detrimental to the pattern of behaviour of the eagles in question.

It was never the intention of the Isle of Arran Distillers to build within the exclusion period, however, the delay in starting building work was due to the company trying to take on board some of the concerns of CDC and the public, reducing the visual scale of the complex in an attempt to lessen the impact on the environment.

Whilst we are not experts in these matters and can only express an opinion, we understand that the Isle of Arran Distillers have discussed the situation with those who are and we understand that the likelihood of disturbance to these birds is likely to be insignificant.

It must be clearly understood that whilst every effort will be made by John Thomson Construction to minimise noise and every effort has been made by ourselves to specify materials and adopt forms of construction which minimise noise, for example the original planning approval allowed for the walls to be clad in steel, however, we have now replaced it with traditional masonry thus reducing noise still further, we are dealing with a building site and as such there is no doubt that a degree of noise will inevitably be present.

Harold Mayes of Lochranza brought the matter to the attention of the public in a letter to the *Banner* on 11 February 1995, but David Hutchison responded that a relaxation of the condition had been applied as 'the condition was put in on planning to safeguard the natural habitat, not specifically the eagle'. He also said that his understanding was that the eagles had not nested in the hills above for three years. Hutchison had clearly had all the delays an architect could take. A week later Mayes was castigating both the editor of the *Banner* and David Hutchison in no uncertain terms.

Sir,
Your mixture of news and comment in your story 'Eagle-eyed' in last week's issue might have been more acceptable had your facts concerning planning conditions for the Lochranza distillery been more accurate.

You stated that the restriction on construction between February 1 and May 31 'was one of several put on by Scottish Natural Heritage and one which, last year, delayed the start of building work.'

Not so. Scottish Natural Heritage in their wisdom may have pressed for the restriction but the conditions of planning consent were determined not by SNH but by the Planning Committee of Cunninghame District Council after the original planning application had been referred back to them by the Secretary of State for Scotland.

So why in your anxiety to curry favour did you not contact CDC to establish why they were permitting work to continue beyond the exclusion date?

Instead of doing so you chose to abandon established editorial practice by relaying the contents of my letter, which at that time had not been published, to Mr David Hutchison, giving him the opportunity to exercise his skills beyond the confines of architecture. Why did you not establish how he could be so sure that the eagles had not nested in the hills above the distillery site for three years? Is his ornithological expertise such that he is unaware that eagles tend to use three separate nesting areas over a period of three years and that this might just be the one when they are returning?

Having then in his apparent wisdom provided that information he chose to give you the benefit of his psychic powers by telling you 'The gentleman

While construction went on, Hal Currie and Gillian McCreadie were on the road selling. A little help from actor Gordon Kennedy was on hand this time. *Arran Banner*

The stills arrive from Rothes, 5 April 1995. *Arran Banner*

[me] is not interested in the eagle.' Not having seen or met him I would like to know how he is pretending to be privy to my innermost thoughts.

If he is as clever in that direction as he would have us believe one can only hazard a guess that he has missed his vocation and should be setting up in Arran as a clairvoyant rather than overseeing the building of a monstrosity.

Nesting or non-nesting eagles aside, the weather began to play its part in the project. During one of the gales that swept off the hill, one of Thomson's Portakabins was turned onto its roof during the night and an entire five-day-old, six-inch block wall was flattened by the force. (In 2015, when Thomsons arrived on site to build the Blending and Tasting Rooms in November, the Portakabins were anchored to the ground.)

While construction went on, relatively unhindered and 'straightforward' as Iain Thomson recalls, Hal Currie and newly-hired graduate trainee Gillian McCreadie were on the road attending events such as London's Ideal Home Exhibition in late March where they marketed the Arran Bond and the Arran Malt Whisky Society. The first issue of the *Spirit of Arran* newsletter of the society was also produced in the spring and sent out to Bondholders on a seasonal basis to keep them up to date with developments and offers. Gillian McCreadie, who had worked at the Lagg Hotel during the summer of 1993, had graduated in

One of the stills is lowered into position.

With the stills in place, construction of the roof is able to be completed. *DHA*

Hospitality Management, Tourism and Marketing from Glasgow Caledonian University and spent the first eight weeks of her time with the company based in London before returning north to the head office in Mauchline then moving on to the island to work out of a Portakabin at the distillery during the first season.

On Wednesday 5 April the wash and spirit stills were delivered on-site from Forsyth's of Rothes and lowered through the steel framework of the roof supports to be placed on top of their brick-built plinths. Their journey had not been without a little difficulty as the u-bend around the bridge at the neck of Corrie's wee harbour meant a delay as the trailer was manipulated until the tractor unit could make onward progress. A ban on using the on-site crane had been lifted on 1 April and the mashtun, made by William Reid Engineering of Forres, had been lowered into position the day before the stills. The wooden washbacks were built on site and in situ by Brown's of Dufftown.

By late April the main distillery building had been roofed over and work on the associated pipework for the stills, underbacks and receivers, tanks, washbacks and mashtun was underway. The man on site for Forbes Leslie Network, the consultant engineers, was Bob Gibson who acted as site co-ordinator and engineer on the mechanical installation.

I was on site from Monday through Friday of each week during construction and I stayed in Lochranza during my time there. My responsibilities were to resolve all mechanical problems as they arose and sort out the connections between civil and mechanical plant, where plinths or openings had to be placed etc. There were no major problems, as usually we resolved all design issues before we arrived on site. I would only stay a few days on site after the system was proved and the plant was running smoothly.

Northern Fabricators of Elgin were there to take care of all the necessary pipework while Advanced Electronics dealt with all the electrical cabling and alarms. Local comment was that the distillery was 'much smaller than expected'. Gordon

The roof structures are in place awaiting installation of the copper-clad cupolas. *DHA*

… which duly arrive on 2 June. *Arran Banner*

Mitchell, the distillery manager, who had resigned his position at Cooley Distillery in December 1994, had arrived on location prior to the installation of the plant, keeping a watchful eye on things as they progressed. He had also brought with him a large supply of Tyrconnell malt whiskey from Cooley which Ewen Fraser, the other Forbes Leslie employee on site, remembers fondly. Andy Scott, the award-winning metal sculptor was commissioned by David Hutchison to create the stunning barley motifs that constitute the iron railings beneath the banisters and balustrades in the distillery.

The Arran Malt Whisky Society also had on offer in their May newsletter a Benrinnes malt at £34.49 and a 1950 Glen Grant at £125 as part of a selection of six whiskies, called, unsurprisingly, Gordon Mitchell's Selection. Gordon

confirmed that, all being well, distillation testing would begin shortly and on Friday, 2 June, three handsome copper-skinned cupola tops arrived on low-loaders and were hoisted into place by the crane to complete the outline of the distillery buildings which has welcomed over a million visitors since they were built.

For the record books the first mashing commenced on Saturday 24 June. By the following Wednesday, after fermentation, the distilled wash was running into the low wines still for the first time to make spirit as part of a trial run to ensure that all the plant was functioning correctly. Bob Gibson and Ewen Fraser kept watch over the commissioning and Gillian McCreadie was also present. Gordon Mitchell thought the spirit was 'very sweet' and asked David Hutchison to come and try it. He takes up the story.

... and are hoisted into position. *Arran Banner*

The wash still is charged for the first time. *Ewen Fraser*

The newly installed low wines still prior to being fired up on 28 June 1995. *Ewen Fraser*

The stills are commissioned, the day before the 'official' first running which Jim Murray attended. Here the frothing wash can clearly be seen in the still through the neck window. *Ewen Fraser*

I was at the family croft over in Knockenkelly when I got a call from him. 'Get up here quick. We have the spirit! Come and taste it!' So I tore over to Lochranza only to totally disappoint Gordon as I hardly ever drank whisky! He would have none of it. 'You must taste this if only once. It's your whisky!' So I did, and I liked it.

On Thursday 29 June new-make Isle of Arran spirit was officially diverted into the spirit receiver for the 'first time'. The event was attended by whisky writer Jim Murray who wrote an article on it in *The Scotsman* of 3 July. In it Gordon Mitchell stated, 'I was very proud of what I made at Cooley. But I suspected this was going to be something special when I sampled the low wines. I just can't

believe how well it has turned out. It's full of character.'

On the following Friday the first casks were filled. Asked by the reporter on the *Banner* how he knew at this early stage that he was making a good whisky, Gordon Mitchell simply replied, 'I put a wee bit on the tip of my tongue and it was very sweet.' The *Banner* went on:

Well, no better way of telling than that. They always say that the cook who doesn't taste the dishes never makes anything right.

Four thousand litres of spirit were made on the first run and then production was shut down to enable the finishing of the building before the official opening in

The commissioning team from left to right: Gordon Mitchell, Bob Gibson and Ewen Fraser. *Ewen Fraser*

Gillian McCreadie shares in a piece of history. *Ewen Fraser*

At last. After 158 years legal spirit is produced on Arran once more. Gordon Mitchell watches on. *Ewen Fraser*

August. In the meantime Andrew Currie had applied for planning permission to erect a temporary Portakabin on site to function as the VC and this was granted on 31 July.

On Thursday 17 August, at 12.30pm Hal Currie addressed several hundred invitees on a stage erected outside the distillery building and was joined by the Lord Lieutenant Major Richard Henderson, Jim Lees, Jim Murray, Iain Thomson, tourism manager Charles Currie, David Hutchison, Mandy Thomson, former Scottish international rugby player and British Lion Gordon Brown and Lachlan MacKinnon, a great grandson of 'the last man to be shot while escaping from the excisemen in Arran and who maintains his connection with the island through a longstanding subscription to the *Banner*'. Jim Murray was ebullient in his praise for the distillery spirit. The *Banner* again:

Production ceased for a while to allow construction to be completed. *DHA*

'I can genuinely say that this is a decent whisky,' he declared, on which he later elaborated, 'It's not just good, it's magnificent. There'll be something special in eight years time.'

Finally it was Gordon Brown's turn. 'How does an Englishman get a job like yours?' he quipped to Mr Murray. Gordon was at least able to claim an Arran ancestry; his great, great grandfather Peter Currie had been born in Kildonan. His witty observations were well received by the crowd and all too soon his speech was over and we were off to the distillery doorway. Major Richard Henderson, Lord Lieutenant of Ayrshire, cut the ribbon to declare the building open and once inside Gordon Brown formally switched over the stills to send the spirit into the receiver. Duties over, Gordon was whisked away in a taxi and the 450 or so guests made for the

buffet. Lochranza brand whisky was available in copious amounts and those who were not driving home were soon taking ample advantage of the hospitality.

For their official opening the Isle of Arran distillers Ltd had laid on a day to remember. Although we understand, that due to the combination of whisky and sunshine, there are a few who may remember very little!

During the day's events a pair of eagles were reported in the next week's *Banner* to have made the start of a series of well-timed appearances above the distillery, but given that they ranged over a vast area and are on the wing a great deal, perhaps a little too much was read into this. Or maybe it was the whisky? Ross Peters thought not and recalled that, 'the eagles reappeared on each subsequent anniversary as if divine providence was the prime factor'.

The VC plans continued with the awarding of a £195,000 grant in November 1995 from the Argyll and Islands Enterprise section of HIE towards the estimated total build cost of £800,000. Some 15 jobs would be created if the company's application for EU Objective One status could be gained. As 1995 closed it was clear another warehouse would be required and once designs were completed, planning was lodged in February 1996 and approved on 9 May.

Gillian McCreadie, now Sales and Marketing Manager, graduated first in Ayrshire Enterprise's management training scheme in April 1996 and in the same month the company received the Royal Mail Scottish Marketing Award for selling over 2,000 Arran Bonds. By the end of the month she had every Stagecoach bus on the island displaying large advertisements along each side endorsing the distillery … 'It's a Dram Good Visit.'

June 1996 marked the first year of production while the new VC rose from the ground, but it was clear that another Portakabin would be required for the rest of the season and another planning application was needed with approval given on 21 June. Gillian McCreadie started looking for more full-time rather than seasonal employees and senior tour guide Sandy Rankin was joined by Bob Fisher from Whiting Bay and Fiona McLaughlin, formerly of the Kinloch Hotel at Blackwaterfoot. Gillian also persuaded charter tourist buses to make the distillery a stop on their island itinerary as Shearings, Wallace Arnold UK Tours and Stagecoach all became regulars in the bus parking area. Gordon Mitchell simply got on with what he knew best … distilling. On 22 June the *Banner* reported:

> With any new project you have to start somewhere and it was clearly the first priority to construct the working distillery and then get around to the visitor centre later. So for the time being the Portakabin acts as office and shop, but across the car park the new Visitor's Centre is rapidly taking shape. Gillian says that they expect the new centre to be partly ready by the end of July, to be followed by a restaurant for next season.

The main buildings soon after completion, 1995. *David Hutchison Associates*

And the visitors are certainly coming to have a look around Scotland's newest distillery. They are already averaging 1500 people a week with 288 on the busiest day last week. The Company certainly won't get fat from the modest tour fee which probably only covers the cost of the whisky samples at the end. What they are still doing though, is selling bonds as investment in Arran whisky for the future. The original Founders Reserve Bond was completely subscribed with 2000 people parting with £450 each to receive 60 bottles of blended Arran whisky in 1998 and 60 bottles of single malt in 2001. But at £75 you can still get a mini-bond entitling you to 12 bottles of Arran malt in 2001, or for £950 a Hogshead of 600 bottles could be all yours.

Across the yard from the reception a couple were having their photograph taken in the Filling House with their own numbered Hogshead. We were surprised when Gillian said that quite a number of bondholders visit their whisky held in the bonded warehouse and actually plan to come and collect it come the liberation day. That is, after they have paid the duty and VAT.

Hal Currie raises a glass of the whisky he had dreamed of creating. June 1995.

The *Banner* reports the official opening of the distillery, 17 August 1995. *Arran Banner*

Gordon Brown (right) switches over the stills. Left is Hal Currie and in the centre distiller Gordon Mitchell.

Cont from Front Page
twelve as the officials took to the stage, the last man to climb the steps was former Scotland rugby captain and current TV pundit Gordon Brown.

tillery doorway. Major Richard Henderson, Lord Lieutenant of Ayrshire cut the ribbon to declare the building open and once inside Gordon Brown formally switched over the stills to send

David Hutchison, Mandy Thomson, Charles Currie of the Isle of Arran Tourist Board and Jim Lees, official opening day, 17 August 1995. *Arran Banner*

71

Gillian McCreadie made sure the message was spread far and wide. *Arran Banner*

The earliest casks (this is no 12) were sent to Campbeltown for maturation before the first warehouse was built. *Alex Dale*

Head Distiller Gordon Mitchell was busy supervising another batch of distilled alcohol in the Filling House. He explained that they had increased production up to 10,000 litres of alcohol a week and his staff were now working night shifts and weekends. Deliveries of milled malted barley from Edinburgh have risen to 25 tonnes a week, and after the distillery process the residue draff goes as pure animal feed to the cows at Glenkiln. Maybe their milk tastes that little bit special!

We were in the basement, and through the grating above Fiona Crawford was taking round another guided tour. Gordon pointed towards a group of builders working at the far side of the building and said that they were preparing the site for another 15,000-litre timber washback tub due to be delivered from Dufftown next week.

And so the Dream Dram which we first reported on as long ago as August 1991 is no longer a dream but well on the way to becoming a reality and providing a whole new visitor attraction for the island.

The first anniversary proper of the distillery was marked by an open day on Saturday 24 August 1996 when several hundred Bondholders and members of the public gathered on a stunning summer day to celebrate. I was one of them as Hal had invited me to attend and say a few words. When the moment came he

Cooper Richard Meakin stencils the cask end of some of the first year's production, June 1996. *Arran Banner*

A staff photograph in the filling store, June 1996. From left to right: Gordon Mitchell, Gillian McCreadie, Duncan Simpson, Richard Meakin, John McMullan. *Arran Banner*

announced that I would speak about the quality of the spirit being produced. I was a little bit taken by surprise but as a whisky historian I instead decided to talk of the contribution Arran would make to the portfolio and heritage of the Hebridean distilleries and then handed over to my colleague John Lamond, Master of Malt, who was far better qualified to describe the new make as a one-year-old. John said that the spirit was 'soft, sweet with a strange tang of oregano', and felt that being so soft it would probably be ready at eight years, but when he returned to it at three years old he noticed it had 'real backbone' and would handle much more maturation in the future. The spirit Gordon Mitchell was producing was

clearly first-class and the next important stage in the company's plan was to get the new VC and restaurant up and running for the 1997 season.

Despite its lowly appearance, the humble Portakabin, according to Hal Currie, had been averaging 150 visitors a day, and on wet days this figure could double so an application had been submitted in March for another Portakabin to be erected to supplement the first. The planning permission issued on 21 June 1996 for it had been granted on the basis that it would be removed by 30 September and the grounds reinstated. There had been only one objector to its installation … Bert Gratton of Mount View Cottage, Ballarie Bridge, just in front of the distillery.

CHAPTER SIX

'Arran Water' Returns

GORDON MITCHELL was one of the last of the traditional Scotch whisky distillers who always maintained that the old-fashioned ways were the best. He spent 50 years in the industry until he retired from Arran in 2007 having started his career in his native Montrose at Lochside Distillery, of which not a trace now survives. He moved on to work with Inver House Distillers at the Moffat distilling complex near Airdrie before going to Cooley Distillery near Dundalk in Ireland in 1989 where an old potato-alcohol plant had been converted by John Teeling into a whiskey distillery, with both patent and pot stills, between 1985 and 1987. This was a familiar set-up for Gordon as Lochside used the same arrangement for many years, although the patent stills had been made redundant in 1974. Cooley was to use double-distillation, instead of the traditional Irish technique of triple-distillation, so Gordon was well suited to his new charge. He recalled his career to me in 2005, when I interviewed him for *Fine Expressions.*

I started in 1957 at Lochside in Montrose as a brewer, which was ironic as the distillery had started as a brewery built in the German Brauhaus style in the 1890s. Joe Hobbs from Fort William had bought it the year before and converted it to distil both grain and malt whisky. It really was a unique place. Nothing there now, of course, all bulldozed for housing. I stayed with them until 1965, the year after Joe died, and I then moved to the Inver House distilling complex at Airdrie near Glasgow. I started as mashman, then stillman, gaining promotion until I was the shift supervisor.

Lochside Distillery in 2002 prior to demolition. *Teimei Horiuchi*

Gordon Mitchell retires and Mike Peirce opens the new warehouse in Gordon's honour, 3 September 2007.

I knew the business inside-out after 30 years, and was then approached by John Teeling and David Hynes who had just converted one of the old Irish wartime potato-alcohol munitions factories at Dundalk into a whiskey distillery. I couldn't resist the challenge and took the plunge, although my wife Evelyn decided I would have to commute to work! Out of that came Cooley Distillery with the Tyrconnell, Locke's, Kilbeggan and Connemara brands, and I stayed there until 1995, when Harold offered me this opportunity on Arran. I think I must be the only living distiller who has been involved in two consecutive distillery start-ups in two different countries!

Gordon had in fact been quietly headhunted from across the Irish Sea after Jimmy Lang, a former Chivas colleague of Hal Currie's, suggested him as being the right

man to get Arran up and running. Gordon arrived at Lochranza as construction was underway and once the plant was installed he conducted pre-production testing prior to the official first running of the stills on 28 June 1995. It was at the first of these early tests that David Hutchison was present to see 'Arran water' flowing again after almost 160 years. Over the next 12 years Gordon gradually built up the stocks of malt as and when he was allowed to, as cash to finance stocks was always scarce in the early years of production.

Not long after I interviewed Gordon he decided to retire and a search for his replacement was begun. That resulted in the appointment of James MacTaggart from Islay who moved to Lochranza in September 2007. Back in 1976 James was working in Bowmore for Strathclyde Regional Council when Harry Cockburn, the Bowmore manager, decided to upgrade the office systems at the distillery and computerise things. James was offered the position of office manager but the

James MacTaggart, Master
Distiller since 2007.

computers never materialised and Harry gave James a job in the warehouses and malt barns instead where he started on 19 October. After Cockburn came the jocular Joe Hughes and then the legendary Jim MacEwan took over after returning from the Springburn operation of Morrison Bowmore Distillers in Glasgow. But James was a young man and knew that his time would come, so he bided it and learnt his craft from top to bottom. Eventually Bowmore became partly computerised as heat reclamation processes were installed and other efficiencies made, so that when he arrived on Arran he felt that he had stepped back in time. Here he could manage everything in a hands-on manner, well away from city-centre control and without having to constantly refer to a large Human Resources department.

His career at Bowmore had lasted over 30 years and with two grown-up sons on Islay, (James jnr working at Caol Ila and Angus being the GP in Port Ellen),

the move to Arran has not presented a problem for him as he commutes back to Islay for the weekends where his wife Mavis maintains the family home. Any hardship is offset by living in the distillery manager's house, just across the road from the Lochranza nine-hole golf course where he enjoys winding down after work.

After lunch in the Casks Café, James took me on a tour of the distillery and carefully explained the way that the process is undertaken at Lochranza. We started beside the two 30-tonne malt delivery bins alongside the weighing bin and four-roller malt mill. Scotch whisky is made of three ingredients: water, yeast and barley, just as beer is (with the addition of hops). Whisky is simply a type of distilled beer, minus the hops! 'People' are often mentioned as the secret fourth ingredient, but the holy trinity remains as it always has. As Arran does not have any malting capacity, the maltsters, Boortmalt, supply the distillery with malted barley sourced in the east of Scotland from Moray, the Mearns, the Lothians and most recently Arran itself. The distillery uses a variety of barley strains which are currently Optic, Oxbridge and Concerto. Barley strains are constantly being evolved and developed to offer brewers and distillers improvements in their respective brewing procedures, primarily to increase the yield of litres of pure alcohol (lpa) per tonne. At the moment Concerto is favoured by the industry for this reason. The typical industry standard yield is around 400 lpa although Arran commonly achieves 410-12.

The yeast strain used at Arran is called Distillery M cultivated by Quest at Menstrie, Clackmannanshire. Some distilleries use brewer's yeast and others a combination of both. The former is less expensive, but Distillery M is preferred in terms of better yield and flavour.

We then moved up to the water source, a short walk away. As previously described in Chapter Two, this emanates from Loch na Davie, some three kilometres up the Easan Biorach in the glen of that name, to the east of the distillery. The lochan is spring-fed ensuring a pure, unpolluted supply which runs down the glen over red granite, supplemented by a number of tributaries from the

One of the two malt storage bins which feed the weighing bin before milling.
Neil Wilson

The purest water on the island feeds the distillery.
Peter Sandground

The water source with the pumping station on the Easan Biorach.
Neil Wilson

flanks of the glen, and is pumped from the caul behind the distillery at a rate of 30,000 litres per hour. Most of this is used as cooling water with about five per cent going into the process. It is probably the purest source of water on the island and tastes delicious. As we return to the distillery James continues to explain the stages of whisky production.

Arran's barley is malted to James' precise specifications at Glen Esk Maltings where it is first 'awakened' in order to start germination. This is achieved by steeping the barley in large tanks for over 40 hours where it goes through soaking and aeration cycles to raise the moisture content to 44%. Then the steeps are drained and the barley is allowed to dry in large rotating drums through which humidified air is blown to create the perfect conditions in which the starch in the barley grain is gradually converted into fermentable sugars. As the tiny rootlets which shoot from the grains can knit together the mass of the barley, the drums are fully rotated every eight hours to keep the grains 'on the move' and stop entanglement. The whole germination process in the drums takes five days.

In past times this process used to be achieved by spreading the barley onto a malting floor, normally joined to a drying kiln, until a consistent blanket about six inches deep (15cm) was created. This was known as the 'piece'. Nowadays, as well as the drum maltings described above, tower maltings are also employed to achieve this on an industrial scale. Six Scottish distilleries still operate floor maltings which are primarily retained for their heritage and tourism values and can be witnessed at Springbank (which also produces malt for Glengyle), Laphroaig, Bowmore, Highland Park, Kilchoman (which, as well as Springbank, malts its entire output) and Balvenie.

Barley contains an enzyme, diastase, which is released during germination and is essential in starch conversion. After five to seven days on a malting floor, the barley has started to grow rootlets and further growth must be halted in order to conserve the starch in the grains; this is done by kilning (drying) the barley. At this stage the barley is called 'green malt' and traditionally was dried on a perforated floor (the haircloth) in a kiln with a peat-fuelled fire below. This imparted a phenolic content measured in parts per million (ppm) to the barley which gives whisky made from it a peaty nose and flavour. In industrial maltings such as at Port Ellen on Islay, the process is carried out in large kilns where a secondary heat source of peat is used to raise the phenolic levels to the customer's specifications. An Islay malt such as Laphroaig will have around 35ppm, while Glengoyne is entirely unpeated (0ppm). Arran's barley is dried entirely by the hot-air process, except for the Machrie Moor malt which is dried with a combination of hot air and peat to a 20ppm phenol level. There are also casks of 50ppm peated spirit maturing at Lochranza from 2011.

The malted barley is now passed through a 'dresser' which neatly removes the rootlets. The barley is now ready to be delivered to the distillery where it is loaded into the storage silo before it passes through another dresser and destoner which removes impurities such as stone chips. Any tiny fragments of metal are removed when the grain passes next to a magnet. After this it is fed into the roller mill which grinds it into a grist. Prior to 2007 milling took place at the maltsters but after a mill and silo were installed by Alan Ruddock Engineering, all the milling has since taken place on site. It is now ready to be made into a sweet, beer-like liquor called 'wort'.

Unlike almost all other Scottish whisky distilleries, all the main processes occur under one roof at Lochranza, as was David Hutchison's plan. Under the gently sloping, twin-cupola-topped roof on the main distillery building, James takes me through the next stage: mashing.

The grist is now mixed with a series of three 'waters' in the large stainless steel mashtun. For each mash a charge of 2.5 tonnes of grist is used and the first water is added from the No 1 brewing tank at a temperature of 64°c. After 30 minutes the wort is allowed to pass through the perforated plates in the floor of the mashtun and is drained off into the underback, leaving the grist behind. The wort is then cooled down to 18-20°c depending on the time of year (it should be cooler in summer and warmer in winter) and then pumped into one of the six wooden washbacks. The water used for cooling the wort then passes through a heat exchanger and becomes the second mashing water from No 2 brewing tank at 78°c. The rotating mash stirrers in the semi-lauter mashtun are used very sparingly to aid the extraction of the remaining sugars as James prefers the wort to be clear, rather than cloudy, as clear wort gives a more fruity flavour.

The water used to cool the remaining wort then passes through the heat exchanger where it is heated to near boiling point then pumped into the mashtun as the third water of the mashing process. This time the liquid extracted from the mashtun does not contain enough sugar to be used for fermentation and is pumped into No 1 brewing tank where it will be used as the first water of the next mash. The spent grist left on the mashtun floor – the draff – is dumped from the base and pumped out into a lorry trailer outside the distillery where it is

David Hutchison's 'everything under one roof' layout is clear in this view. *Neil Wilson*

The mashtun. *Neil Wilson*

either taken to local farmers as cattle feed, or uplifted by them.

In total 13,000 litres of wort are extracted from the first and second waters to fill one washback. It takes approximately seven hours to do this and the turnaround between each mash is 10 hours. At present Isle of Arran carries out 14 mashes per week which is enough wort to create over 14,000 lpa per week.

We move across the room to discuss the next stage of the process: fermentation. Here the sweet sugary wort is converted to alcohol by the addition of yeast. This takes place in the large wooden vessels known as washbacks. Most distilleries now use washbacks made of stainless steel (better known as fermenters) as they are easier to clean and will last indefinitely. However, the washbacks at Isle of Arran are made of Oregon pine as this was traditional practice in the whisky industry and provides more consistent, temperature-steady fermentation. Despite being a 'modern' distillery there was a belief that Arran should make whisky by firmly adhering to traditional methods.

There are six washbacks at Arran, each with a capacity of 15,000 litres, built and installed by Brown & Sons of Dufftown. Each one is filled with the 13,000 litres of wort produced from each mash and is also fitted with a rotating blade (a switcher) which prevents the froth produced during fermentation from spilling over the sides of the washback. A total of 50kg of distiller's yeast is added per washback and fermentation is allowed to take place over the next 52 hours, and this can be as much as 80 hours over a weekend. The yeast reacts with the sugars in the wort to create ethanol as outlined in the chemical formula:

$$C_6H_{12}O_6 + yeast \rightarrow 2\ C_2H_5OH + 2\ CO_2$$

Carbon dioxide is a toxic by-product of this reaction and an alarm is triggered as soon as a level of 1% CO_2 is detected. Fans and extraction ducting disperse this into the atmosphere. At the end of the process an alcoholic liquid known as 'wash',

A new mashing commences. *Neil Wilson*   *Peter Sandground*

basically a type of beer, is created which has a content of approximately 8% alcohol by volume (abv).

Once the wash is ready, the next stage is distillation. A touch-screen control panel at the side of the distilling area shows the whole process and how the still charges are controlled. Malt whisky distillation in Scotland must, by law, take place in copper pot stills. Copper is used as it is not only very malleable but also works to counteract any sulphur compounds which may appear in the distillate that could negatively affect the flavour of the spirit.

Arran single malt is double-distilled in the traditional Scottish style but a few Scotch malts such as Auchentoshan and most Irish whiskeys are triple-distilled or partially triple-distilled (Springbank and Benrinnes are the main proponents of this method in Scotland). The first stage of distillation takes place in the wash still which has a capacity of 7,100 litres. Following fermentation each washback is emptied into the wash charger. From here 6,500 litres of wash are pumped into

the wash still for the first distillation. The liquid is boiled in the wash still by means of internal steam-filled 'fins' and, because alcohol has a lower boiling point than water, it is driven off as a vapour, rising up through the head of the still and down through the lyne arm to a condenser where it returns to liquid form by being cooled. The resultant alcohol spirit known as the low wines appears after 15 minutes and enters the spirit safe at 52% abv.

The stillman can now monitor the entire distillation process as the low wines are run into the low wines and feints receiver until they reach a strength of 0.2% abv over a period of 5-6 hours. The still is then shut off and the remaining liquid in the still, known as pot ale, is then pumped away and given to local farmers for agricultural use. A total of 3,100 bulk litres of low wines are collected from the first distillation and combined with 125 litres of foreshots and 1,825 litres of feints from the previous distillation from the spirit still.

The combined total of 5,050 litres, at a strength of around 23% abv, is then

After the mashtun drains into the underback, the draff is mechanically shovelled out of the base. *Neil Wilson*

The Oregon pine washbacks are another traditional feature on which Hal Currie insisted. *Neil Wilson*

pumped into the 5,200-litre spirit still for the second distillation. After 15 minutes the foreshots (or strong feints) begin to appear in the spirit safe. These consist of many volatile compounds at 74% abv but cannot be collected as true spirit so are diverted into the low wines and feints receiver. After a further 20 minutes the spirit (known as the heart or 'middle cut' of the run) can be collected and is diverted via the spirit safe into the spirit receiver tank. The middle cut lasts for two-and-half hours at the end of which a total of 750 bulk litres of spirit (equivalent to 510 lpa) have been collected at an average strength of 68% abv. Once the middle cut is completed, the remaining weak feints (or the 'tail') are diverted back for a further three hours into the low wines and feints receiver. The combined strong and weak feints will then be used with the low wines from the next distillation to produce the next run of spirit.

As soon as the feints reach a strength of 0.2% abv, the still is shut down and the remaining liquid, this time called the spent lees, is pumped away for agricultural use with the pot ale. It is normally sprayed as fertiliser on farm fields in the south of the island. The spirit is pumped to the filling store vat where it is reduced with water from the Easan Biorach burn to 63.5% abv and is then ready to be filled into oak casks.

From the stillhouse we go out the back of the distillery and into the filling store. By law new spirit must be matured in oak casks in Scotland for a minimum period of three years before it can legally be called Scotch whisky. It is generally accepted in the industry that maturation is the most important part of the production process in terms of the resultant flavour of the whisky. Some distillers would argue that as much as 80% of the final flavour is derived from the cask. Whatever that

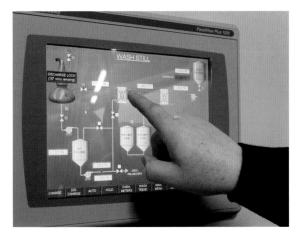

Control of all the processes is now a touchscreen procedure.
Neil Wilson

In the foreground the wash still with the low wines, or spirit still, behind. *Neil Wilson*

percentage might be, it is clear that in order to produce good whisky you must use top-quality oak casks for maturation. Good spirit filled into poor wood will not give you a quality product, but by the same token the best casks will not compensate for badly made spirit. Any nascent problems with the maturing stock were ironed out by former Edrington Group blender Alan Reid when David Boyle was MD and since then the casks used at Lochranza have been top quality.

Seasoned casks are preferred to new oak as the latter can release a lot of tannin into the whisky leading to a bitter flavour. By far the majority of casks used in the industry have previously held either bourbon whiskey from the USA or sherry from Spain. Bourbon barrels are generally made from American white oak and have a capacity of around 200 litres. Legally a cask can only be used once for the maturation of whiskey in the USA, so this provides a constant source of supply

Opposite: The wash still reveals the residues of a long working life.
Peter Sandground

John McMullan oversees another distillation, January 2016.
Neil Wilson

Peter Sandground

for the Scotch whisky industry. Casks are shipped to Scotland either in broken-down form as staves to be re-built in cooperages over here, or as whole casks. American oak casks account for over 90% of the wood used by the Scotch whisky industry for maturation.

Sherry was traditionally shipped to Scotland in cask for bottling, providing the whisky industry with a good source of wood. Scotch whisky matures particularly well in European oak ex-sherry casks and demand for this type of wood, together with the decline in sherry sales worldwide, has pushed prices higher and higher. The majority of casks from Spain have been used to produce oloroso sherry although other types, such as fino, amontillado and manzanilla, have also been used for maturing stocks. Ex-sherry casks traditionally come in two sizes: a hogshead holds around 250 litres whilst a butt is much larger with a capacity of around 500 litres.

New-make spirit is completely colourless and after being filled into casks will derive colour and flavour from the wood as it matures. European oak is tight-grained and tends to give a much darker colour to the whisky and a slightly drier, richer flavour (Christmas pudding, dried fruits) whilst American oak gives a lighter, more golden colour and a fresher, sweeter character (vanilla, coconut and spice). The first time a cask is used to mature whisky it is known as 'first-fill' or 'fresh' and it is during this cycle that the greatest level of flavour and colour is imparted to the whisky. The second or third time the casks are used they are known as a 'first-refill' or 'second-refill' and will imbue the whisky with less colour and flavour than a first-fill. Generally a cask will not be used more than three times depending on the length of each maturation cycle. However, tired casks can be reinvigorated by having them scoured internally and then charred. (This is carried out in commercial cooperages unless there are on-site facilities such as

An early image from 1997 showing the original effluent tanker alongside a skipful of draff about to be taken to local farmers. *Alex Dale*

The effluent tanker delivers another load to a farm at Sliddery, 1997. *Alex Dale*

The wooden receivers can be clearly viewed from outside the distillery. Note Andy Scott's unique iron fretwork. *Neil Wilson*

James MacTaggart, Ben Tattersfield and Gordon Bloy in the filling store. *Neil Wilson*

An ex-bourbon cask maturing in Warehouse No 3. *Neil Wilson*

at Loch Lomond Distillery at Alexandria). This exposes fresh wood with which the spirit can interact. Diageo's state-of-the-art cooperage at Cambus has taken this whole process to a new level.

As a porous wood, the oak casks will 'breathe' as the whisky matures and around 2% of the contents, known as the 'Angels' Share', will be lost each year through evaporation. The exact loss to the Angels will depend on many factors; including the type and size of the cask as well as where the cask is stored in the warehouse and the location of that warehouse. At any one time Arran has over 20,000 casks maturing in six warehouses at the distillery and there are some more casks in bond at Bladnoch and Tomatin distilleries.

Although barrels, hogsheads and butts are the industry standards the following list illustrates how many types of cask are available or have been used in the past. The capacities are merely a guideline as no two casks are ever the same:

Cask Type	Capacity in Litres
Gorda (also called a 'bodega butt')	600
Butt	500
Puncheon	500-545
Hogshead	250
Barrique	225
Barrel	200
Quarter (also called a 'firkin')	45-80

An ex-oloroso cask traditionally racked on the old dunnage system. *Neil Wilson*

Traditional dunnage being put to use in 1997. *Alex Dale*

Both ex-sherry and ex-bourbon casks are used to achieve a more balanced flavour profile. A high proportion of refill casks are used for maturation along with fresh ex-sherry and ex-bourbon as, on their own, they tend to overwhelm the more delicate Arran spirit and mask the intrinsic distillery character. Prior to bottling, the selected casks are vatted together to marry the different flavours and achieve a more rounded style.

A look inside Warehouse No 3 shows that wine cask racking system pioneered by the managing director from 2001, Douglas Davidson, is in full use, but has not been installed in any other warehouses. James has never been enthusiastic about the system and does not think the investment has paid its way; he prefers the old racking systems although Gordon Bloy, who operates the system, can see its advantages. A cursory glance around the bond reveals the VIP casks for Princes William and Harry along with another for Ewan McGregor. We sample a delicious Amarone finish, his personal favourite, as James continues, 'We have some 50ppm laid down but it's a work in progress and my main concern just now is the installation of a new pair of stills in October 2016 and the replacement of the current spirit still which will be a logistical challenge to say the least.' When those new stills are functioning capacity will rise to over 1.2m lpa per annum.

We return to James' office where he gives me a brief summary of Arran's bottling policy. This takes place on mainland Scotland where the standard single malt is reduced to a minimum of 46% abv. Arran is also bottled at natural cask strength which varies from expression to expression. No artificial colouring is added with the result that Arran can be quite pale in colour in comparison to some other brands on the market.

All of Arran's whiskies are 'non chill-filtered'. Chill-filtration is a process designed to clarify the colour of a whisky at the bottling stage. The whisky is filtered at very low temperatures (close to 0°c) to remove a natural haze formed by congeners contained in the spirit. However, these congeners also contribute to the final flavour of the whisky and there has been a move, largely consumer-

The modern racking system employed in the filling store.
Neil Wilson

More commonly palletised storage is used for bulk maturation. *Neil Wilson*

driven, in recent years away from chill-filtration. Whiskies which have not been subjected to this process tend to be bottled at a slightly higher alcoholic strength (normally 46% abv) to reduce the possibility of the haze forming at lower temperatures. The potential loss of a little clarity is more than compensated for, however, by the retention of the flavour and character of the whisky.

While the installation of the three new stills in October 2016 will present some difficulties, it is also an opportunity to shut down the stillhouse and carry out maintenance and repairs on the plant such as the mashtun that requires new plastic 'feet' fitted to the bottom of the stirrers to aid draff extraction after mashing. Cochrane's of Annan will install a new boiler at the same time. 'You never get payback when you increase capacity,' James reminds me. 'We are heading towards 1.2m lpa per annum and that involves gearing up everything so all your associated variable costs increase as well … fuel, malt, casks and so on. Your investment is realised in increased value of stocks and a stronger balance sheet.'

The specialised truck used to retrieve and rack casks in
Warehouse No 3. *Neil Wilson*

The distillery staff, 2016. Left to right: Graham Omand, Gordon Bloy, James MacTaggart, John Dowens,
Ben Tattersfield, John McMullan.

GORDON BLOY

Stillman & Senior Operator

Gordon Bloy is another 'incomer' who has become an Arranach having moved
to the island in 2001 and started a new family with John McMullan's daughter,
Samantha. Born in Grangemouth he spent most of his working life driving
haulage lorries, and for the first six years of his time on Arran worked for the
local firm, Arran Haulage.

It was Gordon Mitchell who eventually persuaded Bloy to join the distillery
staff and he arrived just a month before James MacTaggart started as distillery
manager. Since then Gordon has become James' right-hand man and is a trained
stillman and 'senior operator' which means he can turn his hand to just about
anything that needs to be done.

Wanting to know more about the curious French racking system installed in
Warehouse No 3, Gordon took me over it in detail.

The principle is fine and it allows a sole operator to locate a cask, retrieve
it, and then replace it without any disruption to the other casks in storage.
The problem is that it is not space efficient compared to modern racking.
In this warehouse we have 3,000 casks while number four can hold up to
12,000. Where it would make good sense is if all the privately owned casks
were located in number three so that they could be managed more easily.

Gordon Bloy fills a cask.

Warehouse No 3 and the
French racking system.
Neil Wilson

Five French fabricators installed the racking system that also requires a narrow bespoke tractor to move between the casks to insert and extract them. However, the system constricts the number of casks that can be stored in the available height compared to the maximum seven-high palletised system next door. Somehow I feel that while the system clearly has benefits, it's simply not going to take off as the increased cost of the warehousing space required far offsets the benefits. But is a curiously fascinating anomaly.

And Gordon's favourite Arran dram? 'They're all good. What I really like is watching the eagles if they are around when I am on the early shift that starts at six in the morning.'

The oldest cask still maturing on site. *Peter Sandground*

JOHN McMULLAN

Processor & Operator – mashman, stillman

John McMullan was one of the first employees at Lochranza, having left his job 'on the buses' after an acrimonious dispute when Stagecoach arrived on the island, took over Arran Coaches and renegotiated employees' contracts. He wrote to Hal Currie after he and his wife Diane had attended the public meeting in Lochranza on 6 November 1992 at which she had pleaded with locals to support the distillery. Hal responded immediately to John's approach and when the distillery started operating in June 1995, John joined manager Gordon Mitchell and local recruits Thomas Mackenzie and Duncan Simpson to make up the original team of distillery workers. McMullan explained their roles to me:

We were trained by Gordon to do any job that we needed to. Duncan assisted Gordon with office paperwork and also worked in the filling store. We contracted a truck from John Thomson in Lamlash to transport the spent grain and effluent to local farmers but after Alex Dale arrived in 1996, we got our own truck and a trailer which he drove. Ted Kerr from Corrie joined around the same time as Alex and when Tommy left he was replaced by Danny Watkin who also did the distilling along with me, taking turns about. Then when Alex started working part-time John Graham joined from Thomsons and took over all the driving.

All routine maintenance was done by us unless there was a specialised job that needed certification such as welding and fabrication. Basically we all mucked in depending on what needed doing. We might be distilling one week then building a deer fence the next. There was really no job demarcation. We just got on with it. We couldn't fix casks though, so when Tommy Rogers, the cooper from Govan came over with his assistant Richard Meakin and a new shipment of casks, they would fix any leakers on site.

Nowadays John does an eight-hour shift starting at 6am while distilling and mashing are in progress, followed by John Dowens and then Graham Omand (James' nephew) who moved from Islay to work at Lochranza.

ALEX DALE
Retired Driver

Alex is one of the locals from Pirnmill who worked full time at the distillery from 1996 until 2000 and then part-time for 'three or four years' until he finally retired. He became a great friend of Gordon Mitchell. For three days a week he took the effluent tanker down to Braehead Farm at Sliddery where it was used as field fertiliser. He was also a keen photographer and often captured images of the distillery when unusual jobs were being undertaken. We looked over some of his collection.

Here's one of a cupola being installed after the old one had been lifted clean off the roof and blown smack bang into the road. The wind could be really wild up there. I remember there was one of Thomson's workers, Gavin Mutch, who had a Reliant Scimitar, like Princess Anne once had, and he parked it at the distillery. It had fibreglass panels and a slate was blown off the roof and embedded itself in the bodywork. It would have taken his head clean off if he had been hit.

Gordon loved his Muscovy ducks which used to live around the cooling pond and he introduced the peacocks as well. When the Queen came the security was incredible. Before she arrived the place was in lockdown. One bloke asked me what my truck was so I told him it was the effluent lorry and they promptly took it apart to check it over!

Then when she arrived they stopped us going anywhere that had been cleared so Gordon couldn't even get into his office! He was wandering around pleading, 'But I'm the manager … '

The cupola being replaced after a storm blew it off. Not a job for the faint-hearted! *Alex Dale*

Gordon Mitchell's Muscovy ducks were a permanent feature during the early years of production. *Alex Dale*

When Alex eventually called it a day he retired to his house by the seawall, overlooking the Kintyre coastline, with the memories of his old friend always bringing a smile to his face.

CHAPTER SEVEN

The Visitors Arrive

B EFORE LATE 1997 Andrew Currie had been directing the sales and marketing of the company while based on the mainland. Under him Gillian McCreadie, who had started at the company office in Mauchline in early 1995, was managing sales and marketing on the island and working flat out towards the opening of the new, purpose-built VC. Unprepossessing the Portakabins might have been, but they had managed to attract over 25,000 visitors to the distillery in one season and Isle of Arran has since become one of the most visited distilleries in Scotland with annual figures now in excess of 88,000.

The design of the VC was dictated partly by planning regulations and partly by Andrew Currie's desire to create a novel and innovative experience for the visitor. Once Currie had briefed David Hutchison on what he wanted, the framework and outline were agreed with North Ayrshire Council planners. This new design replicated the profile of the distillery buildings and was markedly removed from the original proposed designs dating back to early 1992. Due to planning and fire authority restrictions this meant that the VC had to appear to be a single-storey building and Currie commissioned a London-based company, The Visual Connection, to 'infill' the atrium spaces with the now-famous barley field and waterfall features that have set it apart from other distilleries. He recalls that one of the earliest visitors to the VC asked if the distillery had been built 'around the burn' and had to be convinced that it was artificial. The rest of the design brief for the mezzanine area, the restaurant bar, shop and tasting bar was handled by Paul Hodgkiss Designs of Glasgow.

While all this work has been progressing Hal Currie knew that the locals had

Front of house staff at the VC, June 1996. From left to right: Sandy Rankin, Fiona Crawford, Gillian McCreadie, Marion Noble and Bob Fisher. *Arran Banner*

Fiona Crawford conducts a tour in June 1996 before the VC was built. *Arran Banner*

to be kept onside and be made fully aware of what the company were proposing as it developed the VC. The lesson he had learnt from the scale and virulence of the objections to the distillery was always to expect opposition, no matter how well the proposals were presented. On Friday 15 November 1996 he invited a number of locals to the distillery in order to bring them up to speed about developments. Terry Crawley, later an employee at the distillery, asked what further works were due to be done and Hal replied that once the VC and second warehouse were completed there would be no further work. He did, however, mention that a bottling plant might be constructed 'in eight or ten years time' but would be 'out of public view'. As it turned out, that development would never come to fruition. Would a restaurant and bar be part of the VC? Yes, but no part of it would function as a pub, Crawley was assured. A Lochranza café owner was

worried what the effect of a fully functioning VC might be on her business but Gillian McCreadie was able to assure her that the 'increase in business generated by the bus companies could result in overflow business to the whole of the Lochranza' and that she could benefit from that. Hal expected a further 10 jobs to be created when the VC opened and that the surrounding grounds would be landscaped and planted to create a 'very attractive' impression for visitors as they arrived. Finally, Hal invited everyone to enjoy some hospitality and presented each one in attendance with a miniature of the one-year-old spirit.

In order to have a fully functioning VC and restaurant, it required a licence to sell and offer alcohol from 9am to 1am to the public and the required application to North Ayrshire Council Licensing Board was made in February 1997. But the councillors were not convinced. Alastair Yates felt it would be unfair to the other pub in the village and Janice Gemmell stated that if Lochranza folk felt that one pub was enough for the village, it should be opposed. On Saturday 8 May Andrew Currie tried to clarify the company's position in the letters' pages of the *Banner*.

Sir

I write regarding our application for a public house licence for the distillery Visitors Centre as we are concerned that this has caused alarm in some quarters. We strongly feel that there is no need for alarm and I hope that once the position is clarified people's fears can be allayed.

In terms of licensing the Visitors Centre is unique. Our main sales of alcohol take place through the shop and therefore we require a licence to sell alcohol during shop hours, opening at nine am. We also wish to serve drinks in the restaurant while people eat and so we need a licence to serve alcohol both in the daytime and during the evening. We also plan to have entertainment in the evenings for private functions and for musical events for our diners. The licensing board has advised us that in order to cover all these requirements we must apply for what is in effect a public house licence. We cannot apply for each of these elements separately and in legal terms they fall under the umbrella of a public house licence.

This does not mean however that we intend opening a pub adjacent to the distillery. That is not our business. Further to that we fully sympathise with any fears that we would be soaking up available custom from the existing two public houses in the area; we are strong supporters of the local community and wish to invest in it, providing to other businesses in the

The foundations are laid for the VC. *DHA*

Some locals join staff for an update in the unfinished VC. Left to right: Bill Scott, Peter Emsley, Gordon, Hal, Alec Dale, Gillian, Terry Crawley, Sandy Rankin, Bob Fisher.

area extra income from the extra visitors we believe we will bring to the north end. Our advertisement for more jobs working as guides as well as staff in the restaurant and kitchen has brought an enthusiastic response. We are delighted to create these extra jobs as it has always been part of our plan to increase employment on the island.

We are very excited about the opening of the Centre which should be ready for Easter and I hope that as many people as possible will come to see what we believe will be the best all-weather tourist attraction in the west of Scotland.

Andrew Currie, Mauchline

Another letter from solicitors, JD&S MacMillan, who had made the application on the company's behalf, also explained the requirement for a full public house licence. However, on Monday 17 March the North Ayrshire Council Licensing Board refused it. There had been 19 objections, most of them stating that they had no objection to a restaurant licence, but were totally against a public house licence. One of the objectors was George Stewart of the Lochranza Hotel. Clearly, the explanation given by Andrew Currie and his solicitors had not carried the day and the objectors 'did not buy this'. Several of them attended to argue their case. One was Terry Crawley, by then the Community Councillor for the village. Had the public house licence been granted he was sure that 'they would have had dancing, discos, entertainment … Lochranza nearly had Arran's first night club.' More worrying for the company was that the vote to reject the application was unanimous. George Stewart, having attended the meeting, withdrew his objection as he felt that he now understood the distillery's intentions. However, Terry Crawley was unmoved.

Let's look at what they wanted. A pub licence with off-sales, extensions common to existing pubs but on a daily basis, a supper hour extension and a restaurant licence so that they could provide music, dancing and entertainment. This would give them the ability to operate from ten o'clock in the morning for off-sales and open as a pub through the day with extensions until one o'clock in the morning. After that they could use a supper hour extension until two o'clock. They informed me there would be music, dancing, entertainment and dining in the evening. In any big city that would be called a nightclub, so that's why there was such opposition. As Community Councillor I was inundated with objections, which, I must admit I agreed with. I made an approach to the distillery with the object of discussing the situation but they refused to see me and informed me that their course of action had been set and was not open for any discussion.

We did not want, and objected to, routine daily extensions, supper hour extensions, roistering until two o'clock in the morning with the consequent disruption and noise made by departing guests until much later. We were left with no alternative but to attend the Licensing Board. I put our objections to the Justices as I have outlined and they refused the licence and instructed the distillery's lawyer to consult with us and return to the next meeting of the Board in three months time. In view of the uncooperative attitude of the distillery management I asked the councillors if one of their number would chair a formal meeting and this was agreed. The meeting was held, agreement was reached and subsequently the licence was issued in the form that is still in force to this day.

With the VC due to start functioning in early April, the result had been another setback at a time when the board thought the objecting was over so Andrew Currie had to convince the locals that there was not going to be a nightclub, even less a pub. On 29 March he received some support in the *Banner* from Brian Miller of Dunira, Lochranza.

Sir,
I was surprised and indeed somewhat dismayed to read that the application

for a full licence for the distillery at Lochranza has been turned down last week. As a resident of the village who lives closer to the distillery than some of the objectors I can assure you that I welcome any additional amenity in the village. While I cannot presume to speak on behalf of Lochranza's residents, I have, in the course of conversation with a number of the local people, come to the conclusion that the objectors constitute the minority opinion in this village.

The most common view of many of the residents of Lochranza is that the distillery is the best thing that has happened to the north end of the island in decades. Not only has the distillery attracted ever-increasing numbers of visitors, but it has already provided full-time employment for five people in the area – a not inconsiderable number in a permanent population of only some 160 people. Moreover, the opening of the new visitor centre this month [April] will indeed add to the number of full-time jobs available. Surely the creation of any employment in an area where such opportunities are very scarce is to be applauded and supported.

Again, it appears that most of the local traders welcome the distillery and do not oppose the extension of the licence. Indeed the prevailing opinion is either supportive or neutral in the matter.

It does seem a pity that a handful of residents (some of whom were not slow to accept the generous hospitality of the distillery during its open nights) and one or two vested interests can delay the plans of a new, enterprising, and valuable amenity in the village. Unfortunately the format of notices for licence applications does tend to encourage objections and to discourage letters of support. However, rest assured that, when the application is renewed in due course, I shall certainly write to the Licensing Court [sic] in favour of the distillery.

A week later another local, Heather McConnachie of Hamilton Cottage, entered the fray with a more impassioned appeal on behalf of the distillery.

Sir,
I write to express my astonishment that Lochranza Distillery was recently refused a public licence for its new Visitors Centre and is unable to serve alcoholic drinks from the bar to visitors to the restaurant.

It seems ludicrous that an enterprise which produces whisky of quality and renown, for sale around the world, cannot offer its guests alcohol with their meals. In common with other residents in Lochranza I am disappointed that my supportive views were not canvassed beforehand and were therefore not expressed to the Licensing Court [sic].

I like the Distillery – I think its buildings are beautifully simple; it's in a spectacular location: the new Visitor Centre is attractive and interesting and the staff are friendly and helpful.

Finally, I think the Distillery is of great benefit to the local economy and I hope that the next application for a public licence will be successful.

Behind the scenes and despite this negative development, a great deal of work had been done in order for the *Banner* to announce on Saturday 12 April that Her Majesty Queen Elizabeth would make an official visit to Arran on 9 August on what was expected to be the final voyage of the royal yacht HMS *Britannia*. The Lord Lieutenant of Ayrshire, Major Richard Henderson, was a near neighbour of Ross Peters and both he and Hal Currie actively pursued the possibility of inviting the Queen to open the VC. The initial approaches to the palace were made some 18 months before the event.

After landing at Brodick, she would open the new sports ground at the annual Highland Games (to be rescheduled to suit HM's itinerary) and then on to Lochranza to officially open the VC, returning later to the yacht which would cruise round the north end and moor in the Kilbrannan Sound. 'To the people of Arran it will be a big day,' the *Banner* opined, 'a day to be remembered long into the future.'

On 12 April something else happened: the first visitors stepped over the threshold of the new VC. Alcohol was not available for sale in the restaurant upstairs but could be bought in the shop downstairs although Gillian McCreadie was quoted a fortnight later saying that the company were not going to appeal the licensing board's decision, but reapply in June when she felt that having dealt with the objections, the decision would be made to approve the public house licence.

The merchandising of Arran retail items such as baseball caps, glassware, T-shirts, polo shirts, rugby jerseys, fleeces, mugs, bags, umbrellas, pens and keyrings was dealt with by Mike Smith and Karen McBride of the Orb Group in Glasgow. Smith recalls that, 'Andrew and I spent a lot of time looking at the range and deciding what would work. This was a combination of all the items and ensuring that they all had sensible retail prices. This ranged from as low as £1 right through to over £100 for decanters. Most of the products were made in the UK and we found that the baseball caps and the glassware were the most popular items.' Nowadays, after whisky, chocolates are the bestselling item.

Twenty-five people were now in employment at the company and tours were being conducted in groups of 15 starting in the atrium in front of the waterfall feature, then through to the 'Crofter's Cottage' for a 15-minute video presentation, and then via the 'Smuggler's Tunnel' to the tasting bar and shop. From there, the tours left the VC to cross to the distillery for a 20-minute tour of the distilling process. They were then returned to the shop to part with some hard cash, but with some items such as a miniature pot still decanter and a bottle of malt on offer for £180, most punters left with items such as books, glasses and quaichs. A bottle of ubiquitous Lochranza blended Scotch could be had for £12.49. It was also to be seen on the gantry in the bar on the set of STV's Scottish soap, *Take The High Road*.

Padraig Ahern, a world-travelled chef originally from Cork who had worked at Sotheby's and Harvey Nichols in London, arrived to take charge of the newly fitted kitchen upstairs at the rear of the mezzanine floor which had been aptly named Harold's Restaurant. Under him he had four chefs, a kitchen porter and

Some of the early merchandise available from the VC after opening in April 1997. *Currie family*

four restaurant staff. He was instrumental in how the kitchen was designed and David Hutchison recalls that 'tens of thousands' were invested in it. Ahern saw the facility as an ideal place for ceilidhs, business meetings and wedding receptions. Gillian again parried concerns regarding taking business from the local hotels and the pub by saying that the first night's event of the local Folk Festival would be held at the distillery 'because the village hall didn't seem to want them'. Ahern qualified further, 'Whatever we do should have a knock-on effect for the rest of the community. People who come here will have to sleep somewhere, get their breakfast somewhere and buy their gifts somewhere … and, of course, we'll have a Burns Night. In a distillery what else could we do!' As it turned out on Tuesday

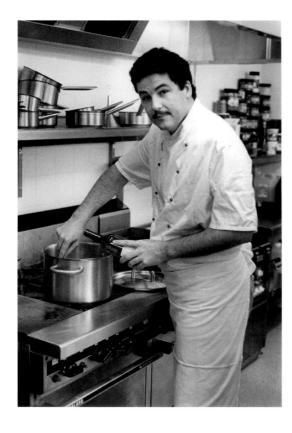

Padraig Ahern, who managed the restaurant 'upstairs' until 1999. *Arran Banner*

Bob Fisher explaining the delights of Arran malt to early visitors Claire and Eileen Anderson from Troon, April 1997. *Arran Banner*

22 April, 38 Lamlash Church Guild members visited the distillery for their annual day out. Approbation of the distillery seemed to be universal.

However, the restaurant still had not received its licence when, on a visit home from Saudi Arabia, Marc Head commented in an otherwise very favourable review of the distillery in the *Banner*:

And now for the small but significant fly in the ointment … the main attraction is our country's newest distillery which has been built along beautifully traditional lines to manufacture a product, which more than any other is synonymous with our part of the world, and yet a visitor cannot

enjoy a dram, a glass of wine or a cold beer while sitting down to a meal. I feel sure that anyone looking round the distillery will realise that the last intention of the management is to turn the area into a large public house – that would completely defeat the concept of both the design and the marketing targets of the project. I personally am not a great drinking man, but I hope that for the sake of those who enjoy a wee nip, the licensing board will look favourably on a future application, and allow a very traditional Scottish venture to develop into a modern international attraction.

Other visitors were of mixed opinions. Anne Bailey of Horsham, who visited Lochranza in mid-June, extolled the whole experience. 'Not only is it attractive and interesting, but the restaurant is such a welcome change from the usual café style that some places make the mistake of opening … it is tasteful in décor, the food is delicious and the staff were extremely helpful and attentive on the day of our visit.' George McAlpine of Stockton-on-Tees was less enthusiastic.

Sir,
My wife and I found your wonderful Island four years ago and have spent time there each year since. We have found the Islanders most friendly and Hotels etc excellent value for money.

It's a darn good ripoff!

Last year my wife and I visited the new Arran Distillery, we paid £1.50 each and for that we were shown round the Distillery, which we found most interesting, at the end of the Tour we were even offered a tasting, if we wished.

This year on June 11th we were joined by friends from the Mainland. As you may recall the weather was rather dampish, no matter; as the husband of the couple was a retired member of Seagrams, and we thought what a good idea to take him and his wife to see the distillery.

On arrival we were charged £3.50 for my wife and I, and owing to age £2.05 for each of our friends, for this we were shown a 12 minute Video, and then we were ushered into no – not the distillery – but the distillery shop! No tour – no tasting!

Maybe Mr Currie time should return to Seagrams to retrain on – 'What's good value for money!'

Quibbling aside, the problem of the lack of a public house licence was solved on a temporary basis when Hal Currie asked George Stewart if he would apply to become licensee for the VC until they had gained approval from the licensing court. By the time HM Queen Elizabeth arrived on Arran on 9 August 1997 for the official opening, the VC was running smoothly and a restaurant licence of sorts was in place. RSVP invitations had been sent out all over the island by the distillery's office manager, Marion Noble, in early July with confirmation letters following on the 23rd. After stepping ashore at Brodick pier the royal party was taken to Ormidale Park where the Queen opened the new sports field and watched part of the Brodick Highland Games. The party progressed on to a huge marquee erected beside Brodick Castle which was filled with large numbers of locals who dined in groups, each one embedded with a security officer, all of them a little short on conversation and chit-chat. Jim Lees, who attended with his wife Shauna and was also due to attend the opening of the VC at the distillery afterwards, recalls that once the luncheon was finished, 'they just seemed to disappear without any of us noticing them go'. The cold luncheon of smoked salmon, stuffed chicken and Arran strawberries and cream was praised by the Queen who sought out the organiser Judy Cook afterwards to compliment her. Arrival of the royal party at Isle of Arran Distillery was scheduled for 2.30pm and her visit was due to be about an hour long. Jim Lees, however, had to hitch a lift in the bus used by the other Ayrshire and Arran tourist board directors as his wife Shauna had left ahead of him in the family car. According to the *Banner*, when they had all arrived:

… some of the other arrangements came a little unstuck. It seems those invited for lunch saw no food until 4pm and guests were checked by security and then a cordon was put between them and the loos, a state of affairs which caused much leg crossing and some people to break ranks and career across the fields looking for the nearest bush.

Andrew Currie's four-year-old daughter, Amber, presented the Queen with a bouquet, but only after board director Patrick Dromgoole had bribed her with a £1 coin to do so. The Queen was then introduced to all of the directors of the

company and their wives in turn – Les Auchincloss, Patrick Dromgoole and Ross Peters along with the Currie family before unveiling a plaque on the wall of the VC as the main reminder of her visit. The *Spirit of Arran* newsletter (Volume 3, number 3) related the rest of the visit as its cover story.

Director Andrew Currie then led her Majesty into the Visitor Centre where she met senior staff, Sandy Rankin, Gillian McCreadie and Padraig Ahern as well as the architect, David Hutchison. The Queen looked at the

whisky exhibits, sniffed the yeast and looked inside the barrels and then went into the crofter's inn [*sic*] where she watched some of the video. She then walked through the crofter's tunnel [*sic*] into the shop where she signed a photograph of herself and our Visitor's Book.

The tour continued into the distillery where Gordon Mitchell told Her Majesty about the whisky making process. The Queen seemed very interested in this and spent some time with Gordon looking inside the mashtuns and watching the spirit safe.

Queen Elizabeth clearly enjoying her visit to Lochranza Distillery, 9 August 1997, when she officially opened the VC.

The Queen appeared very relaxed throughout the visit and completed it with one of her popular walkabouts, personally greeting some of the people who had travelled to the distillery and who were obviously delighted with the gesture. The Royal party then left for Lochranza where the Royal Yacht Britannia was waiting to continue the cruise of the Western Isles on its way to Balmoral.

After the royal visit life returned to normal for the distillery, however Gillian McCreadie was approached by Arran Aromatics to fill the position of marketing manager and so she gave notice and moved on in December that year. Andrew Currie arrived to live next door to the distillery after buying Millhill house, while Marion Noble became his personal assistant as well as being in charge of the mail-order operation and front-of-house staff. Sandy Rankin, who had initially

joined as senior tour guide, became sales manager and financial controller as well as the 'downstairs' manager, while Padraig Ahern controlled 'upstairs'. It was not an ideal management structure and was to become an issue that was not resolved until Paul Currie hired Tom Pearson as the first VC manager proper in 1999 after Sandy Rankin left to go to the Auchrannie Hotel in Brodick. Around the same time Ahern moved on to take up another challenge. Nevertheless some 40,000 visitors were welcomed in the 1997 season in the new VC and trading in the restaurant and shop was encouraging. Terry Crawley summed up the licensing episode that had initially stalled operations:

It was a very unfortunate hiccup in the history of the distillery, the more so as it was totally unnecessary and could have been avoided if discussions had taken place. In practice it meant the distillery could not sell whisky for

Alex Dale and Gordon Mitchell enjoying the party after the Queen's visit. *Alex Dale*

When the Queen opened the VC a display of casks on the ground floor was one of the interactive units for visitors. *Arran Banner*

three months when they really needed to make money.

The impact of the distillery, however, has been positive, not only on the village in particular, but also the island in general. It has been a significant factor in raising the profiles of both Lochranza and Arran nationally and internationally.

On 18 December the company was awarded first place in the final of *The Business Game* on STV when Andrew Currie took home a cheque for £10,000 along with a £5,000 piece of specially commissioned crystal. In a neck-and-neck finish Arran had edged ahead by one point awarded by the three judges, chaired by Sir Rocco Forte, due to the company's 'future prospects'.

By the end of 2001 it had achieved 5-star designation from VisitScotland. Tom Pearson stated in the *Banner* of 29 December that,

I truly believe for us to have achieved this is incredible. We are in a remote island location which comes with its own problems in terms of staffing and the training of the staff. But teamwork and plain hard work paid off. When I arrived here I attempted in my own wee way to galvanise all the strengths we had to make visits here unique and memorable.

The standards were pretty high as they were but we focused on upgrading a number of areas such as front desk presentation and toilet areas. We are now very much a can-do organisation and the visitor centre gets as much benefit as we do.

Pearson and his team had already achieved a 4-star grading after his arrival two years before but the level of visitor experience was subject to varying standards of management after Pearson moved on, not being finally resolved until the arrival

Party time and a night off for the staff in the VC, probably taken in 1998. Among those present were Andrew Currie, Gordon Mitchell, Bob Fisher, John McMullan, Sandy Rankin, John Graham, Fiona Crawford, Marion Noble, Hal Currie, Paul Currie, Lisa Cumming, Padraig Ahern and Alex Dale. *Alex Dale*

The company has always been a strong supporter of local charities. Tom Pearson hands over a cheque to the Duke of Edinburgh's Awards Scheme, April 2001. *Arran Banner*

of Robin Bell in early 2005. Before he retired in 2010 he created a management and training structure which, after he handed over to Faye Waterlow, led to the VC winning the Best Distillery Visitor Experience in the 2014 *Scottish Field* Whisky Challenge, repeating the feat in 2015.

Sheila Gilmore, the Executive Director of VisitArran and its sister charity the Arran Trust, described the impact that the establishment and development of the distillery has had on the island.

I think it followed on from the Auchrannie which started out under Iain Johnston in 1988 as a small country hotel and then was gradually expanded

to offer locals and tourists indoor, all-weather attractions. Arran desperately needed that sort of facility. There was Brodick Castle and its grounds, of course, but that would always remain that sort of attraction … fine if you like castles and heritage. Around the same time other Arran-based entrepreneurs were gradually building local businesses, among them Arran Aromatics and Taste of Arran. These businesses probably didn't think that an Arran brand would necessarily be created but they just worked hard in their own way until, as a group, there was real momentum. The distillery was central to the building of the Arran brand and opened up the north of the island. Before that it was a quiet place to which people just retired and where

The Stagecoach open-top bus which the distillery first sponsored in April 1996.
Alex Dale

the outdoors enthusiasts took to the mountains. As the food sector grew Taste of Arran was developed further and with the cessation of Destination Arran in 2007, VisitArran was established as a partnership amongst all the leading tourism-oriented island businesses including the distillery.

The impact the distillery has made cannot be underestimated. It's one of the jewels in the crown of Arran attractions and has fantastic, open, supportive staff. Above all, it has brought year-round employment to many locals on the island and given that the island's population dropped by hundreds at the last census, that's really important. It has helped raise the bar across the tourism spectrum and Arran now regularly receives awards for the high standards of its hotels and other attractions. When visitors ask me what there is to see and do on Arran, I just reply 'What is there not to see and do?'

The distillery has been generous as well, helping to raise £6000 from the sales of its Millennium Cask to help fund repairs on paths and aid local projects through The Arran Trust.

George Stewart also has nothing but praise for the distillery. Having moved to the island from Dumfries in 1983 after he and his father bought the Lochranza Hotel, he has built up a strong relationship with visitors to the distillery who come from

George Stewart's two most recent Easan Biorach ex-sherry bottlings of the Arran malt, available at the Lochranza Hotel. *Neil Wilson*

abroad and stay over. His cosy bar has an extensive malt menu including some pretty rare drams. These include his own Easan Biorach 10 and 15-year-old bottlings of Arran malt. In 1996 he imported six ex-sherry butts from Spain through personal connections in Malaga. These eventually came to Lochranza by way of Campbeltown on a fishing boat and were filled that year. To date he has bottled five of them at cask strength, the last of which was the 15-year-old. Sometime soon he will bottle the 20-year-old.

The only loss of business we suffered were the coach parties that had lunch here before the visitor centre opened. But it's been no threat to us at all and I thought it was a great idea from the start.

The distillery hasn't just improved the village, it has improved the whole island. The Arran brand profile has been raised by it and the image of Arran around the world is closely tied to the distillery and the success it has achieved.

Endorsements like these are gained because the distillery is the embodiment of the people who are and have been involved in it and the way in which the VC employees are regarded by the thousands of visitors who take the trouble to come to Arran. That effort is not lost on the Arran staff. Here are some of them who, both past and present, have been crucial to this success.

MISS BLACK

FAYE BLACK was a third-generation Arranach who had lived all her life in Lochranza when she started working at the VC when it opened at Easter 1997. She first worked as a waitress in Harold's Restaurant on the mezzanine floor where fine food and wine were dispensed to around 70 customers each evening in the summer months. The food was a cut above the normal distillery fare and she remembers it doing good, steady business. But there were two problems: the quiet winter tourist season and the lack of staff accommodation. Lochranza simply did not have enough available beds to cater for the seasonal staff required and transporting them to and from work on Arran was a logistical nightmare. Faye also confided that there were some historic problems of 'dipping the till' with previous staff who have long since left the distillery's employ. Eventually Harold's Restaurant was remodelled to cater as a drop-in bistro/café for year-round visitors with a much simpler menu and the old name disappeared with the change.

In 1999 Faye was promoted to tour guide and was trained by Bob Fisher who taught her all she knows about whisky.

To be honest, before Bob came along I hated whisky. It was 'the devil's juice' as far as I was concerned. If I tasted it, I had to spit it out. Bob changed all that. After work each day we would spend a half-hour of what he called 'Golden Time' with me in the tasting bar where he started my real whisky education. What he did was take a glass of water and add a few drops of whisky to it. I tasted that, no problem at all, and then he'd tell me something about the process involved. Next day, the same thing would happen except he would increase the dose of whisky! This went on through the summer season for three months until, by the end, I was drinking a proper measure of Scotch and really enjoying it. He called me his 'Girl Friday' as he'd taken me from a state of complete ignorance on the subject to one of complete enlightenment! I owe Bob everything I know about whisky.

When not working at the distillery Faye studied at Aberdeen University before completing her studies at Napier University where she was not only Founding Mother of the Napier University Whisky Society in 2004 (which is still flourishing) but also met her future husband, David Waterlow. Ten years later their wedding day was on 17 May which happened to be World Whisky Day 2014. The reception was held at the only place it could have been … the distillery. Faye even had a special 17-year-old bottling done for the day named Miss Black's Bottle to celebrate her marriage and the 17 years she had spent at the distillery. In less than a month it was one of the fastest-selling special releases Arran have ever done and was gone by 9 June.

In December 2010 Robin Bell, who had become VC manager in January 2005, retired and handed over to Faye who was eventually put in overall charge of the VC, café/bistro and retail area. Nowadays, she also doubles as a Brand Ambassador which has taken her to venues throughout the UK as well as Canada, Italy, Sweden and Germany. Under her direction the VC has been revitalised and now contributes around £180,000 of profit to the company each year, operating on a seven-day basis in summer and a six-day basis in winter with the only closures being for three weeks' maintenance in January. The fact that the Scottish Government's Road Equivalent Tariff (RET), which has effectively halved the costs of the ferry crossing, was introduced in October 2014 has meant that travel onto and off the island for tourists and Arranachs alike has created all-year-round tourism and places like the Auchrannie Resort in Brodick are now operating at 90% occupancy throughout the year.

One of Faye's main responsibilities is creating collaborative marketing amongst like-minded companies operating on Arran. Now that Arran is established as a brand in itself, with cheese, chocolate, perfume, soap, beer, meat, seafood and whisky all falling under the Arran banner, meetings of the VisitArran marketing team take place on a monthly basis. She works closely with Alastair Dobson of Taste of Arran which co-ordinates the marketing of the Arran brands for food and drink.

The distillery also offers staff training to island establishments so that they are better prepared when dealing with visitors and their whisky questions. Several Arran hotels and pubs have very good whisky gantries and just down the road from the distillery, George Stewart's Lochranza Hotel offers over 300 whiskies in the bar. Other Arran locations for the whisky enthusiast include the Drift Inn at Lamlash, the Kildonan Hotel in the south end and the refurbished Douglas Hotel opposite the ferry terminal in Brodick which Sean Henry, who was adopted into an Arran family and went on to make a fortune in property in Russia, refurbished between 2011 and 2013 with a multi-million pound investment. A picture of Faye's father, a Scots Guardsman, hangs on the pub wall as he had trained Sean as

a cadet before he went abroad. Sean has no qualms about spending so much on the Douglas. Faye recalls him telling her, 'If I didn't it would have gone on fast cars and fast women! Besides, I wanted to put something back into the island.'

Other places to visit are the Kinloch Hotel at Blackwaterfoot, the Fiddlers in Brodick and the Ormidale Hotel, also in Brodick. And the Arran Butcher will soon be creating haggis laced with Arran malt whisky while the local chocolatier, Arran Chocolate in Brodick, is currently supplying the distillery with 'half-barrel' chocolates filled with Arran Gold. However, plans for Arran Brewery to produce an ale matured in ex-Arran distillery casks have been dropped.

The 'distillery family', which Faye relates is a truly worldwide one, has a diverse membership. René Helverskov Andersen, a Dane who owns and operates his own furniture-making and decorating business with around 30 employees (Arran's payroll is 35!) is one of them. Each year René arrives in January and spends two weeks working at the distillery undertaking painting and renovation on a *pro bono* basis. His ethos is simply to 'give back'. Others return from around the world as singles to the Arran Malt & Music Festival each year in June, knowing that they will encounter old friends, like minds and forge new and lasting friendships without having to bring their family with them. 'The White Stag Dinner is held then and followed on the last day by the Survivors' Lunch', Faye relates. 'Survivors' Lunch?' I ask. 'You'll have to come and find out,' she replies. As an Arran Bondholder, maybe it's about time I did.

CAMPBELL LAING

Senior Tour Guide

Campbell cuts an imposing figure in his 'work gear'. In his kilt and black shirt he embodies the bold physique of the Highland Scot … except, he's Glaswegian born-and-bred. After 30 years in the Glasgow police, he retired in 1993 to the 'tin-roofed wreck' he had bought three years earlier at Pirnmill and started renovating. He then worked at the CalMac ferry terminal at Brodick for the next

Campbell Laing. *Neil Wilson*

Tour guides, 2016. From left to right: Douglas Coulter, Billy Paton, Gerard Tattersfield, Stewart Dunsmuir, Campbell Laing and Jim Douglas.

13 years until Robin Bell, who had returned as the new VC manager in 2005 after a previous spell as a tour guide, approached him and asked if he'd be interested in working at the distillery. Robin had noticed the way Campbell engaged with the public on the quayside and thought he would make a good member of the team. He took the offer up immediately and over the course of the next seven years rose to senior tour guide and supervisor but now works part-time.

When Campbell started he knew nothing about whisky, and believed that peatiness in Scotch was due to the water used in distillation. He was soon disabused of that common misconception and his command of the whisky production process, its history and heritage is now second to none. Campbell's greatest asset is what is referred to in 'corporate speak' as 'excellent interpersonal communication skills', in other words he has the gift of the gab and immediately makes visitors to Arran feel at home. That's due to Campbell's love of meeting people and his inherent sense of fun. He is comfortable with all nationalities and notes that the most enquiring of them are the French, Swedish and Germans, 'All of them are distilling in their own countries now so their understanding on the process is much greater than most.'

Whenever a group tour is about to be taken round Campbell gathers them in the central atrium of the VC next to the burbling water feature. This is where he 'gauges' them so that he can make the tour as interesting as possible for the less knowledgeable, while ensuring that the 'anoraks' are not bored into

Campbell starts another tour. *Neil Wilson*

The atrium of the VC. One visitor thought the waterfall feature was real … *Neil Wilson*

somnolescence. If a knowledgeable whisky society is taking the tour Campbell does not bother to explain the process at all and instead answers their questions as they raise them.

Prior to 2016 there were three levels of tours called the Oak, Copper and Gold but these have been superceded and the current visitor tour experience at Lochranza consists of another three tours, all of them of 45 minutes duration. The Distillery Tour costs £7.50, as does the Warehouse Tour and the Tutored Tasting costs £15. These three tours are designed to be taken either individually or tagged on to one another. This allows for flexibility where the visitors can choose a short or more in-depth tour depending on the time they have available or the company they are in.

But if you are in a hurry to get to the ferry, the £3.50 'Drop In' tour consists of the video and sampling a dram of Arran at the same time. If you are driving, you'll get a miniature to take home instead.

Some visitors tend not to fit the normal mould. Campbell recalls a group of Norwegians who took the Gold Tour in 2012 and on arrival at the river source promptly stripped off to their underwear and clambered into the freezing water. He was struck dumb until one of the group told him that at every distillery they visited, they always had to seek out the water source and bathe in it! Other visitors have been known to do the same thing in the pool below the water feature inside the atrium. Perhaps the less said about that the better.

Campbell takes me on a quick tour round the well-stocked shop. I ask him what the bestseller is. 'This,' and he hands me a bottle of Arran Gold, the distillery's malt whisky cream liqueur. 'We sell about six or seven cases of this each day in the summer season. The more elderly visitors can't get enough of it.' He hands me a sample and I see what he means. It is extremely moreish and well-balanced. And then I realised I was just past my 60th birthday. Oh, well, maybe not such a bad thing after all …

Eclipse moored off
Lochranza, July 2015.
Glen Sloss

ROMAN ABRAMOVICH

Malt Whisky Enthusiast

In the first week of July 2015 the *Eclipse* sailed out of the Firth of Clyde to begin a tour of the Inner Hebrides taking in Bute, Arran and Islay. Aboard were 60 crew members including security staff and the owner's family (as well as a helicopter and a submarine). The owner was a whisky enthusiast, Roman Abramovich, who also happens to own Chelsea FC and is worth almost £6 billion. After visiting Bute the *Eclipse* moored off Lochranza and dominated the view west to Kintyre. At 536 feet long she was, until recently, the world's largest private yacht and is 124 feet longer than the *Britannia* which also moored off Lochranza in August 1997.

A visit to the distillery was inevitable and a call was duly taken from his staff asking for an appropriate time to come ashore. Campbell Laing conducted Abramovich around and found him to be 'very humble and unassuming generally. He was very pleasant.' Abramovich bought a number of bottlings and the party returned to the yacht. But then the story takes a slight detour from the ordinary.

A Lochranza lady heard about the whiskies Abramovich had bought and decided to take the bull by the horns. Her husband had built up a collection of Arran bottlings over the years and felt it was time to sell them on. She thought that Roman might be interested and prepared a list and added her mobile number and the price they wanted … then she jumped in a kayak and paddled out to the yacht. Met by the ever-present security staff she deftly explained why she was there, so they took the list and thanked her. She thought that would be the end of it all, but a day later Abramovich got in touch, agreed to take the collection for an undisclosed sum and asked her not to contact the press. She kept her word.

Before *Eclipse* sailed on to Islay the crew asked if they could tour the distillery but had to do it in three shifts of 20 as they could not process a group of 60 in one go. Takings in the shop were particularly good that day …

EWAN McGREGOR

Actor

Andrew Currie's contacts in the media led to one of Britain's hottest acting properties appearing at Arran's biggest media event since the Queen's visit the previous year when Crieff's favourite son, Ewan McGregor, arrived in Lochranza on 25 July 1998. This marked the first full three years of production and meant that the new 'Arran water' was now legally Scotch whisky. A large party was thrown with music from Arran Brass, a barbecue and an all-day bar to satisfy the throng of locals who attended. McGregor clearly enjoyed the experience as the *Banner* reported on 1 August.

Ewan McGregor, appeared to be enjoying sampling the whisky tremendously, and even allowed himself to become slightly garrulous when he talked to the press. So much so that his mother, who acts as his agent, had to remind him that he was speaking to journalists. He commented that it was 'beautifully sweet, if not slightly too strong. But if you add a nip of water it is superb'. Although Ewan confessed that whisky was not his usual tipple, it was one of the nicest he had ever tasted. Who knows if beer will remain his favoured drink, as he did receive a hogshead of whisky as a fee!

Andrew Currie and Ewan McGregor at the start of what was to become a very long celebration! *Arran Banner*

Starstruck local lassies queue up for Ewan's autograph. *Arran Banner*

Ewan McGregor toasts the first sampling of three-year old Arran malt, 25 July 1998. *Arran Banner*

It was a major PR coup for the company as journalists from the UK national press had made their way over to Arran to attend a press conference where McGregor played his part to the full but did manage to give an exclusive one-to-one interview with the editor of the *Banner* and reveal his desire the play 007, much in the same style as Sean Connery – 'a serial womaniser who quite enjoys eliminating his enemies'. And his perfect Bond girl? 'Cameron Diaz, she is the best I have ever worked with.'

Despite the attendance of his mum, McGregor was the guest of Andrew Currie at Millhill House that evening where the early hours were whiled away playing poker and drinking Arran malt. The next day, a very fuzzy-headed marketing director arrived at work and was introduced to Gordon Mitchell's ultimate hangover cure. Seeing that Andrew was the worse for wear, Gordon led him to the side of a fermenting washback, opened the hatch, and pushed his head in. 'I thought I'd been punched in the face,' Currie recalled, 'but it worked!'

Takeshi Taketsuru's visit to the distillery was a highlight. David Croll, on the far left of the group, stands behind Takeshi. Whisky writer Michael Jackson is in the centre of the group and Tom Pearson on the right. *Arran Banner*

Masataka Taketsuru and his Scottish wife, Rita. *alchetron.com*

TAKESHI TAKETSURU

Son of Japanese whisky pioneer

In August 2002, the distillery was accorded one of the highest profile visits in the world of whisky. With an entourage of over 20 members of the Japanese press, as well as whisky writer Michael Jackson, the nephew and adoptive son of Masataka Taketsuru (1894-1979), father of the Japanese whisky industry, arrived on Arran. In 2001 his 10-year-old Yoichi single malt whisky had been awarded 'Best of the Best' in *Whisky Magazine*'s World Whiskies Awards, the first time a non-Scottish whisky had taken such an award.

Masataka Taketsuru arrived in Scotland in December 1918 and took a course in organic chemistry at Glasgow University in order to understand how Scotch whisky was made. He lodged with a Kirkintilloch family where he met Rita Cowan and they fell in love and eloped. After taking apprenticeships at Longmorn

on Speyside, Bo'ness grain distillery and Hazelburn in Campbeltown, Taketsuru and his wife returned to Japan in late 1920 by way of the USA. He eventually founded the Yoichi Distillery on Hokkaido Island and the Nikka whisky dynasty. Rita never left Japan and she died there in 1961. Masataka, who mourned his wife's passing every day, was buried next to her above Yoichi Distillery in 1979. Takeshi's tour of Scotland was an attempt to broadly retrace his father's journey some 80 years before when he set out to learn how to make whisky. *The Banner* recorded the party's visit:

After the tour, all members of the ensemble were given samples of the Arran distillery's quality cask-strength malt. Michael Jackson, one of that rare and lucky breed known as 'whisky writers', was present to taste the tipple. Jim Murray has previously described the Japanese Yoichi ten-year-old malt: 'a massive peat surge is immediately countered by an oaky dryness. But soon the peat returns in a kippery, salty style. Massive and chewy with an ever-increasing oiliness and sweetness.' Hoping to elicit a similar response, I asked Mr Taketsuru whether he preferred the Arran cask-strength whisky in his hand to his own world-conquering malt. He commented that the 'malt has an excellent balance'. His translator added that he is 'too polite to say which he prefers'.

Tom Pearson had made meticulous plans to welcome their Japanese friends, laying on amongst other things a banquet lunch of sushi with a 'Scottish smoked salmon twist'. It was a much enjoyed reunion and a fitting tribute to the memory of Father Taketsuru.

ANDREW SMITH, JAN VISSERS & SCOTT BAIN

The legions of Arran fans around the world have their own stories to tell about what makes the island, the distillery and the whisky so special. I contacted three of them and asked if they would like to answer some questions. Andrew Smith hails from Aberdeenshire, Jan Vissers lives in Switzerland and Scott Bain is from Northamptonshire. This is how they responded.

Q: How old are you?
Andy: 31.
Jan: Vintage 1978. I am 37.
Scott: 48.

Q: What is your occupation?
Andy: Veterinary surgeon.
Jan: I run a 1,000-square-metre shop with all kinds of beverages. I specialise in malt whisky.
Scott: Airline Operations Duty Manager.

Jan Vissers

Scott Bain in the stillhouse on the left.

This photo was set up by Andrew Smith and taken by his wife Rachelle. Jaclyn McKie ran a White Stag competition entitled #myfavouritearranmalt where she asked people though Twitter and Facebook to send in photos of their favourite expressions of Arran whisky. Andrew submitted this one as his favourite Arran malt was an ex-sherry cask single malt as pictured. He won the competition and got a weekend at The Douglas Hotel in Brodick with a Gold Tour and bottle of 10-year-old.

Q: Do you in any way have a business relationship with Isle of Arran Distillers?
Andy: No.
Jan: Yes. It started in the early 2000 when I began to sell the whiskies from Isle of Arran Distillery in my shop.
Scott: No.

Q: Are you a White Stag member?
Andy: Yes.
Jan: Yes.
Scott: Of course!

Q: When did you first become interested in Scotch whisky?
Andy: Working as a barman in a castle hotel when I was 18. At that time we had a broad selection of whiskies and I felt I needed to understand them in order to best advise customers on them and try to help them make a selection.
Jan: At the end of the 1990s.
Scott: When I look back on it, whisky has always been there. Visiting Tormore Distillery as a child to listen to the bells chime. Relations living on the Glenury-Royal Distillery site in Stonehaven. My grandmother was housekeeper for one of the Ballantine's executives and there is Inchgower Distillery in Buckie, where the other side of my family come from.

Q: When did you first become aware of Isle of Arran Distillery?

Andy: From the moment the planning application went in. At first I didn't really know what to think of it. At that age I just liked Arran for the wildlife and the bike rides. I began to pay much closer attention to the distillery in about 2005-6 and have followed their story in much greater detail since then.

Jan: Around 2000.

Scott: When they first advertised the Arran Bond. My Uncle took up the offer.

Q: What would you describe your relationship with Arran whisky as?

Andy: It feels like we have another family now, a group of people that in normal life we would have never met, brought together by a shared passion for Arran whisky. As much as we love the whisky itself, it has become much more about the 'family' and we all look forward to meeting up each year at the festival and throughout the year. I feel immensely privileged to have been part of the cask selection panels for the festival bottlings the last few years and an absolute highlight was participating in the White Stag tasting panel to pick the cask for the first White Stag bottling. The Arran staff have always been so welcoming and helpful, I don't know another distillery like it.

Jan: Since 2010 I have been an official and proud Ambassador of Arran Distillers.

Scott: I have watched Arran grow up and mature and have a friendly relationship with the team at Lochranza and Stirling. There is very much a family feel around Arran and you can often find three generations of my family visiting the distillery at the same time.

Q: How many times have you visited Arran?

Andy: I've been going to Arran, and in particular Lochranza, every year since I was born, usually once or twice a year. My dad used to spend his summers there with his family when he was young and it has become a real family tradition. We have our routines … steak from Hugh, cheese from the wee cheese shop, night-time walks to hear the stags, the same walks round to Fairy Dell and up to Loch Na Davie. Regular visits to the distillery have become one of the key parts of that routine now.

Jan: Sorry, I have lost count!

Scott: My mother's side of the family come from Lamlash and we have always visited Arran on a regular basis.

Q: What do you think is the special, unique feature of Isle of Arran Distillery compared to other island distilleries?

Andy: I'd say that a significant part of the unique nature of the distillery is its independence. You get the impression that decisions are made for the best of the distillery and the island, rather than to fit into part of a portfolio. The fact that it is the only distillery on Arran, an island with such an extensive history of illicit distilling is interesting. In addition to this there is the water source; it is one of the reasons for the location of the distillery and whilst water may be a contentious issue these days when it comes to production quality I do strongly believe that it influences the spirit (mash pH, mineral content during fermentation and distilliation, dilution prior to cask filling etc). Having swam in, fished and consumed the clear water I can testify to its clarity and purity! Perhaps the most significant feature for me is a personal one and the feeling of a bond to the island dominates in the same way that I'm sure Islay, Jura, Orkney and Hebridean fans feel about their islands of choice.

Jan: After all the years the company is still independent and it is one big happy family. And the distillery is located in one of the most beautiful places in Scotland.

Scott: Lochranza is the most stunning setting for a distillery and the people of Arran always have a warm welcome. The fact that the distillery is independent, standing on its own two feet makes Lochranza special. Nothing is too much work for the staff and they are always available to help answer any questions or requests. I get a feeling of belonging and being part of something special.

Q: Have you any special memories of visits to the distillery you feel other Arran fans might like to read about?

Andy: I am struggling to isolate a single moment, but getting piped into the warehouses on the eve of the 18th anniversary and witnessing Euan and James opening a cask for us to enjoy that evening had me in goose bumps … the thick smell of oak and spirit in the warehouse and a real feeling that it was a historic moment for the distillery. It was our first visit during festival time and sparked so many new friendships and great memories over that weekend. Some of my fondest memories were spent across the road in the restaurant called the Stag's Pavilion. We all meet there after the festival and have shared some very special bottles of Arran over dinner. This past year we shared one of the very first Arran Malts, a 2012 festival bottling and the sublime White Stag to much cheering and celebration. It's fantastic to share these drams with people who really appreciate it and a delight to see these whiskies being enjoyed as they were intended … a very fine drink rather than an ornament or a commodity to flog at auction.

Jan: I remember very clearly the day in 2010 when I walked into the Visitor Centre and saw my name was on the Ambassadors' Shield. That was a truly emotional moment.

Scott: I have many special memories. Having the opportunity to be involved in the White Stag bottling and the company helping me out to celebrate my eldest son's 18th birthday are a couple that immediately spring to mind. At last year's festival CalMac had gone on strike which left us with the very real possibility of having to miss the Friday night White Stags' meal. Being constrained by both work and travel commitments it looked very likely that we would have to miss it altogether. Then the Arran team came to the rescue. I was phoned by Louisa Young to ask if we would be interested in going over on the Friday morning on a chartered boat they would lay on for a number of us. Of course, I jumped at the opportunity and we made it over in good time.

Q: Is there anything about the distillery you feel could be improved?

Andy: I'm happy to see the distillery grow as long as the quality is maintained and hope that it can continue to be matured on the island. I really think that is vitally important to maintain the character and soul of the whisky.

Jan: Not really. I like the way they are working now.

Scott: Arran is constantly developing the location. They do not stand still. This will only enhance the visitor experience.

Q: Do you think the limited expressions produced each year detract from the standard core range bottlings?

Andy: There is definitely a very fine balance between producing limited editions to satisfy people that are looking for the next new expression for consumption or collection, and for the distillery to maximise the potential turnover from the total production but at the same time retain a solid base in the core production and not to produce so many limited editions that they cease to seem limited at all. If you make too many limited editions not only do some collectors get weary of it but it can reflect badly on the intentions of the distillery.

I personally believe Arran manage to maintain the balance well for a number of reasons. Primarily the core product remains excellent. It is the core that initially attracted us all to the brand and has to remain the heart as that will be most whisky drinker's experience of Arran whisky. At a time when many of the larger distilling companies are chill-filtering, bottling at 40% abv and replacing age statements with flavour-led 'No Age Statement' (NAS) bottlings, much to the dismay of the whisky hardcore, Arran has stuck true to and expanded a great core range. I'm still very happy to enjoy a standard Arran 10 or 14 on an evening and there aren't many other core whiskies I'd still say that about. They also succeed because the creativity behind the limited editions is exceptional, they usually have a story to tell about the island or the distillery and are presented so magnificently.

There is also a strong understanding on the part of the distillery that the contents of the bottle are key and it doesn't matter how utterly majestic the bottle looks, the contents must be equally impressive. Again this harks back to the independent nature, I believe these editions are brought out as part of a passion for their brand and are born of soul and great ideas within the team, not an outsourced marketing exercise.

Jan: No, I think they are a good addition to the core range, some are just stunning, like the new quarter cask, The Bothy.

Scott: Completely the opposite, you only have to look at how quick the White Stag and Smugglers' editions sold out to see how important limited expressions are. This all helps build Arran's reputation and gets the name out there.

Q: Do you have any favourite(s)?

Andy: There's a photo of me in a field drinking one of the premium cask sherry expressions which we took for their photo competition. I still think fondly of this one but in terms of flavour, design and memory I think the White Stag bottling really means an awful lot me. If I could only save one bottle in my collection it would be this one.

Jan: Yes many, but for the moment for sure it is the 1997, 18-year-old Ambassador's Dram, this is the fourth single cask that I have selected from the distillery.

Scott: The last White Stag bottling and the fino sherry bottling from last year's festival in 2015.

Q: Are there other Scotch whiskies that you rank above Isle of Arran?

Andy: I love whisky generally, it is such a diverse drink and such a social one too that I'm always interested to try something I haven't before and further my knowledge and experience. I would say though that I do not have the same emotional attachment to other distilleries. Arran is young so it is difficult to compare, I think in terms of current distillation practice it will be amongst the best although I do have a soft spot for distillation in the era of Golden Promise barley and when high quality ex-sherry casks were plentiful.

Jan: No!

Scott: I just love Arran whisky and all that it stands for. If you look at the whole package of whisky, Visitor Centre and staff – nowhere else in Scotland even comes close.

Q: How would you feel if Isle of Arran Distillers was sold to a large foreign industry concern such as Pernod-Ricard or Beam Suntory?

Andy: I think it would completely transform the company, it would be very difficult to retain the soul and character. So much about the brand is built upon the independent nature of the company.

Jan: I prefer not to think about this.

Scott: I believe what we have at Arran just now is the best of the best. I would not like to see it lose its identity if taken over by one of the majors.

Q: How would you feel if Isle of Arran Distillers was sold to a UK-based industry concern?

Andy: I do fear this scenario. Every time I read an article stating how well the business did in a year part of me is very pleased but a small part is concerned that this is to drum up a buyer! I need a lot longer to save up …

Jan: Let's keep it in Scottish hands.

Scott: I'd feel the same way as the last answer.

Q: How aware are you of the story of how Isle of Arran Distillers was established?

Andy: I've heard the story of Harold Currie at the dinner and the idea of establishing the distillery on Arran.

Jan: Very familiar.

Scott: I have watched Arran grow from being an idea to where it is now.

Q: Do you think there is room for another distillery on Arran?

Andy: I have heard rumours of Isle of Arran Distillers building a second distillery in the south of the island for a peated malt. Whilst it would be good to see the business grow and diversify I hope that it would not detract from the original site and as so much importance was placed on the original location, I'd hope that the same care was taken when considering a second site. If a different company was to establish a new distillery I'd need to have an idea of their plans before considering how I felt about it. We are used to the idea of new distilleries popping up nowadays, Arran was a pioneer of its day though and to have reasonable credibility I'd like to see a project of a similar scale to Arran or Ardnamurchan rather than an off-the-shelf micro-distillery with modified gin stills.

Jan: Why not?

Scott: It's an interesting thought but it would have major problems in trying to live up to what is happening at Lochranza.

Q: Do you think Isle of Arran Distillers should make gin like many other Scottish distilleries?

Andy: Honestly no. I am not a fan of the gin market, packaged as a crafted, artisan product when in the majority of cases industrial gin concentrate is passed through a still with a few wee herbs as some sort of token gesture. I understand the attraction, it is a growing market, there are no fermentation costs/hassles and it is a near instant return rather than needing to wait for years with the product maturing. There is more gin leaving Islay these days than whisky! However I think the market is already very crowded and the addition of a gin to the range would detract from the core. Mashing, fermenting, distilling, maturing whisky is an art – flavouring grain neutral spirit from a factory and bottling it as your own is a marketing exercise.

Jan: Yes. Good idea!

Scott: Personally, I don't think so. Arran is young but has a growing following for all the right reasons – its whisky!

ROBIN BELL
VC Manager 2005-2010

Robin Bell at his home at Bridgend.
Neil Wilson

Robin Bell's journey to the Isle of Arran Distillery was a tough and convoluted one, but when he finally took on the job of VC manager in January 2005, he had the sort of life and work experience that enabled him to sort out the problems that had beset the management and systems over the previous couple of years once and for all.

His connection to Arran stems from the many holidays he and his family spent visiting the island and when the chance came to purchase a house at Shiskine, he and his wife Christine jumped at it. After a working life spent in the North of England and Wales in a number of different disciplines from mining, through machine maintenance, computers, running a fruit and vegetable shop and working as a training officer before ending up analysing access for organisations, Bell felt the time was right for a complete change.

When they arrived on Arran in December 2002 Robin spent the next three months completing his backlog of access reports for his former employers. Their new home came with an annexe, stabling and an acre of land that they planned to convert into a campsite and eventually run as a business. In the meantime he needed to get a job and in March 2003 he began working at the distillery as a 'meeter and greeter' having been interviewed two months before by VC manager Tom Pearson before he left and was succeeded by Alan Reid (not to be confused with the other Alan Reid, who worked as a part-time consultant on the sensory analysis of the maturing stocks from 2000-07).

After three months Bell was made a trainee tour guide to work beside Ray Evans and Peter Handley who had replaced Bob Fisher as senior tour guide after Fisher's retirement in 2002. Learning that no such thing as a training manual existed for tour guides, Bell put one together. Reid then brought in an American called Rosemary Wood to work in the café which was supervised by Jim McConnachie. Somewhat surprisingly, she then took over as VC manager when both Reid and his wife, who acted as bookkeeper, left. Wood, described as a 'loose cannon' by board director Ross Peters, refused access to Bell to check the accounts when Douglas Davidson had asked him to do so. Peters recalled that Wood …

… was her own boss who did as she pleased. Along the kitchen wall of the mezzanine floor of the VC there was a huge mural painted by the Ayrshire artist Gregor Gall that I had commissioned at a cost of £10,000. With a little artistic licence it depicted the shooting of an illicit distiller by the exciseman back in the days of Robert Burns and his words framed it. She had it painted over.

Peter Handley then left in October 2003 and Terry Crawley, who had objected to the original application for a pub licence for the VC, replaced him as a tour guide. Douglas Coulter, an ex-pharmaceutical sales rep was also hired by Wood. However, Bell became disenchanted with the whole working atmosphere and left during the 2004 season. Somewhat ironically, Wood later hired Colin Siddle who had been spokesperson for the objectors to the distillery in the village and she also took on Archie Cummings at the same time.

Bell concentrated on the work required on his home and the campsite at Shiskine but spent two or three days a week for three months selling holiday property rentals for Arran Hideaways and then another three working for some Arran companies, giving tastings and promoting their product on the ferries. However, Wood's reign at the helm was over by December 2004 as she was asked to leave after the accounts were finally investigated. It transpired later that she

The mural painting by Gregor Gall that Rosemary Wood had painted over. *Gregor Gall / Ross Peters*

Detail from the mural. *Gregor Gall / Ross Peters*

123

was a fraudster who had been on the wrong side of the law in the past and the American accent was fake.

After a hiatus at the VC with no manager, the position was eventually reinstated and as he now had the time to spare, Bell was interviewed by Douglas Davidson and his eventual successor, Euan Mitchell, and was back on board for the start of the 2005 season. But he now had to clean up the mess Wood had left behind which took time, but matters improved gradually as did the business relationships with local suppliers who had been spurned by Wood. 'It was a case of winning back hearts and minds', Bell said.

By the end of the 2009 season the VC was running smoothly and as Bell realised that his campsite project at Shiskine was becoming the main focus in his working life, he gave over a year's notice and during that period trained Faye Waterlow to take over from him. And how did Robin sum up his years at the distillery? He paused for a moment, 'Challenging ... but enjoyable.'

KATE HARTLEY

Casks Café & Cleaning Supervisor 2012-2015

Kate's family have been on Arran for over 400 years in her old crofthouse in Lochranza. That croft formed part of a larger property which her maiden grand-aunts owned and she recalls as a child discovering an old secluded illicit still bothy up the back where she would happily play. When her aunts eventually discovered where she spent her days, they had it destroyed along with an iron cauldron which was broken into pieces (see also page 25). Eventually her early unconscious contact with whisky would come full circle when she returned to the island after spending most of her adult life on the mainland.

Kate was born in Brodick and brought up there until she went to St Bride's boarding school in Helensburgh when she was 11. She admits she was not a dedicated student and was happier helping out in her parents' hotel when she was home on holidays. Her interest gravitated to hairdressing and by 19 she was

married and had her first child when she was 20.

She moved away from Arran in 1965 and while bringing up her family (two further children followed) she attended Clydebank Technical College and studied catering. After qualifying she was employed at the old Royal Scottish Academy of Music and Drama in Glasgow for a year, prior to Aramark, an American catering services company taking over the academy catering contract. Six months later she was promoted to the troubled Queen Margaret Union at Glasgow University, which had been losing a lot of money. Once that was running smoothly she was moved to Glasgow School of Art for five years before returning to the RSAMD at its new home in Cowcaddens. She stayed for around eight years as the general manager of catering, cleaning and bars.

Aramark's next move for her was to BP in Grangemouth where she had to manage eight catering and vending accounts but she missed the customer contact of her previous work so she then joined the property and facilities management company MITIE where she worked as Training and Human Resources Officer. After being made redundant at 55 she started her own compliance training company specialising in food hygiene. Eventually deciding to return to Arran, she noticed an advert in 2010 to join the distillery and worked downstairs as a tour guide until February 2012 when she was asked by James MacTaggart to tackle the café which 'was struggling and staffed largely by teenagers who were not coping well'.

The place was not running efficiently and the standards were not as high as they were downstairs. Faye was a fabulous support and we soon had it running like a dream. In my first winter we opened every day except Sundays and we decided to use the café as a means to help to promote the distillery's products. As staff, we all had to really get to know the whisky. We created a menu of five flights of whisky that customers could sample to take them through all the core bottlings. Each flight of four whiskies was priced from £10 to £17. That way we were able to help the customer's understanding of our whisky.

Kate's own favourite is the 12-year-old cask strength and she has even had a bottling named after her, the Dragon's Dram, so named after someone who visited the distillery mentioned Kate on Tripadvisor mischievously describing her as 'a bit of a dragon', something her colleagues were not going to let her forget.

Kate retired at the end of 2015 but she can still be seen helping out by covering any jobs that need doing at the VC when required.

The Casks Café team, 2016. From left to right: Kamilla Panisuik, Peter Dunn, Katie Morrison, Marcin Mazurkiewicz, Mhairi Hartley and Gareth Gregg.

CHAPTER EIGHT

The Business

FOLLOWING THE QUEEN'S VISIT in August 1997, the company's profile was raised significantly while day-to-day management was undertaken by the Curries and their staff, all directed by decisions made at the monthly board meetings. All of this was constricted by the cash the company was generating and trading losses continued. Les Auchincloss had been the main backer of the company and was under constant pressure to prop up the finances. He had his limits though, if not in money then in patience and it was wearing thin.

Paul Currie's efforts to establish exports markets in the early years had created a presence in Japan through David Croll, France through Maison du Whisky and in the Netherlands with Van Wees in Amersfoort. This had led to a large reduction in trading losses in 1996 and 1997, but the year after the Queen's visit the company posted a much larger loss of £362,506 and while Taiwan had been a buoyant market in 1997, some of this business was lost in the subsequent two years and was exacerbated by the loss of supply to Leclerc in France as the margins could not be maintained. Furthermore aged stock for Taiwan could not be sourced.

It was agreed at boardroom level that someone needed to be brought in to oversee some fundamental changes in management accounting and sales in order to turn things around. Hal Currie, now 75, also felt that it was time to relinquish his position as chairman and finally retire. Alan Gray, the Scotch whisky industry analyst was asked to look for likely candidates and in the spring of 1999 he approached Andrew Kettles, formerly managing director of Highland Distillers and The Famous Grouse, who expressed interest in joining the company. An informal, al fresco interview in beautiful weather was conducted at Ross Peters' home at Brae of Auchendrane, Ayrshire, by Les Auchincloss and other members of the board. The result was that Kettles was hired as chairman and in June 1999 it was made public that Hal Currie would step down with Kettles joining the board in July. When Andrew Currie was asked if this move signalled a change in ownership of the company he denied it and stated that he and Paul would continue to fulfil their roles as directors. *The Banner* then enquired if he would not have liked the top job himself? 'Mr Kettles will have more gravitas than me,' he quite reasonably responded. Hal Currie eventually resigned from the board on 22 September along with Andrew who went on to pursue other interests, including restaurants and the creation of Shelter Point Distillery on Vancouver Island. Paul Currie remained on the Arran board as a salaried non-executive director until 2003 and after resigning became involved in other distilling projects. He was a prime mover in the establishment of The Lakes Distillery near Bassenthwaite in Cumbria which opened at the end of 2014. Financial controller, Paul Garwood, was appointed company secretary on the day of Hal Currie's resignation. As of 12 December 1999, Les Auchincloss' Leichtenstein-based management trust LAFOR held 25% of the shareholdings, the Curries 18% and Ross Peters and Patrick Dromgoole 9% between them. The remaining shares were held by 91 other shareholders from around the world.

When Andrew Kettles arrived his initial task was to create a management system that would make sense of the company's trading activities. Until August 1996 his background had been at Highland Distillers and Matthew Gloag & Son based in Perth and he had extensive knowledge of how a modern-day whisky company should be run.

I got monthly management accounts set up and changed the auditors to Grant Thornton who knew the whisky industry well and I also changed our lawyers. A few months after I took up the post I headhunted David Boyle, who had been Regional Manager of The Famous Grouse, to come

Paul Currie beside one of the stills in The Lakes Distillery, Bassenthwaite, which he established in late 2014.
Neil Wilson

in as managing director in October to take over from Paul Currie. David then brought in Kevin Ramsden from Morrison Bowmore Distillers to help him develop sales export markets.

One of my main concerns was to convince Les Auchincloss, who was pumping cash heavily into the company, to regard it as investing ahead of the brand, which was crucial to the long-term future of the business. In due course Les brought Mike Peirce onto the board and they became the main backers while I was there.

David Boyle's tenure as managing director was largely due to his connection with Andrew Kettles when they both worked together at Highland Distillers and The Famous Grouse. They were keen golfers and during one of their regular games Kettles mentioned that Isle of Arran Distillers was looking for some new management and international sales input. Having spent 10 years based in Perth, lately dealing with overseas markets in Northern Europe, Sweden and also worldwide duty free, Boyle decided that a new challenge as part of a younger team was attractive and he joined as managing director in October 1999.

As a native of Kilmarnock Boyle felt that in a sense he was heading back home and that the new job offered him 'the wide prospect of dealing in lots of areas that would be good for me'. In effect David was the second appointment that would diminish the influence of the Curries on the board as Les Auchincloss exerted more authority in order to get the company sorted out. As Paul Currie had been handling management from his base in the south of England until then, the first thing that Kettles and Boyle required was the setting up of an office base in Scotland and they allowed a period of one month to find something suitable and hand over responsibilities. An office was located at Springkerse in Stirling and initially staffed by Garwood, Boyle and Ramsden along with two personal assistants, one of whom, Elke Braun, dealt solely with private cask and Bondholder matters.

Boyle's principal objective was to stem the losses and develop markets abroad but with the bulk of Arran's stocks still maturing in bond, this was a difficult task as much of it was barely over three years old and therefore quite immature. Furthermore, wood management under Gordon Mitchell had been largely a case of purchasing what the company could afford, rather than the best quality available. Mitchell, who was well qualified to analyse the maturing stock, had his hands full managing the distillery and had no time to devote to sensory analysis. Boyle felt that unless they conducted samplings on their bonded stocks soon, they might be building up a huge problem for the future so he turned to someone he knew from his time at Highland Distillers who had vast knowledge in this area.

Blender and sensory analyst Alan Reid had just retired from the Edrington Group where he had worked in the Sample Room on Great Western Road, Drumchapel, when he was approached by Boyle. Would he be interested in doing a complete analysis on the maturing stocks of Arran malt? Over a game of golf at Royal Troon, where Reid was a member, Boyle offered him a part-time consultancy role to analyse the stock at the four locations the distillery was then using for maturation: Lochranza, Springbank in Campbeltown, Broxburn and Bladnoch in Wigtownshire.

Boyle's remit to Alan was to spend whatever time he could afford on the project to sample parcels of casks in order to determine the most appropriate use for the

Alan Reid beside a portrait of WA Robertson, one of the founders of Robertson & Baxter, who was an early Captain at Royal Troon from 1883-87. *Neil Wilson*

contents. The four options were: 1. Retain for blending. 2. Retain for vatting with other casks for NAS bottlings. 3. Retain for single cask expressions. 4. Total rejection and no further use. In reality very few casks fell into this last category. Almost all of the casks maturing when he started the sensory analysis were ex-bourbon American oak.

Reid had studied maturation times in sherry casks while at Edrington by setting up control experiments in a Spanish bodega where comparisons between various ages of maturing sherry samples were analysed. After sampling he found that a period of approximately 18 months was sufficient to ensure good quality finished whisky. With that in mind, once he had determined which of the early four and five-year-old casks were suitable for further maturation as single malt bottlings, he was able to suggest that a further period of five to eight months in sherry wood would be ideal for that age of spirit. This was to become the bedrock of how the bulk of Arran age-statement bottlings were to be developed over the years to follow.

The way it worked was that Reid would travel by car from Troon and park up at the ferry terminal in Ardrossan. After arriving at Brodick he was picked up by Gordon Mitchell and taken to the distillery where 100ml samples had been withdrawn from the parcel of casks to be analysed and laid out in Mitchell's office. Reid and Mitchell then nosed these to determine if they fell into the 'reject' category. If they did not, 10ml of the sample (in the case of a hogshead) and 20ml (in the case of a sherry butt) were then further nosed by them to determine which of the first three categories they would fall into. Job done, Alan was taken back to the ferry and returned to his home in Troon. All of this work was done on a pro-bono basis and he made sure that his opinion was heard at boardroom level if there was any challenge to it.

Trips down to Campbeltown were 'more of a wee day out' as Mitchell and Reid took the summer ferry from Lochranza over to Claonaig and then drove down to Springbank where the sampling was done in bond. Alan remembers those days well:

It was more challenging as a warehouse is not the sort of place to conduct sensory analysis. Gordon had to draw all the samples himself and I just got on with the job. Not ideal, but I still enjoyed those days away. It felt like an adventure. The trips to Bladnoch were the same except I would pick up Gordon at Ardrossan do the driving. We had a lot of fun together and Raymond Armstrong was a great character. Those days were very full and I rarely got back to Troon before seven pm after an early start.

Arran is a gentle malt and most resembles the eight-year-old Glenrothes that we produced thirty to forty years ago at Edrington. Some of the later cask finishes worked exceptionally well but some were not so good.

Reid's involvement lasted until Gordon Mitchell's retirement in 2007 after which James MacTaggart took over the job as part of his remit. The Blending and Tasting Rooms that are due to open at Lochranza will serve as MacTaggart's analysis lab with a facility on the first floor that is drowned in natural light which streams through the two glass-paned cupolas.

The other major problem for Boyle was the quality of maturing stock owned by private individuals.

When I arrived it became apparent that some owners thought they had been sold not only the contents, but also access to it after three years for whatever purpose they thought fit, whenever they wanted. An owner might call us and ask for sufficient malt to be drawn from his cask to fill five bottles, and then individually label them and deliver them to him. On reviewing the terms and conditions of sale, it was clear that the whole offer was far too woolly and open to misinterpretation, so we had to flatly refuse them as it was simply impossible and impractical to do this sort of thing. We than had to redraft all future contracts of purchase.

I even got an approach from the Scotch Whisky Association, though we were not members at that time, asking me what was going on, so I decided

The new Blending and Tasting Rooms during construction, January 2016. *Neil Wilson*

to clarify the situation with the cask owners and wrote to them individually stating what we were prepared to do for them. In a few extreme cases we settled by buying back their casks (if they were amongst the better ones) with some interest paid as well, and giving them some gratis bottles of malt. In other cases we referred them to whisky brokers but Arran was not being traded readily then, so many just held on to them to bottle at a much later date.

Kevin Ramsden had spent his time at Lang's Whisky in West Nile Street, Glasgow, before moving on to Morrison Bowmore Distillers in Springburn where he spent two years. A multi-lingual graduate from Glasgow University, he was an ideal appointment to develop sales leads in Germany and France where he had had

notable success with Bowmore Legend. He took on all the export markets excepting USA, Canada, Japan, Taiwan and the UK which David Boyle retained. The core brands that Ramsden and Boyle had at their disposal were the Arran malt, Loch Ranza blend and Holy Isle Cream Liqueur, and given that the malt was still only five years old at best, all they could do was sell as much as they could and build up their profiles. With a view to reducing costs Boyle repackaged the distinctive blue bottle of Loch Ranza blend to a clear bottle as the original presentation was yielding next to no profit. The blue bottle had been developed by Michael Peters in his London-based design company of which Ross Peters was a non-executive director. It also designed a number of other Arran labels including The Arran Malt, Glen Rosa, Royal Island and Eilandour.

However, a more lucrative development was initiated in 2000 when he contacted Shirley Bell, the Chief Executive of the World Burns Federation and negotiated an agreement, in perpetuity, for the exclusive use of the Robert Burns name on whisky-related products.

I sensed we needed something 'in the bag' for the long term, and it struck me as a very good deal at the time. We launched it on 25 January 2001 with a boxed edition of 1,000 bottles of Arran malt at 40% which included a certificate of authenticity and a facsimile of Burns' poem 'Scotch Drink'. We also did a blended bottling at the same time.

Kevin Ramsden revealed that even in Russia, a market which he did much to bring on board and develop, the Robert Burns' expressions were 'a tough sell' and the cream liqueur, although he thought it superior to the main market leader, was almost impossible to shift overseas. Meanwhile, back at the Springkerse office, the cask ownership problem remained. 'I might take a call from an owner and then spend half-an-hour explaining why we couldn't draw half-a-dozen bottles from it for him,' Ramsden recalls, 'and that meant I had lost time doing what I should have been doing.'

The first trade
bottling of
Arran malt.

The famous
blue bottle.

The early
bottling of a
very fine cream
liqueur.

The French market was less of a problem as Hal Currie's contacts had meant that relationships with the likes of Thierry Benitah at Maison du Whisky were already established. In the Netherlands, Van Wees, Arran's importers, placed their first substantial order for 500 cases and Ronald Zwartepoorte became the company's agent, initially getting around 400 of the cases of Arran malt into Gall & Gall where it would be the Malt of the Month listing in November 2001. Through his contacts at Lang's Ramsden was able to make a better arrangement in Switzerland through Charles Hofer SA, who took the first single cask sales Ramsden made overseas. Jelmoli, the Harrods of Zurich, were one of a number of Swiss customers to take several cases from different cask offerings, also through Hofer.

The late Malcolm Greenwood, ex-Glenfarclas brand ambassador, whisky writer and publisher, also came on board as a freelance representative at trade fairs and helped the brands get some exposure in *Scottish Field*. VC manager Tom

David Croll, who has lived and worked in Japan for many years and whose most recent venture is the Kyoto Gin Distillery, was an early acolyte of the Arran venture and has been involved with the company from the very start. He recalls how he got involved.

During my honeymoon in 1990 I actually visited Lochranza so when I read an article in the Weekend FT about the new distillery three years later, things seem to come full circle. I contacted Hal and I started the conversation thinking I was going to be 'investing' in a few cases of Arran's Founders' Bond offering, but came away having made a more substantial investment in the distillery and also having promised to represent their interests in Japan!

Meeting Hal seemed like a good idea after that, so I made a trip back to Scotland to attend the cutting of the first sod ceremony. We then set up a company called the Isle of Arran Tokyo Information Office, ostensibly to spread the word about the new distillery to the drinks trade and bartenders in Japan. Soon we were also helping to publicise the other Arran offers of inaugural year casks, and then found an Osaka-based importer to take on some of the third-party bottled brands that Arran came out with. That didn't work out so well, so, in 1998, we established our own importing company called Arran Japan. We've been Arran's sole importer since then.

It's been a long journey but Arran really is regarded now as a top-class, very consistent single malt by the trade and whisky lovers, if not yet by a wider public. To be honest, some of the early releases were, perhaps inevitably, a little immature, and there also have been periods where the sheer number of new products was seen as very confusing. That seemed to alienate a part of the customer base for some time, but over the past few years we've seen a huge upsurge in interest in Arran as both new and returning drinkers have discovered the excellent quality and value for money of the range today. Our own sales in Japan of Arran malt have grown 40% in the last year.

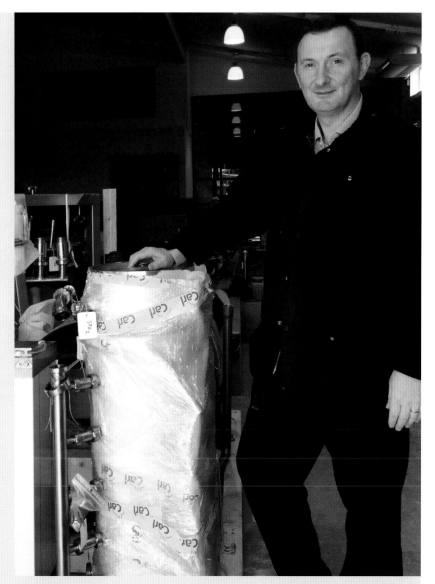

David Croll, Arran's longest-serving business associate overseas, at the start of his new venture, the Kyoto Gin Distillery. *David Croll*

Pearson, reporting directly to David Boyle, continued to sort out the remaining management issues he had inherited after being hired in 1997. There were some lighter moments, however, as Boyle recalls.

After Arran was endorsed by the World Burns Federation we hosted a Burns Supper and on 19 Jan 2001, Joe Kennedy, convenor of the Patrons Club of the WBF of which we were members, came over for the bash. The one thing that I wanted to be sure of was that there was going to be enough haggis. The chef said there would be and the evening got under way following the traditional format. As the haggis was served I saw that the portions were pretty generous so I became a little nervous. Eventually when head table was due to get theirs the portions had been reduced to a small spoonful. I headed to the kitchen to be confronted by the chef surrounded by loads of burst haggises with the stuff all over the place!

Behind the scenes cash flow limitations continued to create problems as some suppliers put the company on stop and as David Boyle had an ongoing difference of opinion with Les Auchincloss regarding the timescale required to bring the company into profitability, he decided to resign. He had also used up a lot of his time becoming involved in a failed takeover bid by Thai Beverages (owners of Chang Beer, the shirt sponsor of Everton FC) in 2001 which deflected him from his primary duties. In the event, as ThaiBev was courting Isle of Arran Distillers they were also looking at Inver House Distillers as a takeover target, eventually deciding on the latter as a larger vehicle for their ambitions. As 'the final part of the jigsaw' before he left, he changed the distribution arrangements for the UK to Derbyshire-based Cellar Trends Limited.

Ramsden was to stay on until July 2003 but during his time had made real progress to establish overseas markets and is gracious in also giving credit to Jim McEwan of Bruichladdich who always ensured that Arran's name was in his conversations with colleagues at trade fairs that they both attended.

With David Boyle's departure a vacancy existed for sales director and after it was advertised export consultant Douglas Davidson applied despite knowing very little about the whisky industry. Chairman Andrew Kettles recognised that Davidson's experience in exports could help the company develop the overseas markets that Paul Currie had started and David Boyle and Kevin Ramsden had expanded and developed. Davidson duly accepted and started work on 10 October 2001. When he arrived at head office he identified improved cost control and expanding Arran's export business as his main priorities. His experience with the Dawson group selling luxury Scottish cashmere abroad stood him in good stead and, somewhat unconventionally, he set about forming alliances with wine companies in Europe in order to gain access to their distribution networks.

In January 2002 Mark Callachan, a logistics and warehousing expert formerly with Drambuie, was hired by Davidson for back-office operations to control the supply chains, packaging requirements and shipments. He joined from Drambuie after a tip-off from Kevin Ramsden that he might soon be available as Drambuie's Kirkliston operation was being closed down. A month later Davidson was appointed managing director and started to undertake a great deal of international travel attending trade fairs at home and abroad and ensuring that the Arran whisky brand continued to be built and actively exposed in overseas markets. He also ensured that Arran's profile was increased in the national press, among whisky writers and trade partners.

He implemented initiatives to increase connectivity with the Arran whisky brand and their customers overseas. Arran's eagles were used as a brand insignia on most of the distillery's wares and following up on the foundation David Boyle had laid in gaining the licence to use the Robert Burns name from the World Burns Federation, Arran's Robert Burns bottlings were promoted widely at the Burns An' A' That festival in Ayr in March 2002.

In December 2002 Davidson travelled to Atlanta, Georgia, with consultant Malcolm Greenwood to launch the Robert Burns single malt at the Atlanta Burns Cottage. Davidson recalls that Greenwood described the malt at the time as 'a whisky Calvados' and this inspired him to look further into cask finishing. On his return from the USA Davidson got in touch with Calvados Christian Drouin and stated that he would like to try finishing Arran malt in their Calvados casks. A deal was agreed and a consignment of empty casks duly arrived at Lochranza, much to the consternation of Gordon Mitchell, who, as a traditional whisky distiller, viewed the whole experiment with great suspicion. However, Davidson was adamant to see the experiment through and simply asked that Gordon fill the casks with seven-year-old Arran malt and then sample them regularly until he felt that the marriage had been made. When Gordon judged it ready the Calvados cask finish was launched in February 2003 at 62.1% abv and the expression, limited to 582 bottles, sold out in six weeks. Whisky writer Dave Broom stated that 'Arran is becoming pretty impressive' after tasting it. The Arran Cask Finish Programme had begun.

Kevin Ramsden left the company in July 2003 to work for Chivas Brothers in Eastern Europe and Euan Mitchell was recruited to replace him in September as European sales director. Although only 30 years old he had considerable whisky trade experience with William Cadenhead, the independent whisky bottler based in Campbeltown, and had impressed Davidson when they had met at trade fairs. Before Mitchell joined however, increased concerns from the board regarding the continued haemorrhaging of cash forced the drastic measure of closing down production at the distillery in an effort to reduce costs, a situation that would remain until the end of 2004 with a solitary break to produce a batch of spirit made from bere barley. In the meantime the company had to rely on revenue from the VC, cask sales and mail order. Ironically, at the end of 2004 Arran took the Best New Exporter Award at the International Business Awards and in April the following year Arran was one of 88 recipients of the Queen's Award for Enterprise: International Trade (Export), the most prestigious of its type in the UK. Clearly, Arran was emerging as a brand with a world-class product.

★ ★ ★

PRESS RELEASE ISSUED on 29 JUNE 2005

**A Great Day in Lochranza
Arran Receives Queen's Award**

Wednesday 29 June 2005 will be long remembered in Lochranza as the day the Distillery came of age. In a double celebration the Company were also presented with the Queen's Award for International Trade by Major Richard Henderson, the Lord Lieutenant.

On a packed day before an invited audience – many of whom were the Company's customers, distributors and suppliers – Lady Jean Fforde read out the Scroll signed by Tony Blair and Queen Elizabeth II – before presenting it to Managing Director, Douglas Davidson.

Major Henderson then presented the Company with a beautiful engraved crystal bowl, together with a Queen's Award flag noting the Company's sales growth from six international markets to thirty during the last three years, with overseas sales rising 147% during that period. He also complimented the Company for increasing their visitor numbers over the last three years to 50,000 – of which approximately 50% came from overseas – noting that this could only be good news for the Island.

Earlier in the day, following a tour of the facilities, Mr Murray – one of the world's top whisky writers, held an enthralling tasting of the first ever Arran 10 Yr old in the Company's Tasting Bar. Noting the Sherry which came through early on the nose, followed by the classic Arran characteristics of honey on the tongue and spice to follow, he declared the Arran 10 Yr Old 'an absolute cracker, all the earlier promise of the Distillery – this is going to be a wonderful whisky' he declared.

Douglas Davidson receives the Queen's Award from Major Richard Henderson.
Douglas Davidson

Accepting the Award from Major Henderson, Managing Director, Douglas Davidson commented, 'For a small Company like Arran to win this Award is a fantastic achievement and reflects greatly the teamwork shown by all our staff who have contributed so much to our success. It is significant that our products are also regularly winning quality awards, attracting three of the world's top spirit producers to participate with us in our Cask Strength Programme. I am also greatly encouraged to hear Jim Murray's opinion of our first ever Arran 10 Yr Old. This bodes well for the launch in September later this year and sends out a strong message to all our markets that Arran is on the move with a further success.

'Our efforts in overseas markets to promote the Island are also paying dividends, with visitor numbers up from 45,000 in 2002 to 50,000 in 2004. Whilst their primary reason may be to visit the Distillery, this can only benefit the rest of the Island – with hotels, b+b's, restaurants and shops all getting a share of the tourist spend. We look forward with renewed energy to 2006 – and beyond – with the launch of the first ever commercial Arran ten year old. We have the products, we now have the markets we lacked three years ago but – most of all – we now have the people on board to carry us forward into the next decade.'

Mr Davidson then passed the flag to Gordon Mitchell, Distillery Manager, who was piped downstairs by Mr Ross Peters, a Director of the Company, to hoist the flag on the Company's flagpole. All was not finished however. At 2.29 p.m. precisely, (the time that the first ever stills were opened 10 years ago), Mr Davidson led the guests in a countdown before passing to Mr Murray to propose a toast to the tenth anniversary of the Company. Fondly recalling those early days back in 1995, Mr Murray was interrupted by a shout from the back of the room.

The Eagles had been sighted, and as the guests watched them soar from the windows of the Eagle's Nest Restaurant, it seemed that they were also giving their seal of approval.

An encouraging omen for the future and another entertaining day at Lochranza was over.

★ ★ ★

The staff at the VC on 29 June 2005 when the company received the Queen's Award for Enterprise. Amongst those present were Archie Cummings, Robin Bell, Rosemary Wood, Douglas Davidson, Calum Green, Matt Edwards, Mark Callachan, Terry Crawley, Jim McConnachie, Miss Bannatyne, Douglas Coulter, Elke Braun, Jaclyn McKie, Euan Mitchell and Gordon Mitchell.

An array of Arran cask finishes on display at a trade fair. *Douglas Davidson*

Following the Calvados cask finish a further 17 individual cask finishes were to be produced up to 2008. The list included Lepanto PX Spanish brandy, Chateau Margeaux, Amarone, Bordeaux, fino sherry, Sassicaia, Moscatel, Madeira and Marsala. More followed with Sauternes, Port, rum and Tokaji (the Hungarian sweet wine). A Champagne-finished expression was produced for the distillery's 10th anniversary from 8-year-old malt finished in French Argonne casks from Claude Giraud. Euan Mitchell related the change to the spirit in *Whisky Magazine*: 'With the Champagne cask finish, it's more the oak character coming through, with a distinct oaky, creamy, toffee character, and honeyed, syrupy sweetness. Citrus notes could be from the champagne, though citrus also appears in Arran. The champagne character is much more integrated, rather than adding another layer.'

During Davidson's time in charge the Ambassadors of Arran scheme was started, a roll of which is displayed on a board in the reception area at the VC. This idea was to say thank you to people who had directly helped to establish Arran at home and in overseas markets and in 2004 listed five recipients, another three in 2005 and a further four in 2006. Up to 2014 a total of 18 Ambassadors had been created.

On another business trip to Tuscany Davidson saw a novel cask-racking system which he was keen to see installed at Arran. Taking along Gordon Mitchell on a

An advertisement for the 10-year-old malt for the Japanese market.
Douglas Davidson

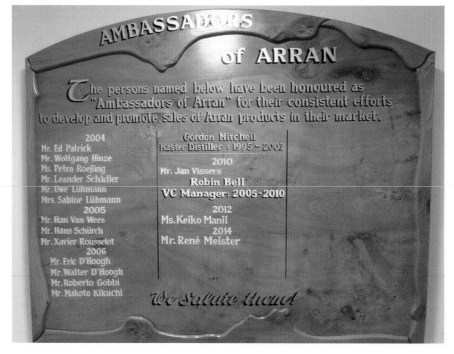

Neil Wilson

subsequent trip they arrived in Bordeaux in March 2007 and visited three or four wine cellars which were using the same unique system. The casks were stacked in fabricated fork cradles with small, integrated rollers incorporated in the arms of the cradles which allowed the casks to be rotated while in place. Removal could be handled by a sole operative with a modified forklift truck, running on rails embedded in the floor, with full articulation to allow it to manoeuvre in the confined space between the racks. Although the system increased capacity from a traditional dunnage capacity of 980 casks to over 3,200, it still fell short of the modern pallet-racking arrangement used in most warehouses. The new system was duly installed by five French workers in the new warehouse (No 3) which opened on 3 September 2007. Since its inception, however, the distillery has not installed the system again and the warehouses built since then employ a pallet-racking system which, while requiring more manual labour, is much more space efficient.

In parallel with the cask finishes the company was actively selling bottlings from single casks with limited expressions made available from 2002 onwards. A mixture of ex-bourbon and ex-sherry casks provided the maturation regime. By 2008 sales were up 33.4% on the previous year with 1,735 cases sold.

In the seven years since 2001 brand sales had doubled to over £2m, bottled malt sales were up by 23% over 2007, and the VC had enjoyed another record year and distillery output was up 13%. Cask finishes were up 29% with sales in 16 countries of 3,865 cases. Davidson had always wanted to retire at 60 and in 2009 gave the board six months notice with control as MD being handed over to Euan Mitchell. He was given a place on the board as deputy chairman which

A promotional flyer produced by Breeze Creative in 2009 for the core range. *Douglas Davidson*

he eventually relinquished when he resigned at the end of 2010.

Euan Mitchell, a graduate in Scottish History from Edinburgh University had started in the whisky industry after seeing an advert for a Trainee Export Salesperson at William Cadenhead, the Campbeltown whisky bottler. After a successful interview with Neil Clapperton at the Cadenhead shop in the Royal Mile in Edinburgh, Mitchell found himself moving to Kintyre where, within a few months, he was transferred to the Springbank sales operation which 'lacked a sales structure'. To gain experience he shadowed workers in every area of Springbank Distillery which gave him experience in all the stages of whisky making including floor malting and bottling. After this induction he arranged trade fairs abroad such as Whiskyfest in the USA, tastings for whisky clubs and visits to overseas distributors, such as Symposion in Sweden. One such visit resulted in a flurry of calls to a radio station from Swedish whisky enthusiasts after Euan was recorded dropping and smashing one of a pair of bottles of 1919 Springbank 50-year-old which had been bought for £10,000. Fortunately it was a hoax set up by the broadcaster but resulted in a lot of free exposure for the distillery.

At the 2003 Whisky Fair at Limburg in Germany he met Douglas Davidson who later contacted him to see if he was interested in joining the company to replace Kevin Ramsden. Initially he was 'sceptical' of the offer but after a trip to

Euan Mitchell.

Lochranza to see the operation he liked what he saw. He then tried a sample of the non chill-filtered, cask-strength malt ('the one with the blue label') and realised that the whisky being produced was first class. His decision was made and in September he joined the company at their headquarters in Stirling as European sales manager. Not long after he recognised how tough things had been for the company when he called Gordon Mitchell at the distillery to ask how production was progressing. 'What production?' was Gordon's answer, 'We're shut down until further notice.' Euan had joined exactly when the distillery had been forced to stop production in order to reduce costs. 'I then realised that things were not quite as rosy as I had thought, but at the end of 2004 we were back in production and things were improving,' he said.

Mitchell believed there had been an over-reliance on the Cask Finishes

Alan Reid, Gordon Mitchell and Euan Mitchell.

programme in terms of brand building and felt that it undermined the excellent distillery character of the ex-bourbon and ex-sherry matured malt that Arran produced. He explained to me how he changed the structure of the product line after he succeeded Davidson.

My two main priorities when taking over as MD were to consolidate our sales in key markets and to bring together a coherent portfolio to build awareness of The Arran Malt brand. The different Cask Finishes we had done over many years had generated much needed income for the company and raised our profile but I felt they were masking the inherent Arran distillery character and so, after discussing the matter with James MacTaggart, we restricted these to three regular expressions, each quite distinct in character: Amarone, Port and Sauternes. My longer-term aim was to create a core portfolio of three aged expressions: ten, fourteen and eighteen years old which would form the spine of the Arran range.

Alongside the core range we would create a series of limited edition

expressions such as the Icons of Arran and the Devil's Punchbowl selection. The first release in the Icons of Arran series, the Peacock, was in my opinion a game-changer for Arran. James selected an amazing batch of casks for this expression and these were all gems maturing away in traditional oak casks which previously held either bourbon or sherry.

The Peacock made a lot of people sit up and take notice of Arran and kickstarted the momentum in growing our sales that we are still seeing today. Consumers who had previously viewed Arran as a whisky used for 'finishing' began to see the real potential of the brand from expressions such as the Peacock and the many single casks we then began to release.

With these commitments made, wood policy was the critical factor and James MacTaggart's input was major.

James highlighted the need to have a more consistent wood policy in the company to ensure the level of quality remained consistently high in the future. Good casks had been purchased in the past but cash-flow restraints also meant some poorer wood had been filled and we set out to change this from 2008 onwards. The more success we had the more we invested in casks to ensure each bottling of The Arran Malt would be of the highest standard for years to come.

One of the most recent limited editions Arran has released is the Smuggler's Series, Volume One – The Illicit Stills which was launched at the end of September 2015 with 8,700 bottles at 56.4% abv and is a blended malt made from four 600-litre Port pipes of unpeated stock, with some ex-bourbon and ex-sherry stock and peated ex-bourbon at 14 and 50ppm. It retailed at £84.99 and in the first hour of release the Arran online shop sold around 200 bottles, making it one of their fastest selling ever. Growth in sales of the core range and limited edition releases such as the Smugglers' Series helped to drive brand sales to over £4m by the end of 2015 as overall company turnover surpassed £6m. And in terms of main markets, where does The Arran Malt stand today?

Europe remains the heart of our brand sales with France traditionally our biggest market. The UK has also bounced back in recent years whilst we have made great strides in developing the profile of The Arran Malt in Asia, particularly Taiwan and Japan, as well as North America. We now sell in over fifty markets around the world but many areas remain untapped and the potential for the future is hugely exciting. Our growing success is entirely down to the collective efforts of our amazing team both at the distillery and Visitor Centre in Lochranza and at our head office near Stirling.

Maintaining that profile and market share has been achieved by taking the core range to a meaningful level and, allied to this, another exciting prospect for the company has been progressing over the past year. A new distillery in the south of the island is in the advanced stages of planning as this book goes to press with the *Arran Banner* of 12 March 2016 announcing the development on its front page. Although lacking a name at present, it is close to being finalised with the final plans submitted for approval on 6 May 2016. These reveal an organic structure with an outline reflecting the rugged northern mountains of Arran, constructed to appear as though it is growing out of the surrounding land, topped with a series of inclined turf roofs. Here the peated spirit output of Isle of Arran Distillers will be created, very close to the original site of the old Lagg Distillery which closed in 1837. This new development will make Isle of Arran Distillers unique and one can only wish that its economic impact on the south of Arran will be as great as its mother distillery has had in the north. It is hoped that subject to approval, production will commence around August 2018.

The frontal elevation of the new distillery at Lagg which is due to come on stream in 2018.

Other key staff at head office at the Touch Estate near Cambusbarron play their part in the smooth running of the company. Many of them are unsung and unseen, but their roles are essential.

LOUISA YOUNG

Senior Brand Manager

Troon-born Louisa Young studied French and International Relations at Aberdeen University, part of which involved spending one year at France's only Lycée Franco Allemand at Buc, near Versailles. During university holidays she also gained experience as an au pair in Chamonix and working on a luxury hotel barge travelling the Canal du Midi. After graduation she worked for the Euro Info Centre before a move to London to take up an events management position with the World Leadership Forum. While attending the now defunct Connect Festival at Inveraray Castle in 2007 she was introduced to some of the whisky exhibitors and later enquired with Euan Mitchell about opportunities within the whisky industry. After a few months a new sales position became available with Isle of Arran Distillers and after being offered the role by the then managing director, Douglas Davidson, Louisa quit London to embark on a new career in the Scotch whisky industry. Apart from a brief interlude after three years at Tullibardine Distillery, which resulted in redundancy after a takeover, she has always been with Arran Distillers working primarily in the Scandinavian, North American and Japanese markets along with UK trade and travel retail.

In the past four years she has been joined by Lucie Stroesser who deals with her native France, Spain, Italy Australia, New Zealand and Asia. Andy Bell, the newest addition to the team, is responsible for Switzerland, Russia, Denmark, Germany and Poland.

Our role is all-encompassing, not only are we ambassadors for the brand but we manage all our accounts, distributors and sales and report accordingly, but it is no burden when you really enjoy the work you do. It's amazing how the Arran presence can get around. I was sitting in the departure lounge at Glasgow airport to go to Amsterdam when I saw a guy with a bottle of Arran ten-year-old so I sidled up to him and we got into a chat. 'Why the Arran?' I asked. 'Well, I'm from Paisley so I thought a local malt would make a nice gift,' he replied. But his accent gave him away, so I asked where he was really from. 'Originally Russia and I am on my way to Jerusalem to see a friend who works in the Russian Embassy there,' he admitted. So that bottle of Arran malt was eventually opened and enjoyed by Russians in an embassy in Jerusalem!

Anyone who has been at one of Louisa's presentations will know how passionate and engaged Louisa is about Arran whisky. 'People know where Arran is now, so I don't have to do the geography lesson any more. It's established and we are here to stay.

'Euan gives us the freedom to do the job we do and make use of our own particular skills. He's good at recognising transferable skills so none of us are one-trick ponies.' Louisa is one of the most engaging whisky ladies I have met and relates some Arran 'tales', many of which cannot be published here. But there are other stories which can.

Do you know the story of how our peated expression got its name? It was in Norway where Arran was the second-largest selling malt behind Glenfiddich. I was doing a tasting and asked the audience if they had any suggestions. That's where Machrie Moor came from.

After Douglas Davidson left the company we had a brainstorming session as to how we should take our limited editions forward and Euan asked for feedback from us. We decided to focus on the distillery, rather than Arran the island. We identified the distillery's resident peacock, Albert, as an iconic symbol of the distillery and decided to work up some ideas around that. Pocket Rocket Creative presented a stunning mock up, so we decided to run with it. Everything proceeded normally with all the logistics in place, the whisky chosen by James MacTaggart and the launch date fixed. Then, a few days before the off, we got a call from James, 'We have a problem. Albert's hidden on the draff truck and disappeared somewhere around Lagg! We're trying to find him.' We kept our fingers crossed and then got another call from James. 'We've found him. He's been knocked down. He's dead!' We had to get another peacock and so Albert II appeared, nobody being any the wiser except the locals because he wasn't timid and rampaged through the village raiding gardens. So James got a couple of peahens to try and calm him down but it didn't work and they ended up fighting all day, so all of them had to go.

The Peacock Icon of Arran became one of Arran's most popular expressions and was followed by the Rowan Tree (look beside the river at the distillery), the Westie (James' West Highland terrier, Ruaraidh) and finally the Eagle.

Is there anything she has not enjoyed during her years at Arran? 'Not really … I would go as far as saying I have one of the best jobs in the world.'

JACLYN McKIE
Sales & Marketing Manager

All of Arran's prowess as distillers would be meaningless without effective sales and marketing management which is where Jaclyn McKie comes in. Another of Douglas Davidson's recruits, she was born in Greenock, raised in Skelmorlie and studied French and Italian at Glasgow University. After graduating in 2001 she returned to Montpellier, where she had spent a year as part of her degree course working in a school and took up a position with a sales and marketing company managing the portfolios of small to medium winemakers and co-operatives. She

Pocket Rocket Creative

Having evolved out of the Glasgow-based BD Network in 2007 when three employees decided to break out on their own, Pocket Rocket have become one of the UK's leading packaging designers and won gongs for Best Packaging at the 2014 World Whiskies Awards ands Best Agency in 2014 and 2016. The agency has had a long relationship with Isle of Arran Distillers after they approached Douglas Davidson to pitch for work before he retired. Gary Dawson, Gary Doherty and Del Sneddon are the founders of the firm and Dawson told me how the agency evolved.

Initially we spent six months talking to potential clients like Morrison Bowmore, Whyte and Mackay and Edrington on new packaging development, until Famous Grouse agreed to take us on. After that we got a bit of momentum and began to work for Douglas Laing, The Macallan and Brugal Rum. Euan gave us the redesign of the Arran core range which until then had a dark and traditional feel to it, so we brought in colour and took it into a more premium area. The first new product range we created was the Icons of Arran and since then we have handled all their limited edition releases. The Devil's Punch Bowl best exemplifies what we are trying to do. It's a sort of Marmite thing, you either love it or hate it, and it does have a dark side, but there is colour as well and is a real stand-out from the competition.

Gary Dawson of Pocket Rocket Creative. *Neil Wilson*

managed the Anglophone markets and helped to introduce many of the wines of Languedoc-Roussillon into the UK market with companies such as Majestic, as well as handling the North American markets and Scandinavia. However, wishing to return to Scotland, she started looking for other challenges closer to home. In 2003 she chanced to see the advert for European sales manager at Arran on an online recruitment website. Although she felt it was perhaps a larger role than she could undertake at that time, she applied anyway only to find that Euan Mitchell had just been accepted. Douglas Davidson did however interview her at the Scotch Malt Whisky Society in Leith and was impressed enough to ask her to stay in touch in the event that something might come up in the future.

That opportunity duly arrived in late 2003 when she was offered the position of sales and marketing assistant which she started in April 2004. Jaclyn's job initially involved a lot of travel over the next five years, but the arrival of children made that much more difficult and she now spends three days a week at head office on the Touch Estate dealing with social media marketing on Facebook, Instagram, Pinterest and Twitter and all the other platforms in popular use. Her posts are always picture-led to get attention and provide a window into the world of the company and its people. At present there are around 12,000 followers on Facebook and 15,000 on Twitter and she works hard to try and pick up genuine followers by interacting regularly with fans and followers, sharing interesting content and offering competition prizes and opportunities to win samples of limited edition expressions.

She also liaises with design and advertising agencies developing point-of-sale material, packaging and briefing photographic studios for location and product shots. One of those agencies, Pocket Rocket Creative, is also based at Touch Business Park and has been working for the company since the core range was redesigned in 2014.

Jaclyn deals directly with the White Stag members and has helped build the community of the club but she admits that, 'sometimes you have to draw the line between Arran as a business and Arran as a friendly community. I have a job to do, and at the same time I don't want to appear remote to Arran fans, which is sometimes difficult as my job and its responsibilities come first.'

The phenomenon of the 2015 White Stag bottling brought this dilemma to the fore. Over the past two years McKie marketed this limited expression on a first-come, first-served basis exclusively to the White Stag membership. However, some members, having secured their bottles, sold them on through eBay and whisky auction sites. This, she feels, diminished the ethos of the product for the genuine Arran enthusiast. The 2015 bottling was an 18-year-old, 53.6%abv, priced at £95 and limited to 214 bottles. One bottle went for £355 on Just Whisky Limited soon after release. 'We learned a lesson with this edition. It was a great shame to see the original, genuine intention behind our carefully thought-out limited edition being misunderstood in some cases by a minority who didn't share in the spirit with which this bottling was created,' she said. Whatever happens with future editions for the White Stag community, it looks as though Arran's quality and popularity is creating the sort of problems which many other distillers would envy.

MAGGIE CORNWALL
Company Secretary & Financial Controller

Maggie Cornwall, a native of the Isle of Lewis, where her parents have a croft at the Port of Ness in the far north of the island, completed Business Studies in Aberdeen before working in the oil industry for a North Sea services company. Seeking a change (Aberdeen is a dark city in winter) she moved to Edinburgh in the mid-eighties, where she had friends, and soon met her future husband. While studying for her accountancy exams she worked as bookkeeper for a publican with a number of bars. After her daughter, Eilidh, arrived in 1990 she moved on to Orbital Software which soon floated on the stock exchange in the dotcom bubble.

Maggie Cornwall, Mark Callachan, Nicole Lie and Gillian Snaddon.

They were ahead of their time, no doubt about that, but ahead of the company being sold I moved to the Scotch Malt Whisky Society in June 2000 where I enjoyed four years. Being close to so many great whiskies was the start of my love affair with Scotch. Balvenie became my favourite.

She arrived just as the SMWS was about to open the Georgian premises it had bought at 28 Queen Street, Edinburgh. This was the first of its members' venues outside its Leith base at the 18th-century JG Thomson vaults at 83 Giles Street. Glenmorangie eventually came knocking to buy the whole operation and she then joined Festival Inns, the chain of pubs and clubs owned by Kenny Waugh jnr (whose father of the same name had been the chairman of Hibernian Football Club from 1982-7) and stayed for a year. She was then hired by Falkirk Football Club just after the club had finally been promoted to the Scottish Premier League having invested heavily in a new ground and stadium. This conformed to the

new regulations regarding a minimum of 6,000 seats and was a joint-venture company between the club's owners and Falkirk Council. After getting things on 'an even keel' she decided that despite her time at Falkirk having been 'enjoyable', it was time to move on.

Obvious Solutions followed, an online graduate recruitment business, which had been taken over by Stepstone ASA in January 2005 and had Microsoft and HBOS on their client list. With a couple of days left before applications closed she heard of the position of company secretary at Arran Distillers and decided to apply. Douglas Davidson conducted her first interview and Andrew Kettles, although no longer an active board member, was supposed to conduct her second but a blizzard prevented him travelling on the day so he spoke to her on the phone later that day. A further 'chat' took place with Davidson and Euan Mitchell and Maggie duly started as company secretary and financial controller on 5 March 2007.

I planned to stay for two years and then move on, but I soon realised that in this job there was never a chance of being bored and there are never enough hours in the day. There were times after I arrived when money was short, however, Les Auchincloss and Mike Peirce always stumped up when necessary. After the financial crash in 2009 our bankers pulled the plug on us so we moved to the Clydesdale Bank. They saw the true worth of our business.

We eventually turned the corner about five years ago and things are now really positive financially and there is still a lot more potential in the company to fulfil. Above all it engenders real passion in the team.

MARK CALLACHAN
Planning Manager

While everyone else in the Arran workforce is getting on with their jobs, Mark Callachan is making sure that all the pieces of the logistical chain knit together to ensure that things run smoothly and on time. A time-served glazier and window fabricator from Bridgend near Linlithgow, 49-year-old Mark moved into the drinks industry after joining family-owned Drambuie at their Kirkliston base at the age of 24. He spent a total of 11 years there, first learning the skills of operating forklifts, hand-loading and a range of other warehousing duties.

After one year he was moved into the compounding department where every Monday Mrs Mackinnon would arrive to make up a vat of the syrup from Drambuie's secret recipe which was then padlocked. From this vat, the production output of the week's Drambuie would be created.

I remember being in charge of a machine that looked as if it had been on the set of Dr Who … all tubes, and flashing lights. Nowadays that job would be controlled from a PC. After a year doing that I was transferred to the Bond Office where I processed sales orders, prepared shipping and export documents and ensured that our movements were complying with customs and excise regulations. But Drambuie decided to close Kirkliston in 2001 to contract out production to Glenmorangie so I had to look for a new job.

Kevin Ramsden, the export sales manager at Arran, lived across the road from the Kirkliston plant and told Douglas Davidson about the closure. Looking for a logistics manager, he contacted Lynne Lineen (wife of the former Scottish rugby internationalist Sean) who was head of Human Resources at Drambuie, and she sent him Mark's CV. Davidson duly contacted and interviewed Mark who joined Arran Distillers in January 2002.

Since then Mark has had responsibility for planning bulk and bottled distribution, ordering glass, and all the other elements that take distilled spirit from the bond to the wholesaler, retailer and export agent. Packaging, labelling, bottle closures, deliveries for overseas trade events and fairs also need to be dealt with. Does anything ever go wrong?

Not if the chain holds. But in late 2014 year we had a glass shortage so our suppliers, O-I, in Alloa could not supply proprietary glass because of a change in production tooling. We needed the new bottles for the redesigns of our three cask finishes, the Port, Amarone and Sauternes, due to be launched in November. We were told there would be a two-week delay, but the labels were late as well, so we hoped it would all come together in the end. Then the labels, when applied, were creased due to a glass imperfection so we had to pull the whole release. As it happened we went to market early in 2015 and it was very successful so gave us an early boost to the trading figures.

Then four or five years ago after one of Chile's frequent earthquakes there was a paperboard shortage and we needed to allow a three-month lead time on supplies, instead of three weeks. Speculation on raw materials on the world markets can alter our cost basis – tin capsules for instance. My job is as much about those sorts of problems as it is about the day-to-day management. But it's how you deal with them that counts.

GILLIAN SNADDON
Bulk Stock Administrator

Gillian began at Arran Distillers in 2006 after answering an advert placed by the then company secretary Calum Green. Previously having had some time out due to the birth of her twin girls, she joined the company from the Diageo complex at Menstrie where she had dealt with customs and excise, LIMS (Laboratory Information Management System) and Sensory Analysis.

Five years were spent at the Arran Stirling head office in Springkerse before the move to the Touch Business Park outside Cambusbarron in 2011. She not only takes care of around 22,000 casks stored at Lochranza, Bladnoch and Tomatin, but also with over 4,000 private casks held in bond for around 2,000 customers and syndicates.

The Arran Bondholder scheme is also part of the role. I asked how problematic it had been. 'I arrived in 2006 as we were starting distribution of Bondholders' Founders' Reserve 10-year-old whisky from a very cramped unit at Springkerse. Each Bondholder had an option on five cased dozens, 60 bottles in total. There was just me doing all the work and it took a lot of time and effort, but there was no alternative.'

And the private casks? 'A high proportion are all stored in Lochranza and most owners want them kept for at least ten or more years. A few don't want them until they are over twenty years old. In the event of the death of an owner, the inheritor is usually approached to see if we can buy back the stock and I suppose in the years to come we might end up with some casks lying in bond with no traceable owner. The French racking system in warehouse number three is actually perfect for private casks as one operator can retrieve a single cask from the system without disrupting any others. Ideally, we could have all the private casks stored on that system with the trade casks kept on the traditional racking,' something that Gordon Bloy is also keen to see.

'Our Private Cask Sales Scheme is a great success. We currently offer two wood types, ex-bourbon barrels and ex-sherry hogsheads of 200 and 250 litres volume with 20 ex-bourbon barrels available for our 20ppm peated spirit on a first-come, first-served basis. The cost of the ex-bourbon is £1,850 and the ex-sherry £2,450 with the peated at £2,200.' However, anyone considering buying a cask needs to look at the forward picture as an ex-sherry hogshead of 10-year-old malt bottled today would result in a total bill of around £8,000 not including printing of labels, applying them, packing, documentation and delivery! That, perhaps, is where a syndicate can make sense.

We have a lot of Swiss buyers and the Danes love Arran as well. The syndicates, from all over the world, are good fun. There's one called Macaulay Culkin and another is White Topps and Fiery Mole. Don't ask me, I don't know why!

Before I finished talking to Gillian, I remembered that as Bondholder number 0479, I had never taken up the option on the 60 bottles of malt due to me. For some reason I assumed that it had lapsed years ago. 'Not at all. I'll check it out,' Gillian assured me. 'Communication with Bondholders on the option petered out a bit when things were in disarray, but we'll have the records.' A day later she emailed me to let me know that I could still take up the option for what was now the 14-year-old Founders' Reserve, matured in ex-bourbon casks and finished in ex-sherry … the classic Arran regime. I did not take long to make up my mind. Sixty bottles would mean that I need not be tempted to buy any other malt for a considerable period. It seemed that all the close shaves and near disasters the company had experienced in the early years had finally become a thing of the past and my 'punt' of £405 when I bought my Bond had finally turned out to be a golden nest egg.

One of the 60 bottles of Founder's Reserve which the author received in late 2015 as one of the original Arran Bondholders.
Jonathan Cosens

149

ISLE
OF
ARRAN
DISTILLERS
LOCHRANZA
1995
ISLE OF ARRAN DISTILLERS LTD.
SINGLE MALT
LOCHRANZA
1995

Company Timeline

1991–1994

FOLLOWING AN AGREEMENT MADE BETWEEN Hal Currie and David Hutchison in the spring of 1991, Isle of Arran Distillers Ltd was registered on 11 November the same year.

The Companies House return filed in 1992 and dated 11 November, records that they were the sole directors and shareholders holding two nominal £1 shares each from an authorised share capital of £10,000. The company made a loss of £11,712 that year due to costs incurred in setting up and undertaking research, meetings, planning and travel.

A further trading loss of £73,651 was posted in the 1993 accounts and on 8 July 1994 Andrew and Paul Currie became directors. At an extraordinary general meeting three days later the authorised share capital was increased to 1,000,000 shares of £1, subsequently converted on 10 November to 2,000,000 shares, each of £0.50 value. This was to ensure that the Curries increased their total holdings and to accommodate the many investors, such as Les Auchincloss, that Ross Peters had approached. On the annual return to Companies House of 11 November 1994 the issued share capital amounted to £84,797.50 represented by David Hutchison with his original two shares, Hal Currie with 61,604, Paul with 64,205 and Andrew with 43,782, totalling 169,595.

When two further share issues were taken up on 15 and 28 November, a total of 961,000 were taken up by 27 new investors with capital of £861,002 being raised, £380,500 of which was at a premium of £0.50 per share. Subscriptions were held open and a further £115,000 was added to share capital in early 1995 with the same amount at premium. Gordon Mitchell, formerly of Lochside Distillery, Montrose and Cooley Distillery, Dundalk, was appointed as Distillery Manager having been recommended to Hal Currie by Jimmy Lang. He was to stay for 13 years.

With the success of these issues and the income from the distillery Bonds, the company was in a much better financial position and construction began on 16 December 1994. The financial loss for the year was £145,364.

1995

BY EARLY 1995 THERE WERE six shareholders in the company: Hal, Andrew and Paul Currie, David Hutchison, Les Auchincloss, who was appointed on the 28 December 1994 following the share issues, and Patrick Dromgoole, a television executive and contact of Andrew Currie who joined on 1 January 1995. Auchincloss, whose shareholding amounted to 312,000, was the largest single shareholder and the Currie family also increased their total holdings to 312,002 shares; David Hutchison did likewise to 10,002. On 14 August Hutchison resigned from the board as he felt that continuing his duties as architect for the project might create a conflict of interest. To this day he has retained his shareholding in the company.

Production commenced in late June while construction was still incomplete and was then stopped until the distillery was in a fit state to function normally. The accounts for 1995 showed a loss of £408,695. This was offset by the share and capital reserves, as previous annual trading losses had been.

1996

ONE OF HAL CURRIE'S AIMS had been to create a distillery that sold only bottled single malt but by 1996 sales of fillings to 'another distiller' were being made and cask sales via a whisky broker for onward sale to 'private individuals' came to an abrupt end when the broker went bust. The company ensured that the purchasers did not lose out, but it was a salutary lesson. Another avenue for the future was the sale of casks to shareholders which could be bought back by the distillery when stocks were required in the future, notably in 2003/4 when production ceased in order to cut costs.

The 'visitor centre' was a large Portakabin, installed in the summer of 1995, but it attracted over 25,000 people that year, something that boded well for the future. A further Portakabin was installed for the duration of the summer season. Ross Peters joined the board on the 1 August as a non-executive director and has remained one ever since. Later that month a gathering of Bondholders took place at the distillery attracting a large number of people to celebrate the first year of production. Construction of the VC proper started after this event, and was scheduled to open at Easter 1997. Branded bottle sales were part and parcel of the revenue generated by the distillery, consisting of Island Prince, Royal Island, Loch Ranza, Glen Rosa, Eileandour and Glen Eason. All the labels for these brands were designed by Michael Peters' Identica Partnership in London. Mail order through the Arran Malt Whisky Society also contributed and it managed to break even that year. These were essential tools for brand building. The trading loss for 1996 was £79,237.

1997

BONDS CONTINUED TO BE SOLD to visitors to the distillery as a customer database was developed, an internet presence established and trading with a new fillings customer was started. Cask sales to private individuals also grew. The market for branded bottled sales was increased with distribution arrangements being put in place in France, Germany, Italy, the Czech Republic, Slovakia, USA, Australia, Thailand, Hong Kong and Japan. Sales for 1997 were 60,000 cases.

The main highlight of the year was the official opening of the VC on 9 August 1997 by HM Queen Elizabeth. This was only the second distillery in Scotland ever to have been visited by the Queen who was at Bowmore Distillery, Islay, exactly 17 years earlier, to the day. Considerable press coverage accompanied her visit helping to make the distillery the most visited attraction on the island next to Brodick Castle. It also achieved 'Highly Commended' status from the Scottish Tourist Board as one of the top four attractions in the West of Scotland. Visitor numbers for 1997 totalled 40,000. The mail order business was struggling to make money but the directors considered it a worthwhile PR tool. On the bright side the first profit after taxation was posted, a modest £34,434 but this was later restated in 1998 as a loss of £63,706 due to a discrepancy in the listing of customers' whisky casks in the stock valuation. Total company employees numbered 25 at the year end.

1998

THIS WAS DESCRIBED AS 'a difficult year' by the directors, primarily due to the downturn in the Far East which halted growth. Nor was the outlook for 1999 considered to offer any more hope for any uplift in business. A bank loan for £1.1m was negotiated to help finances. With the June 1995 stock now over three years of age, Arran finally had malt Scotch whisky in bond at the distillery and some casks had matured well enough to create a limited bottling. A full-blown PR exercise swung into action as actor Ewan McGregor, fresh from the success of *Trainspotting*, opened the first cask on 25 July. Finally, after almost 160 years, legal whisky was being produced on Arran once more. John Lamond was there as well discovering the 'backbone' of the whisky which he felt was more like a five-year-old, so clearly the whisky was top quality. In November, at a gala dinner in Edinburgh, Andrew Currie picked up the Scottish Trade International Award for outstanding export achievement from Sir Ian Wood. On 4 December Martyn

Bridger, a Surrey-based consultant, joined the board as a director. The financial year ended with a loss of £362,506, restated in 1999 as £340,307. Total company employees numbered 27 at the year end.

1999

STRUCTURAL CHANGES AT BOARDROOM LEVEL resulted in the influence of the Currie family being reduced. Hal Currie resigned on 1 June as a director but remained company secretary and president until Paul Garwood took over as company secretary on 22 September when Hal was made Honorary President for life. In July Andrew Kettles had taken over as chairman and later appointed David Boyle as managing director in November. Andrew Currie resigned on 30 September and moved on to new challenges. With the changes in the board came some major changes in strategy.

Three brands would be focused on: Arran malt, Loch Ranza blend and Holy Isle Cream Liqueur. A limited expression called the Painters' Collection was started with labels showing famous paintings of Arran. The first was a 43% abv bottling limited to 3,000 priced at £100 showing Loch Ranza by Perthshire artist William Miller Frazer (1864-1961) who was a lifelong friend of Tommy Dewar, who in turn became his patron. At the end of the financial year Les Auchincloss was in control of 557,752 shares with Paul Currie, Patrick Dromgoole and Ross Peters holding 401,934. In total there were now 97 shareholders in the company which was employing four staff at the distillery, 10 in the VC and eight in sales and admin. The accounts were extended to 13 months to make the financial year end 31 December and showed a loss of £573,148 on turnover of £1,045,530, down by 51% on the previous year, largely due to the 'madness' of price discounting in the large retails chains. However, shareholders' funds stood at a healthy net £1,022,252. Another share issue of 500,000 at £0.50 each was planned for 2000 to raise the authorised share capital to £2.5m.

2000

THE MILLENNIUM YEAR SAW A reduction in visitor numbers to the distillery for the first time but the Arran single bottled malt was available over a full year and sales from this offset the reduced income from the VC. The really disappointing aspect of the year was the continued retail discounting in the large retail chains, the main effect of which was 'that the major players maintain placements and market share at the expense of the small niche players such as Arran'. The result was another loss of £689,063. Despite this, more distribution arrangements were established as the export road map for the future was further developed. Kevin Ramsden was approached by David Boyle and joined as export sales manager in February from Morrison Bowmore Distillers, both having known each other when they were previously with Highland Distillers. An exclusive licensing deal with the World Burns Federation meant that Isle of Arran Distillers gained exclusive rights in perpetuity to use the Robert Burns name on bottled whiskies. This was an initiative that David Boyle secured for a one-off payment during his tenure as managing director and the relationship is still going strong today. The only change in the boardroom was the resignation of consultant Martyn Bridger on 27 May. The shareholding structure changed markedly with the issue of 35m 'B' class ordinary shares of 25p each adding £8.75m to the total authorised share capital of £10m. During the year 2,106,039 shares were issued raising the capital by £553,019 with another £53,019 as share premium. Total company employees numbered 20 at the year end.

2001

NEW DISTRIBUTION AGREEMENTS WERE NEGOTIATED for the UK with Cellar Trends Ltd and Spain along with some other European markets and on 25 January (the birth date of Robert Burns) Isle of Arran Distillers was announced as a patron of the World Burns Federation. However, the overriding influence during the year was the outbreak of foot-and-mouth disease which devastated tourism throughout the UK and lead to another fall in visitor numbers at the VC. It also affected the whisky trade badly. Throughout the UK some £8bn was lost to the economy as the company recorded another loss of £751,966. An abortive attempt at a takeover by Thai Beverages failed but defending it was costly nonetheless. Deliveries to Bondholders continued to create difficulties and the year closed as one of the worst on record. In October Paul Garwood stepped down as company secretary and Calum Green was appointed in his place. David Boyle departed as managing director and Douglas Davidson joined as sales director (he was to take over as managing director in February the following year). Michael Peirce also joined the board as a non-executive director on the same day. He and Les Auchincloss injected a further soft loan of over £120k into the company to help cash flow. By the end of the year distribution agreements in the USA, Italy and Scandinavia were close to being finalised. Total company employees numbered 21 at the year end.

2002

FINALLY SOME RELIEF CAME WITH the VC posting its best year with sales of £360,147 but the loss for the year was £420,682. The first-ever cask-strength release was rapidly taken up by collectors and enthusiasts but the world markets were not so positive with many slowing down due to the war in Iraq. Patrick Dromgoole resigned from the board on 14 February. During the year 898,700 shares were issued which raised a further £449,350 of capital. Total company employees numbered 20 at the year end.

2003

ON 22 AUGUST THE LAST BOARDROOM link with the Currie family ended with the resignation of Paul who subsequently sold his shareholding to Les Auchincloss. Other members of the Currie family, including Hal, were to retain shareholdings to the present day. Sales of branded products increased by 17% with Arran single malt sales up 48%, gaining a silver medal in the Islands (Malt) category at the International Wine & Spirits Competition (IWSC) for the 5-year-old. The Cask Strength 5-year-old was also commended. New distribution deals were put in place to take the total number of export markets to 23 including a listing with the Liquor Control Board of Ontario and its counterpart in Sweden, Systembolaget. An exclusive deal in the off-trade was brokered with Oddbins in the UK but did not match expectations and later reverted to a non-exclusive arrangement. Euan Mitchell, formerly of the independent bottlers Wm Cadenhead of Campbeltown was approached by Davidson and joined the company as European sales manager. In order to cut costs production was halted for much of the year and into the next. Kevin Ramsden decided to leave in July and moved to Chivas Brothers to work in Eastern Europe. The trading losses fell to £297,921 and a further issue of shares was exchanged for £250,000 in cash and £194,488 in whisky stock purchase obligations from shareholders and cask owners after an offer to potential investors in September failed to raise a further £2m and was undersubscribed. Ross Peters explained the reason for this was that 'most potential investors could not accept the valuation basis which they considered was too high given the losses the company made in the early years'. Total company employees numbered 18 at the year end.

2004

THE IMPROVING TRADING PICTURE CONTINUED with a further reduction in losses to £224,952. The directors considered it to be a year of 'solid achievement'. Branded product sales rose by 32% and the VC had its best year to date with sales of £426,093. New markets were opened in Hungary, British Columbia, South Africa, Australia, New Zealand and Ireland. A new arrangement was negotiated for the Czech Republic. The company achieved a 'Best of the Best' award from *Whisky Magazine* and the non chill-filtered malt bottling won an IWSC silver medal. The Holy Isle cream liqueur was relaunched as Arran Gold malt whisky cream liqueur in September. At the end of the year the company was awarded the Best New Exporter Award in the UK by the International Business Awards. Equity for stock buyback also continued. The total shareholdings on 11 November 2004 stood at 102 with over 13m shares in circulation. Production was recommenced during the year and total company employees numbered 21 at the year end.

2005

AGAIN THE YEAR SHOWED IMPROVEMENT with losses stemmed to £113,736 as the company moved forward. Branded sales increased by 11%, malt sales by 28% to total an increase of 72% on all brands. New markets opened in the Philippines, Malaysia and, finally, Greece, after years of fruitless investigation. The Arran Gold cream liqueur and the new Calvados-finished, cask-strength malt won a silver award and 'Best in Class' respectively at the IWSC. Robin Bell returned to the distillery as VC manager in January and began to overhaul its management and systems and started recruiting staff for the new season. A high-profile award ceremony took place in June at the VC for the presentation of the Queen's Award for Enterprise: International Trade. At the same time a commemorative bottling of 1,200 celebrated the first issue of the 10-year-old Arran single malt. Volume of spirit produced for the year ran to 100,000 litres, with a 25% increase planned for 2006. Further stocks were bought back and the launch of the trade bottling of the 10-year-old in the spring of 2006 was planned in line with national advertising for the first time. Andrew Kettles retired as chairman on 30 September leaving a streamlined board of Les Auchincloss, Douglas Davidson, Michael Peirce (who took over as chairman) and Ross Peters. The total number of company employees remained 21 at the year end.

2006

THE COMPANY POSTED A TRADING profit of £106,939. Sales of branded products rose by 21% with a similar gain in malt sales with significant growth in the USA. The distillery ceased selling casks and bulk whisky as a matter of policy but the VC and the mail order business performed well with sales of almost £500k combined. The trade bottling of the 10-year-old malt gained a silver medal at the IWSC awards and capacity rose to 125,000 lpa per annum as planned. A new warehouse gained planning permission to increase bonded capacity and was opened in September the next year. Ray Tully joined the board on 12 December. The total number of company employees remained 21 at the year end.

2007

ARRAN BECAME THE 'Distillery of the Year' in the inaugural *Whisky Magazine* World Whiskies Awards with Arran Gold cream liqueur also being voted World's Best Whisky Liqueur. The company won the Scottish Drinks Producer of the Year from *Scotland Magazine*. The Robert Burns Single Malt and the Arran 100% Proof Single Malt both won silver awards and 'Best in Class' awards at the IWSC. The new £750,000 bonded warehouse received its first casks and production volume rose to 135,000 lpa. Margaret Cornwall, formerly of the Scotch Malt Whisky Society, joined in March as financial controller and to act as company secretary while Gordon Mitchell retired on 4 September, the day after the opening of the new warehouse, which was named after him. A limited edition of 771 bottles, 'Gordon's Dram' marked the occasion. James MacTaggart, previously with Bowmore Distillery on Islay, replaced Gordon as distillery manager.

New markets were opened up in Finland, Quebec Province, Laos and Cambodia and preliminary visits were made to China and India where a distribution arrangement was set up, effective in 2008. The VC welcomed 62,500 visitors and had its most profitable year ever. A re-evaluation of land and buildings was undertaken which added £2,114,000 to the balance sheet but a trading loss of £157,367 was recorded largely due to high interest costs and currency losses. The introduction of obligatory customs strip stamps created a major issue in Russia and trade in the USA fell, so forecast sales were not achieved. Turnover, however, was up by £53,759 to £2,014,652. A share issue was offered in August to raise £2m of investment and total shareholdings stood at 139 with over 15m shares at 11 November 2007. This offer was not fully subscribed for the same reasons as the 2003 issue fell short. In the same document the company also laid bare the options before it.

EXIT STRATEGY

The company has no immediate plans to sell to a trade partner, however it does recognise the need for shareholder liquidity at some time in the future. The Directors believe that the focus on building market share and profitability in the immediate future is the best strategy. We do intend, however, to examine ways in which small shareholders may more easily sell their shares. Although these measures are not yet in place there are pre-emption rights within the Company which allow any shareholder to offer their shares for sale and for all other shareholders to have the right to buy an allocation of these shares in proportion to their current holding.

In the longer term when profitability is at an improved level the Directors will examine the option of a public listing on the AIM market of the London Stock Exchange or a trade sale to a larger company.

As a public company, your board has the duty to consider any offer for the business and give advice to shareholders as to whether that offer should, in the interests of shareholders, be accepted or rejected.

Arran ranked third in cased sales amongst the seven independent distillers that the company considered its nearest competitors. The ranking was: 1. Bruichladdich, 2. Springbank, 3. Arran, 4. Edradour, 5. Benriach, 6. Tullibardine, 7. Benromach. The board felt that the company could overtake Springbank 'in the next few years and challenge Bruichladdich.' Total company employees numbered 22 at the year end.

2008

JAMES MACTAGGART WAS APPOINTED a director of the company on 11 March and Euan Mitchell followed in a like manner on 2 June. The trade 10-year-old single malt bottling surpassed £1m in sales for the first time and the 12-year-old was launched in October. Douglas Davidson was appointed deputy chairman in June and Euan Mitchell took over as MD. Louisa Young joined in January as sales manager with a focus on European markets which were increased with entry into Latvia, Lithuania, Estonia and Poland. New distributors were appointed for the UK, Belgium and the Czech Republic. Arran won the Best Islands Single Malt Whisky (NAS) in the World Whiskies Awards. With the 250th anniversary of the birth of Robert Burns in 2009, a special bottling of the Robert Burns 10-year-old single malt was launched in late 2008 and sold into the UK, Swiss and Canadian markets. The VC had another record year with visitors exceeding 60,000 but the global economic crisis was taking its toll with downturns in most markets. Allied to increased staffing costs this resulted in a loss of £137,101. However, the directors took the view that more stock had to be laid down for the future and that production volume would be increased in 2009. Total company employees numbered 23 at the year end.

2009

THE ECONOMIC DOWNTURN WHICH CONTINUED throughout the year made trading very difficult but there was still growth in a number of markets. The commemorative 10-year-old edition of the Robert Burns malt was released in the UK in January, officially endorsed by the World Burns Federation to mark the 250th Anniversary of the birth of Robert Burns and the Year of the Homecoming in Scotland. The VC welcomed 62,000 visitors and had its best year in terms of sales with turnover up 13%. Sterling was weak throughout the year and Arran's UK distributor, Malcolm Cowen Ltd, collapsed but the company was able to resume with Blavod Drinks Ltd. Sales in the USA grew 53% and three listings with the Norwegian state-controlled alcohol monopoly Vinmonopolet were gained for the 10-year-old Arran single malt, Robert Burns Malt and The Arran Malt Single Cask Series. This raised Arran to the second-most popular malt by volume in Norway, outselling many long-established brands. The 'Icons of Arran' series of the malt was launched and well-received, helping to increase turnover to £2,142,251.

Céline Têtu joined the sales and marketing team to help develop sales in her native France, one of the strongest export markets in which Arran was selling. The weakness of sterling raised tourist numbers and many UK residents holidayed at home, helping the VC throughout the summer season even though the weather was poor. Targets, however, were not achieved but tight cost control helped to mitigate the losses through the year. The decision was also taken to double production volume for 2010 in order to meet forecasts further down the line. Andrew Hogan joined the company from Bruichladdich as regional sales manager to concentrate on growing the North American market. The company ended the year with a small loss of £16,354. Total company employees numbered 23 at the year end.

2010

THE DISTILLERY REACHED ITS 15TH anniversary in 2010 and achieved record growth with revenue increasing 27% and brand sales showing a 42% increase from the previous year. Visitors to the distillery exceeded 67,000 and turnover rose by 4.5%. New expressions included the second in the 'Icons of Arran' series, The Rowan Tree which sold out in advance and a 15-year-old anniversary bottling sold well. Brand sales were healthy with France, Arran's largest export market, posting 55% growth and Norway remained strong while home trade sales were not as good as forecast. However, Internet mail-order sales rose 29%.

An Open Day at the distillery in July would become the first of many as it was decided to hold the event in future on an annual basis, to be renamed the Arran Malt & Music Festival. The official Arran 14-year-old was released in August to replace the 12-year-old expression in the planned core range of 10, 14 and 18-year-olds. The first bottling of the peated (14ppm) expression of Arran, Machrie Moor, was released in early December. Faye Black took over from Robin Bell as VC manager in the same month as it posted its most successful year to date. The company returned a profit of £117,316 which was ahead of forecast. It was decided by the board to increase output for 2011. Douglas Davidson retired as a non-executive director on 31 December with the best wishes of the board. Total company employees including directors numbered 27 at the year end.

2011

AT THIS TIME THE CONFIDENCE that the shareholders had in the future of the company was well-founded as turnover rose 14% to over £3m in 2011 with brand sales rising by 21%. Arran malt brands grew by 24% and a Christmas Gift pack of the 10-year-old malt grew its volume by 38% alone. In conjunction with the National Trust for Scotland (NTS) a special limited bottling of 6,000 called The Sleeping Warrior (an old nickname for Goatfell) was issued and exposed Arran whisky as a brand to 330,000 NTS members worldwide. A £1 donation from each bottle sold raised £6,000 for the maintenance of the footpaths on Goatfell. The 12-year-old cask-strength single malt was introduced to great acclaim and European markets performed well with France, Belgium, Holland and Germany showing strong growth. The Chinese mainland market was entered and sales in Taiwan, the key Far East single-malt market, rose markedly. Sales in Canada were maintained and a new distributor was appointed in the USA effective from January 2012. Visitor numbers, however, were lower than in 2010

with distillery turnover slightly down, but still making a meaningful contribution to profit.

The second distillery Open Day was another success, now renamed as the Arran Malt & Music Festival to run every subsequent year at the end of June. The highest level of production of 350,000 lpa was achieved in order to lay down sufficient maturing stock for the future. This necessitated another increase in warehouse capacity with the planning of a 12,000-cask capacity unit which started to be built in November. A profit of £250,006 was realised which was in line with expectations. Perhaps, finally, the future was set fair for Arran Distillers. Total number of company employees including directors remained 27 at the year end.

2012

TURNOVER ROSE TO £3,649,967, some 18% up on the year before. Sales of brands exceeded £2m for the first time, up 16%. Operating profit also rose by 40%. Soaring demand for the high-margin limited expressions of Arran single malt was largely responsible for this as sales by volume rose by 4.6% while the industry average dropped by 3.2% in this sector. The fourth and final 'Icons of Arran' was released in June – The Eagle, completing the series. The Devil's Punchbowl Chapter 1 was released in June, a limited edition of 6,660 bottles worldwide which quickly sold out. This bottling also received a packaging design award at the World Whiskies Awards. The 14-year-old single malt began to gain momentum in the key markets and the Robert Burns bottlings were relaunched in new packaging. The focus on export markets accounted for 90% of the sales of the single malts with France remaining the distillery's largest market, followed closely by the USA under the new distribution arrangement. Sales in Denmark also profited from a new distributor and a change of distributor in the UK raised confidence for growth in 2013. Russia bounced back after import restrictions in 2010 and 2011 and raised expectations for the future.

A poor summer and the continuing economic downturn resulted in a fall in visitors to the island and the VC but it managed to perform close to the levels of 2011. The distillery and VC had an external makeover, new signage being installed while the café was refurbished at the end of the year. The new warehouse opened in May and permission was sought for further expansion of bonded capacity. During 2012 over 400,000 lpa was produced and a profit of £348,514 was posted. The number of employees and directors remained the same as 2011.

2013

THE POSITIVE TREND CONTINUED DURING the year. Turnover increased by 20% to £4,556,195 and a pre-tax profit of £549,639 was achieved. Brand sales drove this with growth of 28%. In March the 12-year-old cask-strength bottling won a double gold medal at the San Francisco World Spirits Competition. Sales of single bottled malt rose in volume by 21% and in March the 16-year-old at 46% abv was launched as a limited expression of 9,000 bottles, a move designed as a precursor to the introduction of the 18-year-old single malt in 2015. Chapter 2 of 'The Devil's Punchbowl' was released and the introduction of the 'Private Cask' allowed distributors to personalise bottlings for their markets and private individuals.

The USA overtook France as Arran's best export market for single malt sales with further substantial growth expected in the future. Sales in Taiwan soared 130% and the new distribution arrangements in the UK led to increased sales particularly in the independent retail sector. Belarus, Vietnam, and South Africa were opened up and plans were laid for expansion into Latin America where whisky sales were booming. The VC received 6% more visitors than 2012 and turnover was up by 11% to just over £700,000. The three-tier distillery tour system was launched with Oak, Copper and Gold levels so that all types of visitor could be accommodated. The café was renamed the Casks Café & Bar and the fourth Arran Malt & Music Festival took place welcoming Bondholders and visitors from all over the world. The release of 'Staff Bottlings' proved popular

with the first being chosen by senior tour guide Campbell Laing, selling out in a few weeks. Output was maintained at 400,000 lpa for the year. The number of employees and directors was 31 at the end of the year.

2014

THE STEADY GROWTH OF THE company continued with turnover up 21% to £5,514,746. Brand sales drove this with an increase of 23% over 2013, while the industry average in the malt sector for the year was 11%. The final chapter of the 'Devil's Punchbowl' trilogy was released and snapped up quickly while a cask-strength edition of the peated Machrie Moor was also a popular expression. The 17-year-old, limited to 9,000 bottles sold out before release and readied the market for the 18-year-old scheduled to be released the next year. With a core range of 10, 12 and 14-year-old single malts now available to the public, the entire portfolio was repackaged in 2014 and helped boost both shelf presence and sales towards the end of the year. The Lochranza Reserve malt was also added to the range during the year. This NAS bottling allowed access to higher volume sales channels and also meant that there was greater flexibility in use of stock inventory.

France remained the largest export market in general terms but it was outperformed by Germany for single malt sales. Taiwan performed strongly while sales in Japan and mainland China increased and a new importer for Hong Kong was appointed further strengthening Arran's exposure in the Far East. Sales at home grew by over 30%, defying the general market trend of decline. Similarly the US market showed signs of retraction but Canadian sales rose 40% across many provinces. Finally, the Latin American market was entered as the first shipment of Arran malt was realised in December, with more business expected from this market in the future.

Visitors to the distillery rose by 10% to over 65,000 which increased turnover by 14% to £795,000 and contributed £180,000 to the profits. The significant introduction of RET (Road Equivalent Tariff) in October 2014 resulted in reduced ferry fares for visitors and Arranachs alike. Numbers of vehicles coming to the distillery increased by 40% and the traditional summer visiting season was extended resulting in year-round opening of the VC. In November the distillery won the prestigious Best Distillery Visitor Experience in the *Scottish Field* Whisky Challenge for the first time.

Production volume increased to 500,000 lpa with a new warehouse opening in December, increasing storage by 12,000 casks. In July a new filling and vatting storeroom was opened, giving full on-site control of blending and finishing. With an eye to the future two new pot stills were commissioned for installation in October 2016 in order to take capacity to 1.2m lpa per annum.

The net profit posted for 2014 was £831,362, an increase of £281,723 over 2013 and there were 190 shareholdings listed in the company. The number of employees and directors was 27 at the end of the year.

2015

THE YEAR STARTED WITH the VC receiving fresh decoration and signage and a sales team attending The Viking Line annual Cinderella Whisky Cruise in January where the newly packaged core range was introduced along with some other releases. On 23 January a White Stag dinner was held at Oran Mor in Glasgow where the panel selected cask 1997/737, an ex-sherry hogshead which was later released in June as the first official White Stag bottling. February saw the launch of the limited edition 18-year-old Arran malt as a precursor to the core range bottling in early 2016. From 2 March to 2 June the VC hosted a fine art photography exhibition of the work of Ann Holmes. In early April the range of Port, Amarone and Sauternes Cask Finishes was relaunched in new packaging and on the 22 April, Arran's third Tweet Tasting on Twitter took place. During May £1 from every Oak tour, £2 from every Copper tour and £5 from every Gold tour was donated to the Nepalese Disaster Relief Fund and at the end of

the month the VC received another Trip Advisor Certificate of Excellence for 2015.

The Arran Malt & Music Festival kicked off on 27 June and included a food and whisky pairing masterclass which was very successful. The summer shutdown for production staff was from 24 July to 17 August. The same month saw many of the distillery's international distributors visit Lochranza, including the teams from Belgium, Italy and the Czech Republic. The distillery also launched a mini-campaign requesting White Stags worldwide to share their photos of their memories of Arran Distillery over the past 20 years in preparation for a 21st anniversary photo collage to be displayed in the Visitor Centre in 2016. Late August saw the groundwork started in preparation for the construction of the Blending and Tasting Rooms Centre on the west side of the car park. In September the first release in a trilogy of limited edition Arran Malts, The Smugglers' Series, Vol I, 'The Illicit Stills' was made as well as the annual 6th Edition of the regular Machrie Moor and Batch 2 of the cask-strength Machrie Moor.

On 19 October the final limited edition of the year, The Bothy, was released. In November the VC gained the prestigious Best Distillery Visitor Experience in the *Scottish Field* Whisky Challenge for the second year running. A special ex-sherry cask finish Arran malt was produced for the Christmas market exclusively for the larger Marks & Spencer stores. December brought the news that Master Distiller James MacTaggart had been awarded a Highly Commended mention in the category of Master Distiller of the Year in the 2016 Icons of Whisky Competition run by *Whisky Magazine*. In addition to this, the distillery was shortlisted for Brand Innovator of the Year as was Sales Manager Andy Bell for Brand Ambassador of the Year. Turnover for the year was £6.25m and profit realised was just over £1m. The number of employees at year end was 34.

2016

As 2016 OPENED THE COMPANY was able to donate £3,267 to the Kalaa Jyoti orphanage in Katmandu, Nepal, through fundraising from the art exhibition of the orphans' work on display in the VC and organised by local artist Gordon Davidson. The first standard expression of the Arran 18-year-old was released in February, completing the core range of 10, 14 & 18-year-old single malts. The Arran Malt & Music Festival dates were announced as Friday 1 to Sunday 3 July with sales of tickets for masterclasses, ceilidh and the fourth White Stag Dinner commencing on 1 March.

Sadly, March also saw the passing of Hal Currie, one of the company's co-founders and the driving force behind it during its early years and ironically, in the same month, plans were finally made public for the company's second distillery, to be based near Lagg in the south of the island on a 15-acre site. The distillery will draw water from a borehole aquifer flowing at a rate of 227 litres per minute, enough to allow an initial annual output of 200,000 lpa thanks to a recycling process. Denham Benn of Ayr were retained to prepare the initial designs and the planning application for the 1.5m lpa distillery along with six associated warehouses was submitted on Friday, 6 May 2016. Subject to approval, spirit should be running from the stills in the autumn of 2018.

In April the selection process for the 2016 White Stag Tasting Panel was started to enable the 20 winners to select the second White Stag release later in the year. In May the Blending and Tasting Rooms neared completion in time for the 21st anniversary celebrations at the end of June which the publication of this book also marks. Turnover for the year was forecast at just under £7m, with profit to exeed the predicted figure. The number of employees was expected to be 35 at year end.

Expressions

CORE RANGE

10-YEAR-OLD, SINGLE MALT

Date of first release: 2006
46% abv, 70cl, non chill-filtered

Tasting Notes

Nose

Sweet oak and honey are immediately apparent in the aroma. Hints of coconut and candy appear when water is added with butterscotch and liquorice also evident.

Palate

The taste is crisp and malty with a slight nuttiness. With time the malt begins to open and the Arran hallmarks of citrus and sweet fruit emerge to coat the tongue.

Finish

Clean and fresh with a lingering creamy sweetness. Mellow, smooth and bursting with flavour.

14-YEAR-OLD, SINGLE MALT

Date of first release: August 2010
46% abv, 70cl, non chill-filtered

Tasting Notes

Colour

Sunset copper.

Nose

Dried fruits, vanilla and toffee up front. Caramelised fruits indicate a depth of flavour to come.

Palate

An initial burst of freshness leads to warming toffee apples and hazelnuts. A layer of milk chocolate and spiced teacake make the mouthfeel overwhelmingly weighty and full of complexity.

Finish

A trademark Arran finish with cinnamon leading back to where the experience began. The classic island-style fresh wave is balanced by notes of liquorice and pineapple in the lingering finish.

18-YEAR-OLD, SINGLE MALT

Date of first release: March 2016

46% abv, 70cl, non chill-filtered

Tasting Notes

Colour

Honeyed gold.

Nose

Sweet orchard fruits with syrup and toasted oak. Vanilla and light cinnamon.

Palate

Sweetness dances on the tongue with chocolate, ginger, caramelised brown sugar and vanilla. Water uncovers floral notes and aromatic orange fondant creams.

Finish

Long, lingering and luxurious. The classic Arran citrus and orchard fruits mingle with milk brioche and dark chocolate. A memorable depth of character, Arran is fully mature at 18 years old.

LOCHRANZA RESERVE

Date of first release: June 2014

46% abv, 70cl, non chill-filtered

Tasting Notes

Colour

Golden sunshine.

Nose

The fresh island character and citrus notes are immediately evident with fresh pear and honeysuckle.

Palate

Beautifully balanced citrus fruit and light vanilla sweetness with a burst of apple and delicate marine notes.

Finish

Lingering and delicate with sweet oak and spice, softened slightly by a layer of milk chocolate. The fresh island character of Lochranza.

ROBERT BURNS SINGLE MALT

Date of first release: 2001
Date of distillation: NAS
46% abv, 70cl, non chill-filtered

BOTTLED UNDER THE ROBERT BURNS LABEL, this edition of the Arran single malt has been created by combining different ages to create a beautifully rounded whisky that is smooth, malty and sweet with a delicious spicy twist on the finish. The use of mainly American oak ex-bourbon casks in maturation has accentuated the sweet, fruity notes of Arran whilst a smaller proportion of ex-sherry hogsheads add depth and richness. This delicious dram can be enjoyed neat, on the rocks or as part of a classic whisky cocktail. Raise a glass and toast Scotland's national poet and favourite son.

Tasting Notes

Colour

Ayrshire sunshine.

Nose

Sweet and creamy with notes of honey, toffee-glazed pecans and fresh summer fruits.

Palate

A perfect combination of rich malt and lush vanilla notes form a refreshing and smooth palate. Light and sweet at first followed by tantalising spice and oak.

Finish

Clean and fresh with an aftertaste of hazelnuts and milk chocolate. A true drop of liquid poetry and the perfect dram with which to toast the Bard!

LIMITED EDITIONS

15TH ANNIVERSARY SINGLE MALT

Date of release: September 2010
Date of distillation: 1999
Vatting of ex-bourbon hogsheads and Amontillado ex-sherry butts.
Quantity: 5,640 x 70cl
54.6% abv, cask strength, non chill-filtered

In 2008 James MacTaggart selected a parcel of refill ex-bourbon hogsheads from 1999 and re-racked them into eight amontillado ex-sherry butts from the famous house of Valdespino in Jerez, Spain. After two years of secondary maturation in these casks the whisky reached a depth of character which was perfect for toasting the distillery's 15th anniversary.

Tasting Notes

Nose
The aroma is complex with hints of dark chocolate, cherries and ginger. Mint toffee and hazelnut emerge with water.

Palate
Rich and creamy on the palate with classic sherry-wood notes of dried fruit and spice. Confectionery sweetness mingles beautifully with the intrinsic citrus character of the Arran malt.

Finish
Much drier on the long finish with an intriguing peppery note developing.

THE BOTHY

Date of release: September 2015
Date of distillation: NAS
Quantity: 12,000 x 70cl
55.7% abv, cask strength, non chill-filtered

THE BOTHY WAS A LIMITED EDITION of Arran malt which paid homage to the use of small casks that would have played a large part in the Arran whisky trade in the 18th and 19th centuries as they were easier to handle and transport around the island. The malt selected for The Bothy was initially matured in first-fill ex-bourbon barrels before being transferred for secondary maturation into smaller casks, also made of the finest American oak, for a minimum of 18 months. This process produces far greater contact between the whisky and the oak and a faster, more intense maturation. The end result is a full-bodied expression of Arran malt combining power and finesse, full of rich vanilla sweetness and bold peppery spice.

Tasting Notes

Colour

Old gold with straw yellow highlights; as welcoming as a fire's warm glow through bothy windows.

Nose

A warm and comforting aroma. Sandalwood spice and smells of the outdoors; sweet, malty barley and damp oak. Aromas of waxy lemons, melting cane sugar and a hint of cocoa promise intense and complex flavours to follow.

Palate

A luscious, sweet mouthfeel adheres to the palate as a kick of red chilli heat arrives and starts to warm. Distillery character shines as fresh pineapple and green apples with stalks attached come to the fore. Toasted brioche and vanilla ice cream give a round quality to this dram.

Finish

A floral note at the start of a finish that lingers on the palate as tangy citrus notes develop to make the mouth water, bringing the flavour full circle, inciting another sweet sip.

THE SMUGGLERS' SERIES

Volume I — The Illicit Stills

Date of release: June 2015

Date of distillation: NAS

Vatting was made up with a multi-vintage selection unpeated malt from 600-litre Port pipes, 250-litre ex-sherry hogsheads and 200-litre ex-bourbon barrels along with 50ppm and 14ppm peated malt from 200-litre ex-bourbon barrels.

Quantity: 8,700 x 70cl

56.4% abv, cask strength, non chill-filtered

'THE ILLICIT STILLS' PAYS HOMAGE to the island's illicit distillers with an Arran dram of robust body and a heavier peat influence more redolent of the whisky produced on the island in days gone by. The presence of heavily peated Arran malt is perfectly balanced by the sweetness of older bourbon barrels. In the background the rich and fruity influence of maturation in Port pipes has resulted in a fresh, full-bodied and complex dram evocative of the distillery's independent character.

Tasting Notes

Colour

Rusting iron barrel chime rings.

Nose

Subtle peat reek rising from a distant fire hints at a robust character to come. Floral notes bring elegance, sweetness is shown in the form of fresh madeira cake with a maritime oiliness promising rich mouthfeel.

Palate

Juicy plums, spiced with white pepper. Wood smoke of freshly sawn pine. The palate develops with gripping tannin as white grapes begin to show. Pink wafer biscuits and a blast of spicy ginger appear before the finish.

Finish

The flavour of dried apricots fades before salty, maritime notes take over – the dying embers of the smugglers' signal fire on a windswept beach. An Arran dram of true unbridled character, reminiscent of the illicit spirit which gave rise to the illustrious reputation of 'Arran water'.

WHITE STAG FIRST RELEASE

Date of release: June 2015
Date of distillation: 1997
Age: 18 years old
Quantity: 214 x 70cl
53.6% abv, cask strength, non chill-filtered

A LANDMARK BOTTLING for Arran's online community of White Stags was issued as a thank you for their support. The cask was chosen by a tasting panel at an organised 'Stag Night' in January 2015. From five samples provided, the panel chose ex-sherry hogshead 1997/737 which turned 18 years old on 23 May 2015. Sold exclusively on the Arran website to members of the White Stag community only.

Tasting Notes

Nose

Warm and buttery with a subtle pear note. Delicate nuances of vanilla and marzipan lead to a sweeter layer of dried apricots and candy floss reminiscent of a sweetie shop. Typical Arran hallmarks of tropical fruit and mandarins are in abundance.

Palate

Beautifully smooth and creamy with chocolate mousse, toasted marshmallows and orange oil. A few drops of water reveal fragrant marmalade cake and salted caramel.

Finish

Deep, complex and rounded. Chilli-infused dark chocolate dominates with winter spice, figs and honey in the tail. Strong in character with time – an unforgettable experience.

16-YEARS-OLD, SINGLE MALT

Date of release: 2013
Quantity: 9,000 x 70cl
46% abv, non chill-filtered

THIS LIMITED EDITION RELEASE of 16-year-old malt was produced from un-peated malted barley and matured in a combination of ex-bourbon and ex-sherry casks. The whisky was not artificially coloured or chill-filtered to retain the full range of aromas and flavours which typify Arran single malt distillery character. The bottling marked the countdown to the first release of the 18-year-old in February 2015.

Tasting Notes

Colour

Golden syrup.

Nose

Rich, lush honey with hints of ginger and dark chocolate.

Palate

Glides over the tongue in a glorious wave of sweetness and spice. Crème brûlée at first followed by bitter orange and charred oak.

Finish

Long and lingering. Arran shows its decadent side at sweet 16.

17-YEARS-OLD, SINGLE MALT

Date of release: 2014
Quantity: 9,000 x 70cl
46% abv, non chill-filtered

FOLLOWING THE RELEASE of the 16-year-old, this limited edition release was produced from un-peated malted barley and matured in a selection of ex-sherry casks. As is the normal practice at Arran, the whisky was not artificially coloured or chill-filtered. This bottling was the second in a series marking the countdown to the first release of the 18-year-old.

Tasting Notes

Colour

Antique gold with copper highlights.

Nose

Rich warm spices with notes of candied citrus peel, tinned mandarins and golden syrup. The classic Arran orchard fruits of red apple are there with a luxurious layer of honey.

Palate

Plenty of sweet spice with cigar tobacco. A splash of water reveals dark chocolate and orange oil while adding depth.

Finish

The warmth of sherry-wood lingers on with classic sherry wood character coming to the fore, and the slightest puff of bonfire smoke in the tail. This is a sophisticated dram.

18-YEARS-OLD, SINGLE MALT

Date of release: 2015
Quantity: 9,000 x 70cl
46% abv, non chill-filtered

THE FINAL BOTTLING in the trilogy of 16-, 17- and 18-year-old Arran malt, produced from un-peated malted barley and matured in a selection of ex-sherry casks.

Tasting Notes

Colour
Deep polished gold.

Nose
Baked peaches with honey and toasted almonds. Sherry-cask charring and subtle spice.

Palate
Waxy, coating mouthfeel with the warmth of crystallised ginger and sweetness of crème brûlée and caramelised brown sugar. The addition of some water uncovers floral notes, macadamia nuts and Seville orange marmalade.

Finish
Hazelnuts and nougat mingle with lightly toasted brioche and toffee apples.

ICONS OF ARRAN

No 1

The Peacock

Date of release: June 2009

Date of distillation: 1996

Quantity: 6,000 x 70cl

46% abv, non chill-filtered

THE PROUD PEACOCKS that once roamed the grounds at the distillery have become an endearing symbol of Arran's distinctive whisky. Their vivid character is reflected in this single malt, taken from 20 casks chosen by James MacTaggart. This 1996 distillation, aged for 12 years, is typically Arran in style, with orchard fruits and rich vanilla sweetness followed by a spicy twist in the tail, resembling the impressive display of the peacocks.

Tasting Notes

Nose

Sweet oak and honey are immediately apparent in the aroma. Hints of coconut and candy appear.

Palate

The taste is crisp and malty with a slight nuttiness. The malt begins to open and the Arran hallmarks of citrus and sweet fruit emerge.

Finish

Clean and fresh with a lingering creamy sweetness.

No 2

The Rowan Tree

Date of release: June 2010

Date of distillation: 1997

Quantity: 6,000 x 70cl

46% abv, non chill-filtered

THE ROWAN TREE has a special place in Scottish folklore and is believed to ward off evil spirits. This 1997 distillation has been aged for 12 years in 10 ex-sherry butts specially selected by James MacTaggart. Classic Arran in character, this bottling perfectly captures the flamboyant character of the Rowan Tree.

Tasting Notes

Nose

Complex aroma with hints of dark chocolate, cherries and ginger. Mint-toffee and hazelnut emerge with the addition of water.

Palate

Rich and creamy with classic sherry-wood notes of dried fruit and spice. A confectionery sweetness mingles beautifully with the intrinsic citrus character of Arran malt.

Finish

Much drier on the long finish with an intriguing peppery note developing.

No 3

The Westie

Date of release: June 2011
Date of distillation: 1998
Quantity: 6,000 x 70cl
46% abv, non chill-filtered

RUARAIDH (PRONOUNCED ROO-REE) is the West Highland terrier belonging to James MacTaggart. Being of very independent character with a mischievous glint in his eye, he is much admired by visitors to the distillery. This limited edition bottling was drawn from 22 ex-oloroso sherry hogsheads selected by James MacTaggart under the careful supervision of his wee dog. This expression of Arran is rich and warming with a delightful complexity.

Tasting Notes

Nose

A fresh aroma with notes of toasted oak, treacle toffee and orange zest.

Palate

Full-bodied and buttery with an initial rush of vanilla essence and demerara sugar. The sweet character subsides leaving cocoa powder and cardamom seeds.

Finish

Malty and smooth with voluptuous spiciness.

No 4

The Eagle

Date of release: June 2012
Date of distillation: 1999
Quantity: 6,000 x 70cl
46% abv, non chill-filtered

THE PAIR OF GOLDEN EAGLES which nest in the heights above Lochranza are celebrated in this bottling. They have been an integral part of the Arran story since the distillery was built in early 1995 and their logo features on every bottle of Arran malt. This 1999 distillation was drawn from a combination of 14 ex-bourbon barrels and seven ex-sherry hogsheads specially selected by James MacTaggart.

Tasting Notes

Nose

Tropical fruit salad with hints of vanilla pod and caramel-coated hazelnuts.

Palate

Buttery lemon drizzle cake – sweet but with a fresh citrus burst.

Finish

Captivating combination of fresh fruit and the natural sweetness of honey.

DEVIL'S PUNCH BOWL

Chapter I

Date of release: June 2012

Date of distillation: NAS

Multi-vintage vatting of 24 casks. Ex-sherry butts from 1996 (three casks) and 1997 (two casks) and ex-sherry hogsheads from 1998 (eight casks). Ex-bourbon barrels from 1996 (six casks) and 2006 (five casks, peated).

Quantity: 6,660 x 70cl

52.3% abv, cask strength, non chill-filtered

JAMES MACTAGGART lyrically describes the first Devil's Punch Bowl release.

I have selected the casks for the Devil's Punch Bowl with a view to creating a special release of The Arran Malt where the sum is even greater than the wonderful parts. The sherry butts act like the rhythm section of a band; setting the tone and driving the character of the malt. Deep in colour and rich on the palate these casks are the heartbeat of this whisky. The 1996 bourbon barrels add a wonderful honeyed sweetness to proceedings whilst the sherry hogsheads imbue a perfect harmony of aroma and flavour. As a unique twist I have added some of our 2006 peated Arran, in combination with regular un-peated Arran for the very first time, giving the finish a subtle, smoky edge. They say the Devil has all the best tunes but here he has the perfect whisky too.

Nose

Fresh and vibrant. A delightful combination of classic dried fruits, and vanilla essence along with spiced-wood aromas. A touch of butterscotch and orange zest with light peat in the background.

Palate

Dominated by a warm and rich sherry sweetness of prunes and apricots primarily with hints of European oak, nutmeg, white pepper and muscovado sugar. Over time, a subtle touch of tobacco leaf and green tea emerges.

Finish

Lingering sweet and spicy notes with a delicate smoky twist towards the end.

DEVIL'S PUNCH BOWL

Chapter II — Angels & Devils

Date of release: June 2013

Date of distillation: NAS

Multi-vintage vatting of 27 casks. Ex-oloroso sherry hogsheads from 1997 (nine casks) and 1998 (eight casks) and ex-bourbon barrels from 2002 (six casks, unpeated) and 2004 (four casks, peated).

Quantity: 6,660 x 70cl

53.1% abv, cask strength, non chill-filtered

JAMES MACTAGGART DELVED into the darkest recesses of the Arran warehouses to select the casks for the second limited release. Each cask was carefully chosen and by vatting the contents of the 27 casks he created an Arran bottling of depth and rich character where the aromas and flavours dovetailed to perfection. The numbers of every cask chosen were listed on the inside of the presentation box.

Tasting Notes

Nose

The nose is vibrant with the hallmark notes of classic dried fruits, light spice and cigar box as the base of sherry comes to the fore and sets the tone for this complex dram.

Palate

Here the depth of the sherry sweetness comes into its own. Notes of dark chocolate with a layer of delicate butterscotch spice mingle to create a rich initial burst of character. With a dash of water, the lighter shade of the bourbon barrels emerges with soft citrus and vanilla notes dancing on the tongue.

Finish

Over time, the fresh citrus is counterbalanced by the earthy nature of the peated barrels. The intriguing depth of spice and light twist of smoke remains longlasting.

DEVIL'S PUNCH BOWL

Chapter III — The Fiendish Finale

Date of release: June 2014
Date of distillation: NAS
Vatting made from a multi-vintage selection of Arran malt drawn from ex-oloroso sherry butts, French oak barriques and ex-bourbon barrels.
Quantity: 6,660 x 70cl
53.4% abv, cask strength, non chill-filtered

James Mactaggart describes the final release of the Devil's Punch Bowl Chapter III.

I have chosen a brooding selection of Arran's finest aged oloroso sherry butts which set the scene for the final performance. Notes of distinctive dark chocolate and dried fruits give satisfying depth and provide the ideal foundation for this last dram with the Devil. The inclusion of French oak barriques adds a rich layer of spice and toasted oak to proceedings while the bourbon barrels bring the sweetness of honey and vanilla. This final flourish of the Punch Bowl brings the curtain down in dramatic style.

Tasting Notes

Nose

Aromatic and floral, a delicate perfume of white peaches with a background of white chocolate.

Palate

The influence of the barriques is evident almost immediately, the delicate floral notes give way to rich and warming touch of spice which amplifies beautifully on your tongue. Chocolate raisin and cinnamon in the tail give this a creamy mouthfeel. The fresh character of Arran prevails, the typical citrus notes always in the background, complimented with the light vanilla from the bourbon barrels which adds a layer of sweetness.

Finish

Long, lingering and luxurious. The final curtain falls with long-lasting notes of sweet spice and mandarin.

MACHRIE MOOR

Sixth Release

Date of release: September 2015

Date of distillation: NAS

Vatting of peated Arran malt drawn from ex-bourbon barrels aged since 2004.

Quantity: 15,000 x 70cl

46% abv, cask strength, non chill-filtered

Phenolic content: 20ppm

Tasting Notes

Nose

Earthy, hints of bonfire smoke, caramelised citrus and sweet orchard fruits.

Palate

All the original fresh island character of Arran with warm cereal notes
on a backdrop of citrus fruit.

Finish

Long and enduring, with the trademark Arran citrus notes complimented
beautifully by the delicate puff of smoke in the tail.

MACHRIE MOOR CASK STRENGTH

Second Edition

Date of release: September 2015

Date of distillation: NAS

Vatting was made up with a multi-vintage selection of peated Arran malt drawn from ex-bourbon barrels.

Quantity: 9,000 x 70cl

58.2% abv, cask strength, non chill-filtered

Phenolic content: 20ppm

Tasting Notes

Nose

Wood smoke is apparent straight away over a background of delicate tropical notes.

Palate

Berry fruits, luxurious sweet brioche with the ever-present robust peat smoke giving it strength and depth.

Finish

Fresh Arran character with a touch of salted caramel and vanilla. Long-lasting and memorable.

BIBLIOGRAPHY

Adamson, Gregor, *An Examination of Illicit and Licensed Whisky Production on the Isle of Arran from 1700 to the Present Day*, Stirling University dissertation, 2015

Burrel, John: *Arran Journal*, Vols I & II, (1776-1782), reprinted privately as a facsimile edition, 1982

Cowley, Colin: *Annals of Arran Isle, Vols I & II*, Colin Cowley, 1996

Fairhurst, Horace: *Exploring Arran's Past*, Kilbrannan Publishing, Arran, 1982

Hume, John R & Moss, Michael: *The Making of Scotch Whisky*, James & James, Edinburgh, 1981

MacBride, Mackenzie: *Arran of the Bens, the Glens and the Brave*, TN Foulis, London & Edinburgh, 1911

MacCulloch, John: *The Highlands and Western Islands of Scotland* (Vol IV), Longman, Hurst, Rees, Orme, Brown, and Green, London, 1824

Mackenzie, WM: *The Book of Arran* (Vol II), Arran Society of Glasgow, Glasgow, 1914

Martin, M: *A Description of the Western Islands of Scotland*, Bell, London, 1703

Milne, Allan Paterson: *Arran: An Island's Story*, Kilbrannan Publishing, Arran, 1982

Paterson, J: *Account of the Island of Arran. Prize-Essays and Transactions of the Highland and Agricultural Society of Scotland*, 1837

Smith, Gavin D: *The Secret Still, Scotland's Clandestine Whisky Makers*, Birlinn, Edinburgh, 2002

Smith, Graham: *Robert Burns – the Exciseman*, Alloway Publishing, Ayr, 1989

Newspapers and Journals

Arran Banner, issues from 1991 to 2002

The Scots Magazine

Edinburgh Courant

Caledonian Mercury

The Scotsman

The Herald

The Wall Street Journal

Governments Acts and Papers

House of Commons Papers

An Account of the Names of All the Distillers in Scotland for Home Consumption from 10th November 1818 to 5th April 1819, House of Commons, 24th May 1819

Licensed distillers. Returns of the number of licensed distillers, informations laid, and names and residents of all persons licensed to distil or rectify spirits, who have been convicted in the several Courts of Exchequer, from the 1st January 1827, 1847

Malt Spirits. A return of the quantity of malt spirits distilled by each distiller, upon which drawback was payable under 4 Geo. 4, c. 94 and 6 Geo. 4, c. 58, 1831-1832

Report from the Select Committee on Petitions complaining of the additional Duty on Malt in Scotland, House of Commons, 31st May 1821

Spirits – An account of the total number of gallons of wash distilled by each distillery in Great Britain and Ireland, for the years end 10th October 1826, and October 1827, respectively, and for the half year end 5th April 1828: An account of the total number of proof gallons of spirits made from malt only, by every distiller in Ireland and Scotland, for the same periods, 1831

Seventh Report of the Commission of Inquiry into the Excise Establishment, and into the management and collection of the excise revenue throughout the United Kingdom. British Spirits: Part II, 1835. Command Papers

The Population Act, 51 Geo III, 1811

Internet Resources

British Library Newspaper Archive

Companies House (Beta service)

Archives

Ayrshire Archives, Customs and Excise records, CE76/1/15-34, CE76/1/48, CE76/2/5, CE76/4/11

Glen, Dr IA: *Robert Armour: A Maker of Illicit Stills*, published in Scottish Studies, 1970

List of Arran Tenants Summoned to Appear at the Excise Court on the 9th, 10th and 12th July 1802

Robert Armour, Plumber and Coppersmith in Campbeltown: Account Books, 1811-1817

Arran Estate Offices

Letter from John Murphie to James Lamont, Arran Castle, 1806

Letter from Mr Macleod Bannatyne, Edinburgh, to Mr William Stevenson, Arran Castle, 15 June 1796

Warrant of John Hendry, Hugh MacKenzie, Hugh Kerr and Neil MacCook, April 1803

INDEX

numbers in *italic* refer to captions

A

Abramovich, Roman 113; *113*

Adamson, Gregor 15-18, 21-22, 25

Ahern, Padraig 100; *101, 106*

Andersen, René Helverskov 110

Arran Bondholder scheme 28, 32, 37-39, 53-55, 70, 72; *54, 56-59*

Arran Malt Whisky Society 53, 54, 64, 66, 152; *59*

Arran, Isle of
    Ambassadors of *138*
    geology 28-31
    Society of Glasgow 8

Auchincloss, Les 55-6, 103, 127-9, 134, 147, 151-5

B

Bain, Scott 117-122; *117*

Balvenie Distillery 79

Bannatyne, Miss *137*

Bell, Andy 142, 160

Bell, Robin 122-124; *122*

Bell's, Scotch whisky 40

Benitah, Thierry 132

Bennan 17-19, 23; *19*

Benrinnes Distillery 79

Black, Faye
    see: Waterlow, Faye

Bloy, Gordon 90-91; *90-91*

Bowmore Distillery 76-77, 79, 153, 156

Boyle, David 128-129, 134

Bramble, Forbes 41

brands, Arran 131; *132, 137-139, 144, 149*
    expressions (bottlings)
        core range 163-167; *163-167*
        limited editions 168-180; *168-180*

Braun, Elke 129; *137*

Britannia (royal yacht) 103

Brown, Gordon (former rugby player) 68-69; *71*

Bridger, Martyn 153, 154

Brodick Castle 15, 16, 102, 106

C

Callachan, Mark 147-148; *137, 147*

Campbell, Daniel, of Shawfield 14

casks 82-88; *72-73, 87-92*

Chivas Bros
    see: House of Seagram

Cooley Distillery, Dundalk 66-7, 75-6

Cornwall, Maggie 146-147; *147*

Coulter, Douglas 123; *111, 137*

Cowan, Rita
    see: Taketsuru, Rita

Crawford, Fiona 72; *96, 106*

Crawley, Terry 96-98, 104-5, 123; *97, 137*

Croll, David 61, 127, 133; *62, 116, 133*

Cumming, Lisa *106*

Cummings, Archie 123; *137*

Cunninghame District Council (CDC) 37, 39, 50, 61, 63
    Planning Department 46, 55-57, 63

Currie, Andrew 5, 53, 128; *7, 62, 106*
    Arran Bondholder scheme 28, 32, 37-39, 53-55

Currie, Barbara 4-6; *7*

Currie, Charles 68; *71*

Currie, David 5

Currie, Harold (Hal) 127-128; *33, 62, 64, 71, 97, 106*
    House of Campbell 7-8
    House of Seagram 5-6
    Légion d'Honneur 4; *6-7*
    Rigby & Evans 4
    St Mirren FC 7
    World War II, involvement in 1-4; *2-7*

Currie, John 5

Currie, Paul 5, 53, 128; *7, 106, 128*
    Arran Bondholder scheme 28, 32, 37-39, 53-55

customs duty
    see: excise collection and duty

D

Dale, Alex 92, 93; *97, 105-106*

Davidson, Douglas 88, 123-124, 134, 139; *136, 137*

Dawson, Gary 145; *145*

Distillers Company Ltd 7, 28

distillery bond
  see: Arran Bondholder scheme

distillery buildings, construction and design of
  35-37, 39-51, 55-59, 61-73; *26, 36-37, 39, 47,
  50, 60, 64-70, 131*

distillery closures 7, 28, 40

distilling, illicit see: illicit distillation

Dobson, Alastair 110

Dobson, Graham 49

Douglas, Jim *111*

Dowens, John 93; *90*

Dromgoole, Patrick 102-3, 128, 152-4

Dunn, Peter *125*

Dunsmuir, Stewart *94, 111*

E

Easan Biorach 29, 33, 37, 40; *30-32, 38, 78*

Eclipse (yacht) 113; *113*

Edrington Group 83, 129, 130, 145

Edwards, Matt *137*

Elizabeth, HM the Queen, visit by 99, 102-104;
  103-104

Emsley, Peter *97*

excise collection and duty 11-25; *20*

Evans, Ray 123

F

Febry, G 44

Ferguson, Sir Alex 7

Fforde, Charles 31-32, 45

Fforde, Lady Jean, The 135

Fisher, Bob 70, 109, 123; *96-97, 101, 106*

Forbes Leslie Network 65-66

Fraser, Ewen 46, 66; *68*

G

Gall & Gall, importers 132

Gall, Gregor, artist 123; *123*

Garwood, Paul 128

Gemmell, Janice 97

Gibson, Bob 65-66; *68*

Glengoyne Distillery 79

Glengyle Distillery 79

Glenshant Distillery 15

golden eagles 50-51, 55, 61-64, 69, 91, 134, 136

Gooding, Sam 46-48

Goodwill, L 43

Gordon, HJ 54-55

Graham, John 92; *106*

Gratton, Bert 44-46, 73; *50*

Gregg, Gareth *125*

Green, Calum 148, 154; *137*

Greenwood, Malcolm 132, 134

Greyhound, The (excise cutter) *20*

Grouse, The Famous 40, 127-129, 145

H

Halliburton, Lorna 39-40

Handley, Peter 123

Hartley, Kate 25, 124-125; *124*

Hartley, Mhairi *125*

Head, Marc 101

Henderson, David 40-43

Henderson, Richard (Major) 68-69, 99, 135-136; *136*

Highland Park Distillery 40, 79

Hodgkiss, Paul, Designs 95

Hofer, Charles, SA 132

House of Campbell 7-8

House of Seagram 5-6

Hutchison, David, & Associates (DHA) 50, 55-56, 62; *30*

Hutchison, David 8, 27-28, 66-67; *33, 47, 62, 71*

Hutchison, Mark 28-31

Hutchison family croft *9*

I

Identica Partnership 152

illicit distillation 13-25; *9, 19, 25*

Isle of Arran Distillers Ltd, formation and development of
  32, 151-161

Isle of Jura Distillery 40

K

kelp, harvesting 15

Kennedy, Gordon, actor *64*

Kettles, Andrew 127-129, 134, 147, 153, 155

Kilchoman Distillery 79

Knockenkelly 8, 67; *8*
Knox, Tom, councillor 49-50, 61; *62*

L

Lagg Distillery 8, 16, 22-23, 141; *21, 141*
Lagg Inn *24*
Laing, Campbell 110-112; *111-112*
Lakes Distillery, The *128*
Lamlash Bay *16*
Lamond, John 73
Lang, Ian (MP) 49-51
Lang, Jimmy 54, 76
Laphroaig Distillery 79
Lee, Mick 57
Lees, Jim 31-32; *33*
Légion d'Honneur 4; *6-7*
licensing issues at distillery 96-98
Lie, Nicole *147*
Lochranza, choice as distillery location 29-33; *31, 50*
Lochside Distillery, Montrose *76*
Lonie, Rob 46
Lowe, John 46
Lowe, May 46
Lynch, James M 40, 48-49

M

Maison du Whisky 132
malt riots, Glasgow, 1725 14
Malt Tax, the 13-14
McAllister, Main 49

McBain, Stewart 54
McBride, Karen 100
McConnachie, Heather 99
McConnachie, Jim 123, 137
McCreadie, Gillian 64; *68, 72-73, 96-97*
McGillivray, Neil 50
McGregor, Ewan 114-115; *114-115*
Mackenzie, Hazel 49
McKenzie, Thomas 92
McKie, Jaclyn 143-146; *118, 137, 143*
McMillan, Mrs
    see: McMullan, Diane
McMullan, Diane 47, 92
McMullan, John 47, 92-93; *90, 106*
MacTaggart, James 76-77; *77, 90*
Mazurkiewicz, Marcin *125*
Mayes, Harold 63-64
Millar, John 32
Miller, Brian 98-99
Mitchell, Euan 135-140; *139-140*
Mitchell, Gordon 66, 75-76; *68, 71, 73, 76, 97, 105-106, 140*
Morrison Bowmore Distillers 77, 145, 154
Morrison, Katie *125*
Murray, Jim 67-69, 116, 135-136

N

Neil, John 47
Noble, Marion 102, 104; *96, 106*
North Ayrshire Council 95, 96

O

Omand, Graham 93; *90*
Orb Group 100

P

Panisuik, Kamilla *125*
Patton, Billy *111*
Pearson, Tom 104-106, 132, 134; *106, 116*
Peirce, Mike 128, 147, 154-5; *76*
Pernod-Ricard
    House of Campbell see: House of Campbell
Peters, Michael 131
Peters, Ross 55, 59, 69, 99, 103, 123, 128, 131, 136, 151-3, 155
planning objections
    see: distillery buildings, construction and design of
Pocket Rocket Creative 145; *145*
Primrose, Janet 46
production processes at distillery 77-89; *78, 80-92*

Q

Queen's Award for International Trade 135-136; *136-137*

R

Ramsden, Kevin 128, 131, 134-135
Rankin, Sandy 70, 103-104; *96-97, 106*
Reid, Alan (blender and sensory analyst) 129-130; *129, 140*

Reid, Alan (VC manager) 122-123

Rigby & Evans 4

Roberston, Iain M 49

S

salt, tax on

   see: excise collection and duty

Sampson, Derick & Partners 35; *39*

Sannox Estate 32-33

Scotch Malt Whisky Society 146, 147, 156

Scott, Andy, sculptor 66

Scott, Bill *97*

Scottish Natural Heritage (SNH) 48-50, 55-59, 63

Shelter Point Distillery 128

Siddle, Colin 41, 46, 51, 123

Sillars, Evelyn, councillor 32

Simpson, Duncan 92; *73*

Smith, Andrew 117-122; *118*

Smith, Mike 100

smuggling 11, 14-25

Snaddon, Gillian 148-149; *147*

Spirit of Arran newsletter 64, 103-104; *115*

Springbank Distillery 79

St Mirren FC 7

Stewart, George 98, 102, 107

Stroesser, Lucie 142

T

Taketsuru, Masataka 116-117

Taketsuru, Takeshi 116-117; *116*

Taketsuru, Rita (née Cowan) 116-117

Tatlock & Thomson, RR 37; *38*

Tattersfield, Ben *87, 90*

Tattersfield, Gerard *111*

tax on malt (see also Malt Tax) 12

Thomson, Iain 61, 64, 68; *62*

Thomson, John, (construction company) 59, 63, 92

Thomson, Mandy (architect) 61, 68; *62, 71*

Trickett, Joe 41, 43, 46, 48

V

Van Wees, importer 132

Villers-Bocage, battle of 2-4; *3*

Visitor Centre (VC) 35, 68, 70-73, 95-108; *96-97, 100-101, 103-108, 111-112, 123, 125*

Vissers, Jan 117-122; *117*

Visual Connection, The 95

W

water purity, sources 28-33, 37-38, 40, 43, 46, 50, 77; *78*

Waterlow, Faye (VC manager) 106, 109-110, 124; *109*

Whitehouse, Lamlash, licensed still 15

Watkin, Danny 92

Whyte & Mackay 145

Wilson, Brian (MP) 61; *62*

Wittmann, Michael, SS-Obersturmführer 2-4; *2*

Wood, Rosemary 123-124; *137*

World War II, Hal Currie's involvement in 1-4; *2-7*

Y

Yates, Alastair 96

Young, Louisa 142-143; *142*

Z

Zwartepoorte, Ronald 132